D0872061

50(

Scientific Progress

*A philosophical essay on
the economics of research in natural science*

NICHOLAS RESCHER

Scientific Progress

*A philosophical essay on
the economics of research in natural science*

University of Pittsburgh Press

Published in Great Britain 1978 by
Basil Blackwell and Mott Limited

Published in the U.S.A. 1978 by
the University of Pittsburgh Press,
Pittsburgh, Pa. 15260

ISBN 0–8229–1128–0

Library of Congress Catalog Card Number 77–74544

PRINTED AND BOUND IN GREAT BRITAIN

1. Science – Philosophy

Title

Contents

B. THE PHENOMENOLOGY OF DECELERATION

E. RAMIFICATIONS AND IMPLICATIONS

I wish to dedicate the book to nine contemporary writers on the inauspicious subject of the futurology of science. Though in each case I disagree with their position, I have found in their ideas a source of stimulus and provocation, incurring a debt which I acknowledge with gratitude.

Richard Feynman, physicist
Gerald Holton, historian
Ernan McMullin, philosopher
Peter B. Medawar, biologist
Derek J. Price, historian
Gunther S. Stent, biologist
Alvin R. Weinberg, science-administrator
John Wheeler, physicist
Eugene P. Wigner, physicist

Preface

More than a century has now passed since Emil du Bois-Reymond delivered his celebrated lecture "On the Limits of Natural Science" (*Ueber die Grenzen des Naturerkennens*) in 1872, soon followed by the even more widely influential address on "the Seven World-Riddles" (*Die Sieben Welträtsel*, with which he opened the Leibniz celebration of the Prussian Academy of Sciences in Berlin in July of 1880. Over the ensuing century, the theme of the limits of science has constantly been on the public agenda. But at no time has this theme been more pressing and topical than today, when influential voices sound all around us with predictions of an imminent end to scientific progress. For in recent years a growing recognition of the massive difficulties and obstacles to the continuation of rapid progress in scientific inquiry has developed on many sides and, as will appear in Chapter II, this has engendered a great deal of defeatism and failure of nerve within the scientific community itself.

The scientific "establishment" of the present day appears to be undergoing a crisis of self-confidence strongly reminiscent of that decline in the sense of legitimacy which enervated the French aristocracy in the closing decades of the old régime. On reading the comments of many of the most thoughtful scientists of the day, one might well think that Spengler's gloomy vision of the setting of the formerly bright sun of Western civilization and its intellectual heritage is on the brink of realization. My main aim in writing the book is to vindicate in the face of this defeatism the Leibnizian vision of an open and hopeful future for scientific inquiry. For one cannot but feel that the end-to-progress theory has tragic implications for the human condition. Leibniz was surely right: the essence of human happiness resides not so much in any attainment, completion, and accomplished possession as in "a continued and uninterrupted progress" (*dans un progrès continuel et non interrompu*).[1]

Not that our view of the prospects of scientific progress is unqualifiedly rosy. For while we shall reject the theory of scientific *stoppage*, we shall support one of scientific *deceleration*. Very likely, this view will displease everyone—it is too tame for those of the doomsday school and too negative for the partisans of wholly unfettered scientific progress. All the same, the truth of the matter appears to lie in this middle ground. A just view of the future of science will accordingly be neither over-sanguine nor apocalyptic, but *realistic* in its conception of the long, hard haul that lies ahead.

To be sure, the futurology of science is an enormously risky enterprise. And here, as elsewhere, today's wisdom proceeds by correcting the imperfections of yesterday's. We shall make no advance if we shirk from contributing our own quota of errors to the venture. (As my father's drill sergeant wisely told him during officer's training in 1914: *Die Fehler sind ja da um gemacht zu werden.*)

The present study will have to be substantially oriented towards the economic dimension of natural science—a scrutiny of the *productive* aspect of inquiry in this sphere in terms of inputs and outputs. As such it has two major inspirers: Gottfried Wilhelm Leibniz and Charles Sanders Peirce.

It was Leibniz who first clearly conceived of science as a *productive enterprise*. Throughout much of his many-sided activity he was concerned to put science on a businesslike basis. He sought to organize and systematize scientific work (in his academy projects), to secure its financial support (in his demarches upon princes), and to inventory systematically its stock-in-trade (in his projects of encyclopedism and of a *scientia universalis*). Leibniz plumbed in full depth the implications of Francis Bacon's prophetic vision and saw that scientific inquiry can and must be rationalized as a productive venture.

---

[1] *Nouveaux Essais*, Bk. II, ch. 21, sect. 36. Leibniz's ideas on this head may well take their lead from Hobbes, who writes in *Leviathan* that: "There is no such thing as perpetual tranquility of mind while we live here, because life itself is but motion and can never be without desire, or without fear, no more than without sense" and concludes that "there can be no contentment but in proceeding." Lessing later on put the matter as follows: "Not the truth he has or thinks himself to have constitutes the real worth of man, but the actual effort he has exerted to uncover the truth. For his powers are expanded not by the possession but by the inquiry after truth, wherein alone his ever growing fulfillment consists. Possession makes him relaxed, lazy, proud. . . ." (*Theologische Streitschriften*, 1778).

Peirce, on the other hand, was the first to concern himself with the specifically economic aspect of scientific research. He proposed the founding of a new discipline, the *economy of research*, and gave it a central place in his theory of knowledge.[2] He thought it important to explore the implications for scientific practice of the fact that science, like other human enterprises, must prominently exhibit a specifically economic aspect, and was the first to regard scientific inquiry in terms of the concepts and categories of technical economics.

Almost as important as the debts of *inspiration* are those of *information*. Here three sources tower above all the rest:

Pierre Auger, *Current Trends in Scientific Research* (Paris and New York, 1961; UNESCO Publication).

F. H. Wertheimer *et al.*, *Chemistry: Opportunities and Needs* (Washington, D.C., 1965; National Academy of Sciences/ National Research Council Publication).

D. A. Bromley *et al.*, *Physics in Perspective, Student Edition* (Washington, D.C., 1973; National Academy of Sciences/ National Research Council Publication).

These three documents of the "government report" type present a magisterial overview of the current situation of the physical sciences. I am not a professional scientist myself, and would have felt lost in ranging over the deliberations crucial to the argument of this book without the navigation aids provided by these splendid surveys—and in particular their very vivid picture of the relation between theory and technology in modern physics and chemistry. In a way, the present book can be regarded as a philosophico-economic commentary upon these three works.

The genesis of the book lay in an invitation extended in 1973 by the University of Otago in Dunedin, New Zealand to deliver a series of De Carle Lectures as Visiting Professor for the spring of 1975. I accepted this invitation with pleasure and set out to prepare materials for these lectures. As it turned out, the birth of my daughter Catherine prevented my going to New Zealand that spring, and the present book thus fills the gap left by these undelivered lectures. However, a part of this material was ultimately presented in a set of lectures I gave in the School of

---

[2] See my essay "Peirce and the Economy of Research," *Philosophy of Science*, vol. 43 (1976), pp. 71–98.

Literae Humaniores of the University of Oxford during Michaelmas Term of 1975. I am grateful to the Subfaculty of Philosophy for inviting these lectures and to Corpus Christi College for its kindness in affording me an academic foothold during my stay in Oxford.

Many people have aided my work on this book. William C. House, my research assistant during 1974–1975, helped in assembling documentation, and Barbara Hill, my research assistant during 1975–1976, read a draft of the manuscript and made suggestions for its improvement. Carl G. Hempel, James V. Maher, Jr., Gerald J. Massey, Arnold Pacey, Mark Perlman, Friedrich Rapp, and Peter F. Brown each read parts of the manuscript and offered useful criticisms and suggestions. Kathleen (Mrs. Edward) Reznik prepared the typescript through what I am sure must have seemed an endless series of revisions. Virginia Chestek, Jay Garfield, and Allen Janis helped to check the proofs. I am most grateful to all who helped.

Pittsburgh
January 1976

I

The Future of Scientific Progress

In the year 2000 A.D. it will be possible to answer many fundamental questions concerning which we can merely guess at present. If there is progress it will be mass progress, measurable in averages and susceptible of graphic presentation.

CHARLES BEARD (1932)

1. METHODOLOGICAL PROSPECTUS

The future prospect of scientific progress constitutes the principal theme of this book. Are the days of scientific discovery numbered? Is there good reason to think that the *fin de siècle* theorists (old or new) are right in holding natural science to be approaching the completion of its work? Is there indeed no genuine prospect of "scientific revolutions forever" (to quote the title of a recent article)?[1] These are the sorts of problems at issue here. And it must be stressed that our attention will be focused upon the *natural* or *physical* sciences. These—physics, chemistry, biology, and their "laboratory science" congeners—are alone at issue whenever *science* is spoken of here (except in a few instances where the context of the discussion will make it quite clear that the term is being used in its more general application).

A prime task of the discussion is set by the question: What features of the physical world account for the fact that the historic course of scientific inquiry into its workings has proceeded with the actually realized rate and volume of results? No one has to my knowledge heretofore posed—let alone attempted to answer—this pivotal question regarding the metaphysical foundations of natural science. However imperfectly it may achieve this goal, the present book at any rate *endeavors* to provide a rationally cogent basis for considering a range of

---

[1] William Kneale, "Scientific Revolutions Forever?", *British Journal for Philosophy of Science*, vol. 19 (1967), pp. 27–42.

issues that have heretofore been left to the tender mercies of instinct and intuition.

A simple but far-reaching *idée maitresse* lies at the basis of these deliberations: the thought that if it requires (as over the past century or so it has) an exponentially increasing *effort* to maintain a relatively stable *pace* of scientific progress, then in a zero-growth era of constant effort science will enter a period of logarithmic deceleration. The thesis of this book is thus Malthusian in its structure. The resource-requirements for continuing the accustomedly smooth linear course of scientific progress increase in geometric proportion. But the resources made available in the zero-growth world which now lies around the corner will cumulate only linearly. One knows full well the destined outcome of such a race between an exponential and a linear function.

It will be argued that despite these somewhat harsh realities, the prospects of scientific progress in principle remain literally limitless. However, the cost of scientific inquiry rises faster than the returns from it, and hence a deceleration will come not because of the ending of the frontier but because of the increased difficulty of pushing it further out. But even to hint is to anticipate.

The theme of "the limit of scientific progress" has been broached many times before by philosophers and by scientists—sometimes very eminent ones, as we shall see. Nevertheless, the topic does not seem auspicious, and many of these discussions have generally been stale and unprofitable. There is a very simple explanation for this, one which (hopefully) enables the present book to avoid the deficiencies of many of its earlier congeners. Most earlier writers on the subject have construed the limits of science to operate predominantly on the side of man and to be the result—primarily and in the first instance—of human failings and deficiencies (in intellect, learning-power, memory, imagination, will-power, etc.). The present analysis abandons this approach, and sees the limits of science to reside ultimately in the limitations—be they physical or economic—that are imposed upon us by the nature of the world. The acquisition by man of knowledge about the workings of nature is clearly a matter of *interaction*—a transaction in which *both* parties, man and nature, must play a crucial role. This shift away from a primarily anthropocentric perspective will—so it is hoped—afford greater promise of illumination and fruitfulness.

The theory of scientific progress to be unfolded here is empirical in character and thus capable of confirmation or disconfirmation through its predictive consequences. Yet, the book is a venture of futurology in only a very limited sense. No attempt is made to predict the *content* of the course of future discovery in science, but only its *magnitude*.

An indeterminacy-principle of sorts seems to operate in the sphere of prognostication. Thus let

r = the range or extent of the claims being made
e = the level of exactness of detail at issue

Then a relationship of the form

$$e \cdot r < c \qquad (c \text{ a constant})$$

obtains to circumscribe the region of feasible prediction as per Figure 1.

Figure 1

PREDICTIVE INDETERMINACY

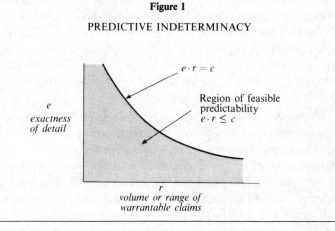

Extensive forecasts in human affairs are attained only at a cost of diminishing exactness—making low demands on the exactness-of-detail side of the specificity/generality divide. Our present predictions regarding scientific progress will conform to this futurological indeterminacy relationship. Designed to cover a wide range of claims, they are necessarily confined to a high level of generality, relating to future findings at an externalized, quantitative level, without any pretence at detail as regards their internal, qualitative content. For it must be stressed that it would be quite unreasonable to expect detailed prognostications about the specific *content* of scientific discoveries. It may be possible in some cases to forecast *that* science will solve such and such a problem, but *how* it will do so—in the sense of what the specific nature of the solution is—lies beyond the ken of those who antedate that discovery itself. To enunciate not merely the *that* but the *what* of a scientific innovation would require that we already have this discovery in hand—or at least are able to conjecture its precise content. This is beyond the range of reasonable expectation in a domain where innovation is preeminently *conceptual*. However, our present concern is thus not so much with the *nature* of scientific progress as with its *amount*. Above all, the questions of *the volume and the rate of future innovation in science* lies at the center of this inquiry.

The discussion accordingly proceeds in the highly aggregate manner familiar from economics. In predicting the general movement of an economy—or even the more specific movements of its constituent industrial sectors—the economist need not say anything about the activities of a particular factory, the fate of a particular product, or the dealings of a particular company. His deliberations can, nay must, proceed on a far more generalized and aggregated level.

To be sure, the available data needed for even this relatively modest project are fragmentary and imperfect.[2] And the analysis will have to stretch these deficient data to their reasonable limit—perhaps beyond it. The paucity of the data and the complexity of the phenomena preclude any claim to finality. Inevitably, our model of scientific progress is a very rough first approximation. No doubt the real situation is not *just* as in our all-too-detailed account, but merely *something* like this. Here, as in other branches of science, one simply does what one can, hoping that the encouragement of one's successes—or annoyance at one's mistakes—will goad others into making a better job of it. This conceded, it remains to be said on behalf of the model that it has three significant merits: (1) it is consonant with the available information, (2) it produces a generally plausible account, and (3) it is sufficiently precise so that it can be put to the test.

[2] For a useful (though now somewhat obsolete) overview see Steven Dedijer, "Measuring the Growth of Science," *Science*, vol. 138 (1962), pp. 781–788. A recent report of the Organization of Economic Cooperation and Development has remarked that "most countries have better statistics on poultry production than on the activities of their scientists and engineers." (Quoted in Harvey Brooks, "Future Needs for the Support of Basic Research," *Basic Research and National Goals* [Washington, D.C., 1965; A Report to the Committee on Science and Aeronautics, U.S. House of Representatives, by the National Academy of Sciences], pp. 77–110 [see p. 78].)

2. SPECULATION ABOUT THE FUTURE OF SCIENCE

The conception that headway is made in the study of nature over the course of time was not unknown to the ancients (though it was certainly not a commonplace among them).[3] Seneca, for example, predicted that the solution of then unsolved problems would be regarded as simple by future generations.[4] Still, discovery and improvement in knowledge is not yet *progress*, which, after all, requires a wide-ranging and systematic advance. The able British historian of *The Idea of Progress*, J. B. Bury, dates the establishment of the theory of progress from the seventeenth century:

> So long as men believed that the Greeks and Romans had attained, in the best days of their civilization, to an intellectual plane which posterity could never hope to reach . . . a theory of degeneration held the field, which excluded a theory of Progress. It was the work of Bacon and Descartes to liberate science and philosophy from the yoke of that authority.[5]

No sooner did the idea of progress gain acceptance, than men began to speculate about its future course with respect to knowledge. And perhaps no seventeenth-century thinker had a clearer vision of the bright prospects of the fututre—of science advancing arm in arm with a betterment of the material circumstances of human life—than that great optimist Leibniz. Writing around 1680, he projected a plan to assure the smooth progress of science under the supportive stimulus of government:

> [W]ould it not be fitting to make at least a trial of our power before

[3] On the early history of the idea see Edgar Zilsel, "The Genesis of the Concept of Scientific Progress," *The Journal of the History of Ideas*, vol. 6 (1945), pp. 325–349.

[4] *Veniet tempus, quo ista quae nunc latent, in lucem dies extrahat, et longioris aevi diligentia: ad inquisitionem tantorum aetas una non sufficit: veniet tempus quo posteri nostri tam aperta nos nescisse mirentur* (Seneca, *Nat. quaest* VII, 25; cf. 31, and see also J. B. Bury, *The Idea of Progress: An Inquiry into Its Origins and Growth* [New York, 1932], p. 13). Seneca adduces an example: the explanation of comets.

[5] J. B. Bury, *ibid.*, p. 66. Thus Pascal wrote that:

> The experiments which give us an understanding of nature multiply continually . . . from whence it follows . . . that all men together make continual progress in them [sc. the sciences] as the universe grows older. (*Fragment d'un traité du vide*, quoted in Charles Frankel, "Progress, The Idea of" in *The Encyclopedia*, ed. Paul Edwards, vol. 6, p. 484a.)

despairing of success? Do we not see every day new discoveries. . . . I shall be told that so many centuries have worked to small avail. But considering the matter closely, one sees that the majority of those who have dealt with the sciences have simply copied from one another or amused themselves. It is virtually a disgrace to the human race that so few have truly worked to make discoveries; haphazard experiences apart, we owe nearly everything we know to a handful of persons. . . . That is why with all the learned men we have today I believe, if a great Monarch would make some powerful effort, or if a considerable number of individuals of ability freed from other concerns would set to work properly, that we could make great progress in a short time, and ourselves enjoy that fruit of our labors which, in the cool and sluggish way we proceed presently, will be reserved for posterity.[6]

Like Bacon before him, Leibniz believed in the power of organized inquiry, but only he foresaw the necessity and desirability of public interest and governmental sponsorship.[7] He had a keen sense of the awesome magnitude of the enterprise. But given the right conditions of collaboration and coordination, he saw vast prospects of progress lying ahead.

By the eighteenth century, the progress of knowledge was no longer a matter of ardent hope but one of confident expectation. The "age of reason" was prepared to brook no impediments to the swift and sure perfecting of man's knowledge and capabilities. We thus find Goodwin declaring towards the close of the century that "The extent of our progress in the cultivation of human knowledge is unlimited. Hence it follows . . . that human interventions are susceptible to perpetual improvement. . . . Intellect has a natural tendency to proceed."[8]

This issue of the future prospects of scientific progress—of the eventual fate that may be presumed to lie in store for the ongoing development of science—is the central problem of the present book.

3. MODELS FOR THE FUTURE COURSE OF SCIENTIFIC PROGRESS

Five major alternatives for theories regarding the long-range future of

---

[6] L. Couturat (ed.), *Opuscules et fragments inédits de Leibniz* (Paris, 1903), p. 334.
[7] Much of Leibniz's activity in the promotion of "projects" (not least the founding of academies) falls under this rubric.
[8] William Goodwin, *Enquiry Concerning Political Justice* (London, 1793).

scientific discovery are readily discriminated. They are distinguished by the way in which the choices built into the following schema are resolved:

The prospect of ongoing scientific discovery is <limited/ unlimited>. In the former case of a limitation, the limits of innovation will eventually be <finally attained/asymptotically approached>, and these limits are due to the finitude and limited complexity of <nature/man>.

Five alternative theories arise through the variation of the factors at issue here. They are summarized in Table 1.

Table 1

VIEWS OF THE FUTURE OF SCIENCE

Name of Theory	The Horizons of Scientific Innovations are
I. Nature Exhaustion	limited by the inherent finitude of nature and ultimately attainable
II. Nature Saturation (Asymptotic Completion)	limited by the inherent finitude of nature but only approachable asymptotically
III. Capacity Exhaustion	limited by the inherent finitude of man and ultimately attainable
IV. Capacity Saturation (Asymptotic Incapacitation)	limited by the inherent finitude of man but only approachable asymptotically
V. Unlimited Horizons (Potentially Unending Progress)	unlimited

---

Let us examine these five theories in turn:

Case I: Nature Exhaustion (Ultimate Completion)

In an initial surge of hopeful expectation, the major seventeenth-century thinkers entertained the hope that scientific progress would come to an end with an all-embracing true theory of nature.[9] This case is rendered graphic by the picture of Figure 2:[10]

[9] Bacon, Galileo, Descartes, and Boyle all tended to assume a definitely realizable ideal of scientific knowledge, viewing this as something achievable which, once attained, would be bound to endure forever.

[10] This way of depicting the matter in terms of a monotonic increase without retrogressions does not involve any inextricable commitment to a cumulative view of scientific progress. It is quite compatible with the view that today's big discovery is the

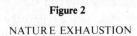

Figure 2

NATURE EXHAUSTION

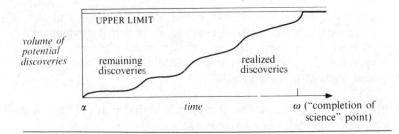

This picture of the matter has it that major innovation in science will come to an end as regards further discoveries of a very high level of intrinsic significance and fundamental importance. (It is, of course, such *major* discoveries that will be at issue when one moots the prospect of an end to scientific innovation. No one wants to deny the prospect that there will always be minor details to be filled in—blades of grass that remain uncounted, as it were.)

On such a view, science has a finite history. It begins at some juncture *alpha* (α)—presumably with the mathematics, astronomy, and medicine of the ancients—and continues until an ultimate point *omega* (ω) when "all returns are in" because nothing of really fundamental importance remains to be discovered. This theory views scientific progress in terms of *discovery exhaustion*. Its paradigm is the case of geographic exploration: a point is ultimately reached when all that was once *terra incognita* is charted. The stock of potential scientific discoveries that reveal the "secrets of nature" is like the apples on a tree, all of which eventually get picked off, or like a vein of ore that eventually becomes exhausted.

Along these lines, the eighteenth-century French encyclopedist Denis Diderot (1713–1784) already propounded the idea that discovery might actually be grinding to a halt in what was the most active branch of science in his day:

---

undoing of yesterday's. What increases monotonically is simply the *number* of discoveries, and this implies nothing about the cumulation of their *content*. Quantitative discovery-cumulation at the numerical level is something very different from qualitative discovery-cumulation at the contentual level, and increase as regards the former is compatible with annihilation in the latter respect.

I dare virtually to guarantee that before one hundred years have passed one will not find three great mathematicians in Europe. That science will come to a dead stop pretty much where a Bernouilli, an Euler, a Maupertuis, a Clairaut, a Fontaine, and a D'Alembert and a La Grange have left it. They have erected the pillars of Hercules beyond which there is no voyaging. Their work will stand in the centuries to come like the pyramids of Egypt, whose massive surfaces surcharged with hieroglyphics arouses in us a frightening idea of the power and the capacities of the men who have erected them.[11]

A similar outlook pervades the teachings of Immanuel Kant's *Critique of Pure Reason* (1781). His position is roughly as follows: The sciences move one by one towards a position of completed finality. Already, logic, arithmetic, and geometry have effectively attained this state—at least as regards their major doctrines. Physics and its congeners (especially astronomy and cosmology) have virtually been brought to the same condition by Newton and his successors. The other sciences will eventually have their day as well.

On a view of this sort one envisages an eventual exhaustion of the manifold of unrealized cognitive possibilities. A point will eventually be reached when science "has no future" as an innovative enterprise because its work of discovery is done. The Nature Exhaustion model envisages *the task-completion of science*, the day when science will have plumbed the bottom-most depths of the finite pool of "secrets" that nature has at her disposal.

Case II: Nature Saturation (Asymptotic Completion)

One acute contemporary analysis of physics moots the prospect of its ultimate completion in the following terms:

It is possible to think of fundamental physics as eventually becoming complete. There is only one universe to investigate, and

---

[11] *De l'interpretation de la nature*, sect. iv; *Œuvres complètes*, ed. by J. Assezat, vol. II (Paris, 1875), p. 11. And compare Laplace's speaking in 1820 of "the perfection which [modern science] has been able to give to astronomy," bearing in mind that perfection entails finality. (*A Philosophical Essay on Probabilities*, English tr. from the 6th French, ed. by F. W. Truscott and F. C. Emory [New York, 1951; Dover reprint].)

physics, unlike mathematics, cannot be indefinitely spun out purely by inventions of the mind. The logical relation of physics to chemistry and the other sciences it underlies is such that physics should be the first chapter to be completed. No one can say exactly what completed should mean in that context, which may be sufficient evidence that the end is at least not imminent. But some sequence such as the following might be vaguely imagined: The nature of the elementary particles becomes known in self-evident totality, turning out by its very structure to preclude the existence of hidden features. Meanwhile, gravitation becomes well understood and its relation to the stronger forces elucidated. No mysteries remain in the hierarchy of forces, which stands revealed as the different aspects of one logically consistent pattern. In that imagined ideal state of knowledge, no conceivable experiment could give a surprising result. At least no experiment could that tested only fundamental physical laws. Some unsolved problems might remain in the domain earlier characterized as organized complexity, but these would become the responsibility of the biophysicist or the astrophysicist. Basic physics would be complete; not only that, it would be manifestly complete, rather like the present state of Euclidean geometry.[12]

Extended from physics to natural science in general, such a position is as depicted in Figure 3:

Figure 3

NATURE SATURATION

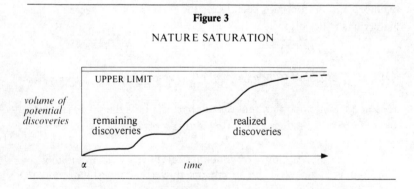

Like the previous case of possibility exhaustion, the present case also views the realm of potential discovery as one of limited proportions.

[12] D. A. Bromley, *et al.*, *Physics in Perspective: Student Edition* (Washington, D.C., 1973; National Research Council/National Academy of Sciences Publication), p. 26.

However it takes the view that this realm is never wholly and completely exhausted: the total exploration of nature is achieved only gradually and "in the limit," because the upper limit of potential scientific discovery is never actually reached but only approached asymptotically over "the long run" of scientific progress. On this view of saturation rather than exhaustion, there is no final *Götterdämmerung*, and natural science does not come to a stop in a final blaze of definitive innovation that extinguishes all prospects of further discovery for the rest of time. But, nevertheless, science as an innovative enterprise comes to an end for all practical purposes—it simply goes out with a whimper rather than a bang.

A position of just this sort was maintained by the great American philosopher Charles Sanders Peirce (1839–1914). Peirce, in effect, saw the history of science as progressing through two stages: an initial or preliminary phase of groping for the general structure of the *qualitative* relations among scientific parameters, and a secondary phase of *quantitative* refinement—of filling in with increasing precision the exact values of parameters that figure in equations whose general configuration is determined in the initial phase. Once the first phase has been gotten over with—as Peirce believed to be the case in his own day, at any rate with regard to the physical sciences—ongoing scientific progress is just a matter of increasing detail and exactness, of determining the ever more minute decimal-place values of quantities whose approximate value is already well-established.[13]

On such a view, science undeniably "has a future" because there will always be worthwhile discoveries to be made. But discoveries take place within a setting of over-all limits—the magnitude of their intrinsic importance becomes ever smaller. New discoveries will not fundamentally modify our overall understanding of processes of nature. It is a matter of increasing the accuracy or sophistication of a basically determinate view of the world, of making adjustments and refinements which—however difficult and important the work of discovery itself might be—still produce only marginal adjustments in our intellectual world-picture. Scientific progress does not ever quite *reach* a situation that is completed, final, and statically unchanging because the domain of potential discovery has been completely exhausted—rather, it moves

---

[13] The background of Peirce's position will be described more fully in the next chapter.

towards this position by way of *asymptotic approximation* to a finally
adequate picture of the world.

Case III: Capacity Exhaustion (Impassable Barrier)

This case is rendered graphic by the picture of Figure 4:

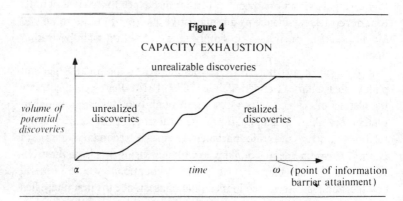

Figure 4

CAPACITY EXHAUSTION

Like the condition of possibility-exhaustion, this case envisages a
termination juncture ω for the enterprise of scientific progress. But this
is *not* reached because the area of possible major discoveries has been
exhausted—quite the reverse, a theoretical possibility of further
advance definitely remains open on the side of the possibilities afforded
by the workings of nature. A termination is reached solely because of
limits and limitations on the side of man's information-acquisition
capabilities. Progress stops because an *information-barrier* has been
reached: our capacities for obtaining data about the world have been
pushed to their limit and the restricted data thus obtained have been
exploited *au fond* by theorizing intelligence.

To be sure, the circumstances of the case are such that further
findings could be made IF these information-gathering limits could be
removed, but this is a visionary and unrealizable circumstance. The
enlargement of knowledge in natural science comes to an ultimate stop
with a limitation of *ne plus ultra* beyond which lies a *terra incognita*
whose secrets our meager powers are too feeble to penetrate. We can
push the scientific enterprise only "up to a point"—it is not our privilege
to reach the final truth.

This discovery-barrier theory was mooted as a realistic prospect by the historian of progress J. B. Bury, who sketched this possibility in the following terms:

> Science has been advancing without interruption during the last three or four hundred years; every new discovery has led to new problems and new methods of solution, and opened up new fields for exploration. Hitherto men of science have not been compelled to halt, they have always found means to advance further. But *what assurance have we that they will not one day come up against impassable barriers*? The experience of four hundred years, in which the surface of nature has been successfully tapped, can hardly be said to warrant conclusions as to the prospect of operations extending over four hundred or four thousand centuries. Take biology or astronomy. How can we be sure that some day progress may not come to a dead pause, *not because knowledge is exhausted, but because our resources for investigation are exhausted—because, for instance, scientific instruments have reached the limit of perfection* beyond which it is demonstrably impossible to improve them, or because (in the case of astronomy) we come into the presence of forces of which, unlike gravitation, we have no terrestrial experience? It is an assumption, which cannot be verified, that we shall not soon reach a point in our knowledge of nature beyond which the human intellect is unqualified to pass.[14]

The prospect so vividly posed by Bury presents what we have characterized—in his very words—as the *impassable barrier theory*.

Case IV: Capacity Saturation (Asymptotic Incapacitation)

This case is depicted in Figure 5. Like the Nature Saturation case of asymptotic completion, the present case envisages the ultimate stabilization of our scientific knowledge. But it takes the view that this is so not because the range of potential discovery is being exhausted, but rather because man's ability to press into the heretofore unexplored regions of this range is increasingly impeded. As with the "impassable barrier" envisaged by Bury, there is a limit "beyond which not"—but a limit that is actually not ever *reached*, but merely *approached*.

---

[14] J. B. Bury, *op. cit.*, pp. 3–4 (my italics).

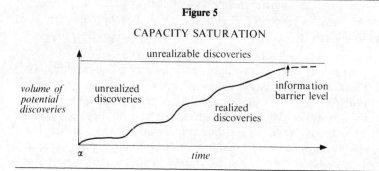

Figure 5

CAPACITY SATURATION

Case V: Unlimited Horizons (Potentially Unending Progress)

This case is rendered graphic by the picture of Figure 6:

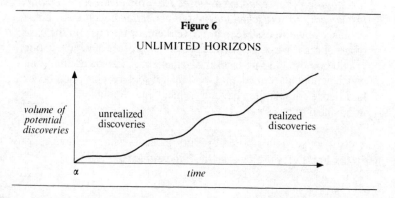

Figure 6

UNLIMITED HORIZONS

On this view there are no confining boundaries to the range of scientific progress, nor are any inherent limits to the expansion of knowledge imposed by the limitations of man.

There is little doubt that this is the traditional view held—or at any rate supported—by many of the greatest natural scientists from Newton to our own day. Newton's famous simile of the little child picking up pebbles on the seashore, while a great ocean of truth lay unexplored before him set a seemly model of modesty that sees the progress to one's own day as a vanishingly small fraction of the realm of potential knowledge. Kelvin struck just the same note. "I know," he said on the day of his jubilee, "no more of electric and magnetic force, or of the relations between ether, electricity, and ponderable matter, or of chemical affinity, than I knew and tried to teach my students in my first session."[15] To be sure, neither of these statements says flatly that the pool of unrealized discoveries is literally infinite, a thesis which—as we shall see—also finds its share of advocates.

These five models for the course of scientific progress indicate the problem-area of the present book. Its task is to assess where (if indeed anywhere in the region defined by them) the truth of the matter in fact lies—or at any rate, the best-supported conjecture about it that can be made on the basis of present indications.

4. THE CENTRAL THESIS

It will be the main thesis of this book that the latter-day prophets of doom who espouse a model of saturation or exhaustion are wrong—that the demise of science is being grossly exaggerated, and that the situation we actually confront is not one of the *termination* of science but merely one of its *deceleration*. The keynote of our analysis is an optimism chastened by realism.

An important preliminary stipulation must be made. This issue of the limits of science will be treated here in a way that abstracts altogether from the historical finitude of the human race. To be sure, we shall be concerned about human science, *our* science and not that of hyperintelligent creatures of some other galaxy. Like everyone else, we too presume that life on earth will come to an eventual end in some cosmic cataclysm, even if mankind manages to avoid hastening the process by suicidal intervention. But we propose to postulate the effectively unending continuity of human effort, and implore the reader to grant a suspension of disbelief in this regard. For *this* sort of termination to the scientific enterprise is not of much theoretical interest. Our concern is with other possible modes of cessation whose workings are more concretely informative about the prospects of innovation and novelty in science. In particular, it would be of the

[15] Quoted by S. P. Thompson, "The Kelvin Lecture. The Life and Work of Lord Kelvin," *Annual Report of the Smithsonian Institution for the Year* 1908 (Washington, 1909), pp. 745–768 (see p. 768).

greatest value if it proved possible to develop some illuminating insights into the nature of science itself, and not just to rehearse some trite facts about human vulnerability.

Nor shall we worry about any limitation to the capacity of the human intellect in learning or intellectually utilizing scientific information. For when a plurality of possible blockages arises, the crucial issue is that of *which of them is encountered first.* Now over and above the limits of *man's intellect* and of *time for humanity at large* there looms the issue which concerns us here, that of the physico-economic limits on *knowledge-yielding interactions* with nature. And we shall argue that these are in fact the urgently pressing limits, whose effects are not remote by centuries or millennia but by decades (if even by that much). In the final analysis, it is harmless to disregard intellectual or biological limits in a context where—as we hope to show—it is the physico-economic limits and limitations that play the decisive role.

II
Historical Stagesetting

We are most of us much more apt to congratulate ourselves upon what we have accomplished than to contemplate and compare with it what remains to be done.

GEORGE GORE

1. FIN DE SIÈCLE

Before setting out on our inquiry, a closer scrutiny of the historical background is useful. In the middle years of the last century thoughtful minds looked confidently forward to the unfettered advance of science. George Babbington Macaulay, speaking of the scientific method as "the Baconian philosophy," said of it:

> It is a philosophy which never rests; which has never attained, which is never perfect. Its law is progress. A point which yesterday was invisible is its goal to-day, and will be its starting-point to-morrow.[1]

And in even purpler prose than Macaulay's, Baden Powell (Savilian Professor of Geometry at Oxford) wrote:

> To the truly inductive philosopher, the notion of a limit to inquiry is no more real than a mirage which seems to bound the edge of the desert, yet through which the traveller will continue his march to-morrow, as uninterruptedly as to-day over the plain.[2]

---

[1] Essay: "Lord Bacon" (1837).

[2] *Essays on the Spirit of Inductive Philosophy* (London, 1855), p. 107. Compare:

Science and knowledge are subject, in their extension and increase, to laws quite opposite to those which regulate the material world. . . . [T]he further we advance from the origin of our knowledge, the larger it becomes, and the greater power it bestows upon its cultivators, to add new fields to its dominions. Yet, does this continually and rapidly increasing power, instead of giving us any reason to anticipate the exhaustion of so fertile a field, place us at each advance, on some higher eminence, from which the mind contemplates the past, and feels irresistibly convinced, that the whole, already gained, bears a constantly diminishing ratio to

However, as the progress of science continued over the ensuing decades, a more cautious spirit began to prevail. Indeed, by the final quarter of the last century, a widespread belief was abroad that the position of science was one of eventual exhaustion or saturation. Towards the beginning of this period, one acute observer—the English physicist and chemist George Gore (1826–1908)—put the matter as follows:

> Although we know but little of the actual limits of possible knowledge, there are signs that nature is not in every respect infinite. It is highly probable that the number of forms of energy and of elementary substances is limited. . . . Not only does it appear highly improbable that an unlimited variety of collocations of different atoms, united to form different substances, can exist; but many combinations and arrangements of forces are incompatible, and cannot co-exist. From these considerations, therefore, there is probably a limit to . . . the amount of possible knowledge respecting them. The number of laws also which govern a finite number of substances or forces must themselves be finite. (Pp. 15–16.) The future limits of human knowledge seem to be infinitely distant; the exertion of creative power in developing and improving mankind appears to be infinitely far from being exhausted. It is highly probable that there remains to be discovered a vast number of scientific truths, of which we are at present totally ignorant, because very large gaps are evident in all directions in our present system of knowledge. . . . From these and many other circumstances we have great reason to believe that we are still surrounded on every side by an immense number of natural phenomena which we do not perceive, or of the existence of which we have but little conception. . . . (Pp. 22–23.)
>
> We are most of us much more apt to congratulate ourselves upon what we have accomplished than to contemplate and compare with it what remains to be done. Our knowledge is finite, but our ignorance is nearly infinite. . . . The amount of discovery in the future appears likely to be vastly greater than that of the past. . . . Not a single science, even of the mathematical ones, is

---

that which is contained within the still more rapidly expanding horizon of our knowledge. . . . When time shall have revealed the future progress of our race . . . it may possibly be found that the dominion of mind over the material world advances with an ever-accelerating force. (Charles Babbage, *On the Economy of Machinery and Manufactures* [4th ed., London, 1835], pp. 386–390.)

probably yet complete either in principles or details. There is not a single force, nor even a single substance, yet completely understood. . . . [A]s the whole realm of attainable knowledge appears immensely great in comparison with the powers of the human mind, the unfolding of it will probably require an almost infinite amount of labour, and therefore a vast period of time. . . . Another reason for concluding that the future of science is immense is because, in a very large proportion of new experiments, we are unable to predict the results successfully. Knowledge of principles and laws enables us to predict effects; and the extent to which we are *unable* to predict successfully indicates, in a rough sort of way, the proportionate amount of such principles and laws yet to be found. If . . . in 100 proposed new experiments we can only predict successfully the result of 10, the knowledge necessary to enable us to predict successfully the remainder has yet to be obtained. . . .

As the human mind has discovered the present stock of scientific truth, and is rapidly finding more—and we fully believe that what remains to be ascertained must be of essentially similar character—it is reasonable to suppose that in course of time a vast deal more will be found; but how far man, with his finite intellect, will in the future be able to explain the phenomena belonging to the various parts of the universe, and successfully predict effects, no one at present can even guess. It is, however, reasonable to suppose that as the whole of nature is systematically framed in accordance with intelligent design, nothing in it is essentially inscrutable to intellectual powers, and that the vast expanse of truth which remains unknown is only temporarily inscrutable, until the prior knowledge necessary to its discovery is obtained. And as ceaseless activity is a necessary condition of human existence, we may also conclude that new and improved intellectual processes of research will be invented, and that the entire universe of scientific truth will [eventually] be investigated and discovered. (Pp. 26–29.)[3]

[3] George Gore, *The Art of Scientific Discovery: Or the General Conditions and Methods of Research in Physics and Chemistry* (London, 1878). George Gore, F.R.S., L.L.D., 1826–1908; author of original researches in various branches of physics and chemistry (especially electrometallurgy); lecturer at King Edward's School, Birmingham; civil list pensioner 1891; writer on the relation of science to society. (Data from *Who Was Who: 1897–1915* [London, 1920].) On Gore see also R. M. MacLeod, "Resources of Sciences in Victorian England: The Endowment of Science Movement, 1868–1900" in P. Mathias (ed.), *Science and Society: 1600–1900* (Cambridge, 1972), pp. 111–166 (see pp. 129–131).

Gore's position is clear and straightforward: The domain of physical knowledge is finite, but science nevertheless still has a brilliant future because we have as yet explored only a minute fraction of this finite domain.[4]

As the nineteenth century moved to its close, however, and brilliant new headway continued to be made in every branch of natural science, a less expectant tendency of thought came to predominate: perhaps science might actually be drawing near to completion. While there was some divergence of opinion as to the reason for this view, a *fin de siècle* consensus seemed to form to the effect that scientific progress, in the *natural* sciences at any rate, was fast approaching its end and that these sciences were nearing their completed state.

Consider some examples of this phenomenon. In 1880 the German physiologist, philosopher, and historian of science Emil du Bois-Reymond published a widely discussed lecture on *The Seven Riddles of the Universe* (*Die sieben Welträtsel*),[5] in which he maintained that some of the most fundamental problems regarding the workings of the world were insoluble. Reymond was a rigorous mechanist. On his view, nonmechanical modes of inquiry cannot produce adequate results, and the limit of our secure knowledge of the world is confined to the range where purely mechanical principles can be applied. As for all else, we not only *do not* have but *cannot* in principle obtain reliable knowledge. Under the banner of the slogan *ignoramus et ignorabimus* ("we *do not* know and *shall never* know"), Reymond maintained a sceptically agnostic position with respect to basic issues in physics (the nature of matter and of force, and the ultimate source of motion) and psychology (the origin of sensation and of consciousness). These issues are simply *insolubilia* which transcend man's scientific capabilities. Certain fundamental biological problems he regarded as unsolved, but perhaps in principle soluble (though very difficult): the origin of life, the adaptiveness of organisms, and the development of language and

---

[4] Compare Thomas A. Edison's (purported) remark that we know only one-millionth of one percent of what there is to be known. (See Louis Gottschalk, *Historical Understanding* [New York, 1956], p. 212.)

[5] This work was published together with a famous prior (1872) lecture *On the Limits of Scientific Knowledge* as *Ueber Die Grenzen des Naturerkennens: Die Sieben Welträtsel—Zwei Vorträge* (11th ed., Leipzig, 1916). The earlier lecture has appeared in English tr. "The Limits of Our Knowledge of Nature," *Popular Scientific Monthly*, vol. 5 (1874), pp. 17–32. For Reymond cf. Ernest Cassirer, *Determinism and Indeterminism in Modern Physics: Historical and Systematic Studies of the Problem of Causality* (New Haven, 1956), Part 1.

reason. And as regards the seventh riddle—the problem of freedom of the will—he was undecided.

The position of du Bois-Reymond was soon and sharply contested by the zoologist Ernest Haeckel in a book *Die Welträtsel* published in 1889,[6] which soon attained a great popularity. Far from being intractable or even insoluble—so Haeckel maintained—the riddles of du Bois-Reymond had all virtually been solved. Dismissing the problem of free-will as a pseudo-problem—since free will "is a pure dogma [which] rests on mere illusion and in reality does not exist at all"—Haeckel turned with relish to the remaining riddles. Problems of the origin of life, of sensation, and of consciousness Haeckel regarded as solved—or solvable—by appeal to the theory of evolution. Questions of the nature of matter and force, he regarded as solved by modern physics except for one residue: the problem (perhaps less scientific than metaphysical) of the ultimate origin of matter and its laws. This "problem of substance" was the only remaining riddle recognized by Haeckel, and it was not really a problem of science: in discovering the "fundamental law of the conservation of matter and force" science had done pretty much what it could do with respect to this problem—the rest that remained was metaphysics with which the scientist had no proper concern. Haeckel summarized his position as follows:

> The number of world-riddles has been continually diminishing in the course of the nineteenth century through the aforesaid progress of a true knowledge of nature. Only one comprehensive riddle of the universe now remains—the problem of substance. . . . [But now] we have the great, comprehensive "law of substance," the fundamental law of the constancy of matter and force. The fact that substance is everywhere subject to eternal movement and transformation gives it the character also of the universal law of evolution. As this supreme law has been firmly established, and all others are subordinate to it, we arrive at a conviction of the universal unity of nature and the eternal validity of its laws. From the gloomy *problem* of substance we have evolved the clear *law* of substance.[7]

[6] Bonn, 1889. Tr. by J. McCabe as *The Riddle of the Universe—at the Close of the Nineteenth Century* (New York and London, 1901). On Haeckel see the article by Rollo Handy in *The Encyclopedia of Philosophy* (ed. by Paul Edwards), vol. III (New York, 1967).

[7] Haeckel, *op. cit.*, pp. 365–366.

The basic structure of Haeckel's teaching is clear: science is rapidly nearing a state where all the big problems have been solved. What remains unresolved is not so much a *scientific* as a *metaphysical* problem. In science itself, the big battle is virtually at an end, and the work that remains to be done is pretty much a matter of mopping-up operations.

It is interesting to note that the quarrel between Haeckel and du Bois-Reymond actually rested on a point of agreement at the deeper level. On both views, science was coming pretty near the end of the road. On du Bois-Reymond's theory it was approaching the impassable barrier of an exhaustion of human powers on the Capacity Exhaustion model. On Haeckel's view it was nearing its ultimate completion in the portrayal of the laws of nature on the Nature Exhaustion model. But both theories have the same fundamental structure: they agree in that both predict that science will reach a point beyond which it will not go—either because on the one hand (du Bois-Reymond's) it *cannot* do so, or because on the other hand (Haeckel's) it *need not* do so.

The idea of an eventual end to scientific innovation played a decisive role in the metaphysics of the great American founder of philosophical pragmatism, Charles Sanders Peirce—it provided the basis for his theory of truth. The "real truth" about the world, Peirce taught, is the position at which the community of inquirers would arrive in the limit of scientific inquiry carried out over the indefinite long run. The real truth is accordingly a *focus imaginarius*—an idealization located at an infinitely remote point which we never actually attain, just as we can never give the full decimal value of π. The knowledge-in-hand that we actually possess at any concrete stage of inquiry is ever fallible, always inaccurate. The imprecision of our measuring instruments prevents our ever arriving at an exactitude and precision that is final and complete. At just this point Peirce's theory of truth flows over into his theory of scientific knowledge. At the current stage of scientific knowledge, further scientific progress is solely a matter of increasing accuracy—it consists in filling in with increasing refinements and ever more accurate determination the details of a picture whose formative outlines become increasingly clear and well-defined. Future progress is a matter of providing increasingly fine-grained detail within a context whose course-grained structure has already been determined. Thus Peirce wrote ca. 1896 that there is plausible reason to think, judging by the content of current science, that "the universe is now entirely explained in all its leading features; and that it is only here and there that the fabric of scientific knowledge betrays any rents."[8]

In regard to physics, above all, a widespread conviction was abroad in the 1875–1905 era that the days of major innovations were over, that all the really big discoveries had been made. Some of the most able physicists of the day shared this conviction that the discipline had reached its more or less completed form and that little remained to be done, apart from work on relatively minor issues.

Thus in a dedication address delivered at the Ryerson Physical Laboratory at the University of Chicago in 1894, A. A. Michelson (America's first Nobel Laureate in science) remarked:

> While it is never safe to affirm that the future of Physical Science has no marvels in store even more astonishing than those of the past, it seems probable that most of the grand underlying principles have been firmly established and that further advances are to be sought chiefly in the rigorous application of these principles to all the phenomena which come under our notice.
>
> It is here that the science of measurement shows its importance—where quantitative results are more to be desired than qualitative work. An eminent physicist has remarked that the future truths of Physical Science are to be looked for in the sixth place of decimals.[9]

---

[8] *Collected Papers* (Cambridge, Mass.; 8 vols., 1931–1958; ed. C. Hartshorne *et al.*), vol. I, 1.116.

[9] Quoted in *Physics Today*, vol. 21 (1968), p. 56. See also Charles Weiner, "Who Said It First?", *Physics Today*, vol. 21 (1968), p. 9. Compare the somewhat ampler statement in A. A. Michelson's *Light Waves and Their Uses* (Chicago, 1961):

> The more important fundamental laws and facts of physical science have all been discovered, and these are now so firmly established that the possibility of their ever being supplanted in consequence of new discoveries is exceedingly remote. Nevertheless, it has been found that there are apparent exceptions to most of these laws, and this is particularly true when the observations are pushed to a limit, i.e., whenever the circumstances of experiment are such that extreme cases can be examined. . . . Many other instances might be cited, but these will suffice to justify the statement that "our future discoveries must be looked for in the sixth place of decimals." It follows that every means which facilitates accuracy in measurement is a possible factor in a future discovery. . . . (Pp. 23–24.)

The "eminent physicist" who is the supposed author of this claim is presumably Lord Kelvin (compare the exchange of letters in *Science*, vol. 172 (1971), p. 111, as well as p. 52 of Badash's paper cited in footnote 11). I have not succeeded in verifying the attribution. The sentiment does not square with his oft-repeated view (cf. pp. 14–15 above), and the common perception of Kelvin as a prime exponent of *fin de siècle* confidence in the completeness of science does him a grave injustice.

Michelson's gloomy forecast was echoed by T. C. Mendenhall, formerly a physics professor, at the time a college president, and soon to be both president of the American Association for the Advancement of Science and Superintendent of the United States Coast and Geodetic Survey. In his popular text on electricity (1887), he maintained that:

> More than ever before in the history of science and invention, it is safe now to say what is possible and what is impossible. No one would claim for a moment that during the next five hundred years the accumulated stock of knowledge of geography will increase as it has during the last five hundred. . . . In the same way it may safely be affirmed that in electricity the past hundred years is not likely to be duplicated in the next, at least as to great, original, and far-reaching discoveries, or novel and almost revolutionary applications.[10]

This *fin de siècle* sentiment that the great heroic deeds of physical science were over was by no means confined to a few eccentric notables, but was rather widely current.[11] Thus in his 1956 Presidential Address to the American Physical Association R. T. Birge reported as follows about his own first physics teacher at the University of Wisconsin in 1906:

> To him physics was an incomparably beautiful, but *closed* subject. There was nothing in his lectures to suggest that there were things still to be discovered in physics, and hence no incentive to enter the field except to become a teacher and in turn show these same beautiful experiments to one's own students.[12]

An even more remarkable instance of the same phenomenon is given by the strikingly parallel report of Max Planck:

> As I was beginning to study physics [in 1875] and sought advice regarding the conditions and prospects of my studies from my

[10] T. C. Mendenhall, *A Century of Electricity* (Boston and New York, 1887; revised 1890), p. 223.

[11] For an interesting (but very incomplete) study of this idea see Lawrence Badash, "The Completeness of Nineteenth-Century Science," *Isis*, vol. 63 (1972), pp. 48–58.

[12] Raymond T. Birge, "Physics and Physicists of the Past Fifty Years," *Physics Today*, vol. 9 (1956), pp. 20–38 (see p. 20).

eminent teacher Phillip von Jolly, he depicted physics as a highly developed and virtually full-grown science, which—since the discovery of the principle of the conservation of energy had in a certain sense put the keystone in place—would soon assume its finally stable form. Perhaps in this or that corner there would still be some minor detail to check out and coordinate, but the system as a whole stood relatively secure, and theoretical physics was markedly approaching that degree of completeness which geometry, for example, had already achieved for hundreds of years. Fifty years ago [as of 1924] this was the view of a physicist who stood at the pinnacle of the times. (Max Planck, *Vortäge und Erinnerungen*, 5th ed. [Stuttgart, 1949], p. 169.)

Such sentiments represent a widespread tendency—at least common if not actually typical of the tenor of scientific opinion in the 1875–1905 era. The very fact that the most "advanced" science of the day—physics—seemed to be nearing "the end of the line," together with a contemplation of the enormous strides being made all across the scientific frontier—in biology, medicine, chemistry, etc.—opened up the seemingly plausible prospect that science stood pretty much at the last frontiers and that the course of progress in scientific knowledge—so dramatically explosive since its first great flourishing in the seventeenth century—was now nearing its completion. Natural science was approaching its final and completed state for really major innovations and discoveries—be it abruptly or asymptotically. From the teacher of Planck in the 1870's to the teacher of Birge in the first decade of the present century, a substantial group among those working physicists who thought about the issue at all took the view that the potential range of physical knowledge is finite, and moreover held—with such notable exceptions as George Gore—that the proportion of the known to the unknown sector of this finite range was seen as relatively large.

One aspect of this phenomenon warrants note: The predominant ethos of science during the closing quarter of the last century was one of success and self-congratulation—decidedly not of failure. To speak of a *fin de siècle* spirit seems to imply a sentiment of let-down, weariness, exhaustion, failure of nerve, perhaps even feelings of impotence. This was by no means the case in the present connection. The dominant sentiment in metascientific theory was one of elation, of pride in the face of immense strides—feelings of a power approaching *hubris* that the intellectual conquest of nature was virtually complete.[13]

This sort of view resonates sympathetically to fundamental facets of the human condition. It reflects the natural tendency of a mortal creature to revert to the melancholy thought that all good things must come to an end. With the 20–20 vision of hindsight we clearly see how absurdly premature this view in fact was. But that does not alter the fact that this belief, given the situation of the day, was far from being wildly unreasonable at that time, and was actually rather plausible in the mid-1890's. For what we now call "classical" physics had indeed reached something like a definitive state. The discoveries that marked the close of this period—the experiments on electrical discharges in gasses, the experiments to measure the "ether drift" caused by the motion of the earth, and the discovery of Roentgen rays and radioactivity—were just getting underway. It was these researches which were to provide the wholly new data and methods that rapidly produced a total reconstruction of the basic concepts for understanding the physical world. As matters stood, the *fin de siècle* view was, not without reason, seriously adopted by many of the best scientific minds of the day.

2. THE MID-CENTURY ETHOS OF LIMITLESS PROGRESS

The *fin de siècle* spirit was a transient phenomenon. As Rutherford's teacher, J. J. Thomson already observed in his presidential address to the British Association in 1909:

> The new discoveries made in physics in the last few years, and the ideas and potentialities suggested by them, have had an effect upon the workers in that subject akin to that produced in literature by the Renaissance. Enthusiasm has been quickened, and there is a hopeful, youthful, perhaps exuberant, spirit abroad which leads

[13] Thus for Ostwald the "progress in discovery we experience anew from day to day . . . affords a guarantee that in the course of time one wish after another will be satisfied and one possibility after another will be realized, so that science will approach the ideal of omnipotence with rapid steps." (Wilhelm Ostwald, *Die Wissenschaft* [Leipzig, 1911], p. 47.) Compare the following passage from a well-known textbook: "All branches of theoretical physics, with the exception of electricity and magnetism, can be regarded at the present state of science as concluded, that is, only immaterial changes occur in them from year to year" (Charles Emerson Curry, *Theory of Electricity and Magnetism* [New York and London, 1897], p. 1). (I owe this reference to Martin Curd.)

men to make with confidence experiments which would have been thought fantastic twenty years ago. It has quite dispelled the pessimistic feeling, not uncommon at that time, that all the interesting things had been discovered, and all that was left was to alter a decimal or two in some physical constant. There never was any justification for this feeling, there never were any signs of an approach to finality in science. The sum of knowledge is at present, at any rate, a diverging not a converging series.[14]

Beginning in the first decade of the twentieth century, the outlook on the prospects of the physical sciences changed dramatically, and soon a wholly new outlook prevailed. The reason for this change of view is all too plain when one looks down the list of the Nobel Prize-winners in physics during the era from Röntgen to Yukawa.[15] The revolution wrought by these men in our understanding of nature was so massive that their names became household words throughout the scientifically literate world. Nor was progress confined to the sphere of theory. By the end of World War II, physics had reached awesome heights of technological impact in the atom bomb and the prospects of peaceful uses of nuclear power that lay just around the corner. Given all this, it was inevitable that a drastic alteration in informed views of the prospects of science should have come about. By the 1920's this phenomenon was well under way, and it reached its hey-day in the years immediately following World War II.

The destruction of the classical "Newtonian" world-view was— curiously enough—seen by one acute contemporary observer (Oswald Spengler) not as a new beginning but as an omen of termination; not as a sign that physical science was entering upon new open vistas of major progress, but as an indication that physics was entering its last and final phase:

Western physics is drawing near to the limit of its possibilities. . . . This is the origin of the sudden and annihilating doubt that has arisen about things that even yesterday were the unchallenged

[14] J. J. Thomson, "Presidential Address to the British Association," *British Association for the Advancement of Science, Report, 1909*, p. 29.

[15] Röntgen (1901), Lorentz and Zeeman (1902), Becquerel and the Curies (1903), J. J. Thomson (1906), Michelson (1907), von Laue (1914), W. H. and W. L. Bragg (1915), Planck (1918), Einstein (1921), Bohr (1922), Heisenberg (1932), Dirac and Schrödinger (1933), Fermi (1938), Pauli (1945), Yukawa (1949).

foundation of physical theory, about the meaning of the energy-principle, the concepts of mass, space, absolute time, and causality-laws generally. . . . If we . . . observe how rapidly card-houses of hypothesis are run up nowadays, every contradiction being immediately covered up by a new hurried hypothesis; if we reflect on how little heed is paid to the fact that these images contradict one another and the "classical" Baroque mechanics alike, we cannot but realize that the *great style of ideation is at an end* and that, as in architecture and the arts of form, a sort of craft-art of hypothesis-building has taken its place. Only our extreme mastery in experimental technique—true child of its century—hides the collapse of the symbolism.[16]

Spengler goes on to draw a rather apocalyptic conclusion:

In this very century, I prophesy, the century of scientific-critical Alexandrianism, of the great harvests, of the final formulations, a new element of inwardness will arise to overthrow the will-to-victory of science. Exact science must presently fall upon its own keen sword.[17]

But the advance of science towards new triumphs of explanatory and experimental success was so massive that Spenglerian scepticism could not be sustained. The inter-war years saw the development of a new ethos—not of *fin de siècle* finality, not of Spenglerian *Götterdämmerung*, but of immense hopefulness in the prospects of ongoing discovery and innovation.

Thus by the end of World War II a totally different vision of the future prospects of science was in possession of the field. In surveying the concept of scientific progress in 1945, one perceptive observer wrote:

The modern scientist looks upon science as a great building erected stone by stone through the work of his predecessors and his contemporary fellow-scientists, a structure that will be continued but never completed by his successors.[18]

---

[16] Oswald Spengler, *The Decline of the West* (Munich, 1918; U.S. edition; New York, 1926), pp. 417–420.

[17] *Ibid.*, p. 424.

[18] Edgar Zilsel, *op. cit.* (p. 5), p. 325.

Given all that had transpired in the interim, the *fin de siècle* view of two generations before seemed ludicrously naive from the vantage point of a mid-century perspective.[19] As the twentieth century progressed, a new view became firmly entrenched, a vision of unending progress—and progress at an uncompromisingly rapid pace.

One of the clearest and most notable spokesmen of the new attitude was Dr. Vannevar Busch, longtime President of the Carnegie Institution of Washington and Chairman of the U.S. National Defense Research Committee during World War II. His epoch-making 1945 report to the President—a document that was to lay the blueprint for the massive post-war thrust of U.S. governmental support for scientific research and education—typified the new outlook in its very title: *Science: The Endless Frontier*.[20] In the wake of the extremely successful wartime application of science—following hard upon the massive progress of science itself in the inter-war period—it was only too tempting to see a straight road of unending scientific progress stretching ahead.

The historical situation may be summarized in graphic form. It is tempting to define a ratio (ρ) of relative informedness along the following lines:

$$\rho = \text{extent of perceived knowledge} \div \text{extent of perceived ignorance}$$

This ratio reflects a key facet of the intellectual *Weltanschauung* of an era with respect to the current state of knowledge regarding the natural world. The historical situation with respect to this parameter is sketched

[19] Compare the situation in technology:

In periods of depression the voices of prophets of technological stagnation were usually listened to with greater attention, and repeatedly over the last hundred years persons recognized as authorities at the time told the world that all important inventions had already been made and no further inventions of great import could be expected. Such pessimistic predictions of the future of technological exploration look particularly comical to a reader who has the advantage of hindsight: for they were made before the automotive, electrical, radio-magnetic, and nuclear revolutions of technology had occurred. Thus the predictions were surely wrong at the time they were made. There is little inclination to accept such predictions as correct at the present. (Fritz Machlup, "The Supply of Inventors and Inventions," *Weltwirtschaftliches Archiv*, vol. 85 (1960), pp. 210–252 [see pp. 237–238]. Cf. E. Jantsch, *Technological Forecasting in Perspective* [Paris, 1967; OECD Publications].)

[20] Washington, D.C. (U.S. Government Printing Office), 1945. Regarding the influence of this document see D. K. Price, *The Scientific Estate* (Cambridge, Mass., 1967), pp. 2–3. See also Vannevar Busch, *Endless Horizons* (Washington, D.C., 1946), esp. the final chapter, "The Builders," which eloquently develops the image of the construction of a building of unending proportions.

in Figure 1. It yields no one definite trend or tendency, but a roller-coaster of violent fluctuations.

Figure 1

THE CONTEMPORARY ASSESSMENT
OF SCIENTIFIC COMPLETENESS

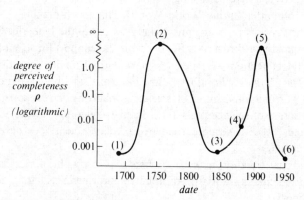

(1) Newton, 1675 (see p. 14)
(2) Kant and Diderot, ca. 1775 (see pp. 8–9)
(3) Macaulay, 1836 and Baden Powell, 1855 (see p. 17)
(4) Gore, 1878 (see pp. 18–19)
(5) The *fin de siècle* school (see pp. 24–26)
(6) Mid-twentieth century optimism (see pp. 26–29)

Note ρ = extent of perceived knowledge ÷ extent of perceived ignorance

---

3. *FIN DE SIECLE* AGAIN: THE NOBEL SYNDROME AND THE ESCHATOLOGY OF
SCIENTIFIC PROGRESS

The euphoric vision of endless vistas of scientific progress along limitless horizons which opened up with the great burst of turn-of-the-century innovation in physics was short lived, lasting for around fifty years (say from the end of the 1900's to that of the 1950's). In mooting the future prospects of scientific progress in a retrospective mood, one acute recent commentator has written:

If possible barriers to scientific inquiry loom on the horizons today, it would not be because science is finished, but rather because it could not (in some specific instance) go any further. It is not definitive; it is just as tentative as ever. Even statements about barriers will be tentative, hypothetical. What has happened is simply that the feeling of unlimited horizons characteristic of the earlier part of our century is being succeeded by a more hardheaded look at the actual prospects.[21]

What has the upshot of this hardheaded look been? For over the past decade now, a new, muted tone of voice has sounded in these discussions, and the pendulum of current thinking has swung back towards the *fin de siècle* view. Recent winners of the Nobel Prize have afforded particularly prominent examples of this persuasion.

The opening gun on the new spirit of doubtfulness and loss of élan was sounded by a lyric and poignant paper on "The Limits of Science" published in 1950 by the Princeton physicist Eugene P. Wigner (Nobel laureate in Physics for 1963).

> Can we see even today signals of the crisis in science? Perhaps. The difficulty in penetrating to the frontiers of physics has been mentioned before. It is already so serious for the average human mind that only a negligible fraction of our contemporaries really feels the force of the arguments of quantum and relativity theories. . . . The clearest sign of the growing realization that the capacity of our intellect limits the volume of science is the number of queries which we hear every day, whether this or that piece of research "is worth doing." . . . It is depressing for every scientist and for every person to have to conclude that his principal motive, or that of his epoch, is not here to stay. However, humanity's goals and ideals have shifted already several times during our known history. In addition, it must fill us with pride to believe that we are living in the heroic age of science, in the epoch in which the individual's abstract knowledge of nature, and, we may hope, also of himself, is increasing more rapidly and perhaps to a higher level than it ever has before or will afterwards. It is uncomfortable to believe that our ideals may pass as the Round Table's illusions disappeared.[22]

[21] Ernan McMullin, "The Limits of Scientific Enquiry" in *Science and the Modern World*, ed. by J. Steinhardt (New York, 1968), p. 68.

[22] Eugene P. Wigner, "The Limits of Science," *Proceedings of the American Philosophical Society*, vol. 94 (1950), pp. 422–427.

The eminent Australian immunologist Sir MacFarlane Burnet (Nobel laureate in Medicine, 1960) after surveying work in many areas of science—with special attention to the biological sciences, wrote: "I believe that in all the major sciences the general picture has been completed and in broad outline completely delineated by 1970."[23] With respect to his own speciality in particular, Burnet writes:

After working for a year on the present book I cannot avoid the conclusion that we have reached the stage in 1971 when little further advance can be expected from laboratory science in the handling of the 'intrinsic' types of disability and disease. There will always be possibilities of improvement in detail but I am specially impressed by the fact that since 1957 there has been no new thought on the handling of cancer, of old age, or of auto-immune disease. The only real novelty has been kidney transplantation. . . . None of my juniors seems to be worried as I am, that the contribution of laboratory science to medicine has virtually come to an end. The biomedical sciences all continue to provide fascinating employment for those active in research, and sometimes enthralling reading for those like me who are no longer at the bench but can still appreciate a fine piece of work. But the detail of an RNA phage's chemical structure, the place of cyclostomes in the evolution of immunity or the production of antibody in test-tubes are typical of today's topics in biological research. Almost none of modern basic research in the medical sciences has any direct or indirect bearing on the prevention of disease or on the improvement of the medical care.

A more widely based and disturbing opinion about the laboratory sciences themselves quite apart from their bearing on medicine has been voiced by two near contemporaries of mine, Gunther Stent and Niels Jerne, both of them distinguished experimentalists. They feel that both biological and physical science may have passed the era of the great discoveries. I have to agree with them and can quote a statement I made elsewhere, that future historians may speak of an age of scientific discovery that started with Galileo in 1586 and ended something less than four hundred years later. If one looks at the volume of competent scientific work being produced in all fields in 1971, that statement may seem utter nonsense. There is more than ever before and the general technical competence with which the experimental work

[23] *Genes, Dreams, and Realities* (New York, 1970), p. 219.

has been done is higher than ever. But the new discovery when it comes usually has an air of triviality for anyone not actually working in the field in which it has been made. Compared to the great days of the 1930s for particle physics or the 1950s for molecular biology, the late 1960's were not very productive.[24]

And again Richard Feynman, the American 1965 Nobel physics laureate who is by any reckoning among the best physicists of the day, has written as follows:

What of the future of this adventure? What will happen ultimately? We are going along guessing the laws; how many laws are we going to have to guess? I do not know. Some of my colleagues say that this fundamental aspect of our science will go on; but I think there will certainly not be perpetual novelty, say for a thousand years. This thing cannot keep on going so that we are always going to discover more and more new laws. . . . We are very lucky to live in an age in which we are still making discoveries. It is like the discovery of America—you only discover it once. The age in which we live is the age in which we are discovering the fundamental laws of nature, and that day will never come again. It is very exciting, it is marvellous, but this excitement will have to go. Of course in the future there will be other interests . . . but there will not still be the same things that we are doing now. . . . There will be a degeneration of ideas, just like the degeneration that great explorers feel is occurring when tourists begin moving in on a territory. In this [present] age people are [perhaps for the last time?!] experiencing a delight, the tremendous delight that you get when you guess how nature will work in a situation never seen before.[25]

This perception is by no means confined to Nobel laureates, but has gradually become prevalent among a much wider range of students of contemporary science, as such passages as the following attest:

I am not about to claim that scientific enquiry is nearing its end. . . . My aim is a modest one really: to argue that some limits on the future progress of scientific enquiry are possible, and certain

[24] *Ibid.*, pp. 217–219.
[25] Richard Feynman, *The Character of Physical Law* (Cambridge, Mass. and London, 1965), pp. 172–173.

among them probable. The aim is modest, yet if it be achieved, it would challenge one of the most pervasive convictions of twentieth century man: that the progress of science is likely to remain the steady and inevitable affair it seems recently to have become.[26]

Or again:

If we note carefully the dates of these major . . . scientific breakthroughs of the twentieth century, we will immediately discover their tendency to localize in the first thirty years of the century. In fact it would appear that the basic techniques—the fundamentally new ideas . . . were born and nourished in the years 1900–1925, and that we, the beneficiaries of these new discoveries and developments, have been living off the original ideas of a previous age.[27]

Sentiments of this sort abound in the recent literature and can be cited from writers of virtually every level of scientific sophistication.

One particularly interesting and well-developed statement is that of the biologist Gunther S. Stent, *The Coming of the Golden Age: A View of the End of Progress*. The following quotation will convey the flavor of Stent's fascinating book:

I want to consider what I believe to be intrinsic limits to the sciences, limits to the accumulation of meaningful statements about the events of the outer world. I think everyone will readily agree that there are *some* scientific disciplines which, by reason of the phenomena to which they purport to address themselves, are *bounded*. Geography, for instance, is bounded because its goal of describing the features of the Earth is clearly limited. . . . And, as I hope to have shown in the preceding chapters, genetics is not only bounded, but its goal of understanding the mechanism of transmission of hereditary information *has*, in fact, been all but

---

[26] Ernan McMullin, *op. cit.*, pp. 35–84 (see pp. 37–38).
[27] George J. Seidel, *The Crisis of Creativity* (Notre Dame and London, 1966), p. 3. Compare:

The most satisfactory way to assess "quality" [in scientific work] would be if we could measure the rate of progress in the understanding of the subject. Have there been vastly more "break-throughs" in recent years? I see nothing to suggest anything other than a fall-off in the appearance of work of this exceptionally high quality in many fields of science. (Kenneth Mellanby, "The Disorganization of Scientific Research," *Minerva*, vol. 12 [1974], pp. 67–82 [see p. 73].)

reached.... [To be sure] the domain of investigation of a bounded scientific discipline may well present a vast and practically inexhaustible number of events for study. But the discipline is bounded all the same because its goal is in view. ... There is at least one scientific discipline, however, which appears to be *open-ended*, namely physics, or the science of matter. ... But even though physics is, in principle, open-ended, it too can be expected to encounter limitations in practice ... [for] there are purely physical limits to physics because of man's own boundaries of time and energy. These limits render forever impossible research projects that involve observing events in regions of the universe more than ten or fifteen billion light-years distant, traveling very far beyond the domain of our solar system, or generating particles with kinetic energies approaching those of highly energetic cosmic rays.[28]

Bentley Glass made newspaper headlines in December 1970 with his presidential address to the Chicago meeting of the American Association for the Advancement of Science, posing the question "Are there finite limits to scientific understanding, or are there endless horizons?"[29] His answer ran as follows:

What remains to be learned may indeed dwarf imagination. Nevertheless, the universe itself is closed and finite. ... The uniformity of nature and the general applicability of natural laws set limits to knowledge. If there are just 100, or 105, or 110 ways in which atoms may form, then when one has identified the full range of properties of these, singly and in combination, chemical

---

[28] Gunther S. Stent, *The Coming of the Golden Age* (Garden City, 1969), pp. 111–113. One notable exception to this view is that of the eminent Russian physicist Peter Kapitsa. After surveying various fundamental discoveries of the past he writes:

If we honestly extrapolate this curve we see it does not have any tendency towards saturation and that in the very near future many more such discoveries, which give us the possibility of increasing our control over nature and put new strength in our hands, will be made. Subjectively, it seems that we know all there is to know about nature. However, when we read the works of scientists of the Newtonian era we see that they felt precisely the same. We can, therefore, be sure that further discoveries must still be made. ("The Future Problems of Science," in M. Goldsmith and A. Mackay [ed's], *The Science of Science* [London, 1964], pp. 102–113 [see pp. 105–106].)

This reflects standard, "party-line" thinking in the U.S.S.R. See pp. 123–131 below, and also see footnote 33.

[29] Bentley Glass, "Science: Endless Horizons or Golden Age?", *Science*, vol. 171 (1971), pp. 23–29.

knowledge will be complete. There is a finite number of species of plants and of animals—even of insects—upon the earth. We are as yet far from knowing all about the genetics, structure and physiology, or behavior of even a single one of them. Nevertheless, a total knowledge of all life forms is only about 2×10^6 times the potential knowledge about any one of them. Moreover, the universality of the genetic code, the common character of proteins in different species, the generality of cellular structure and cellular reproduction, the basic similarity of energy metabolism in all species and of photosynthesis in green plants and bacteria, and the universal evolution of living forms through mutation and natural selection all lead inescapably to a conclusion that, although diversity may be great, the laws of life, based on similarities, are finite in number and comprehensible to us in the main even now. We are like the explorers of a great continent who have penetrated to its margins in most points of the compass and have mapped the major mountain chains and rivers. There are still innumerable details to fill in, but the endless horizons no longer exist.[30]

Again, in a fascinating 1974 article on "The Universe as Home for Man" the physicist John Archibald Wheeler interestingly deploys the image of balance-scale that weighs past and future discoveries:

Hang up a balance with its two pans. Into one load all the captured insights of the last five centuries. . . . Look into the other scalepan, now quite empty, and ask what will be laid upon it in the next 500 years. Are the riches that we see and celebrate in the one pan only the prelude to still greater prizes to pile up in the other in the next five centuries? Or are the discoveries yet to come destined to be secondary? . . . Have we seen the last of the great revolutions in our view of man and the universe? If more than three-fourths of all the investigators who ever lived are now alive, are they and their successors to achieve nothing more than extensions and applications of what we already know?[31]

Wheeler, like Glass (and George Gore before them), sees science as an inherently *finite* enterprise, albeit one which—like an iceberg—

---

[30] *Ibid.*, p. 24.
[31] John Archibald Wheeler, "The Universe as Home for Man," *American Scientist*, vol. 62 (1974), pp. 683–691 (see p. 683).

is such that the part open to present vision is by far the smaller.[32]

As one reads these discussions one gets the strange *déjà-vu* feeling of having seen it all before. Wheeler and Glass echo George Gore's view of a vast but ultimately finite potential for scientific discovery—albeit one that is at present only partly exhausted. And the whole cycle of the *fin de siècle* drama is being replayed in what has the appearance of something akin to a conspiracy of pessimism in agreement on the end-to-science thesis—with Nobel prize winners in the forefront. The same range of positions is once again maintained. Wigner—like du Bois-Reymond before him—holds a theory of Capacity Exhaustion: man's intellect is limited in ways that will block his access to intrinsically available findings. Feynman (like Haeckel) holds to a theory of Nature Exhaustion: the whole gamut of the secrets of nature is rapidly being uncovered. All these views agree in envisaging the approaching end of the scientific adventure. Indeed, this view seems at present (i.e., in the mid-1970's) to have become an integral part of a more pervasive and widely diffused end-to-growth ethos.[33] Our present discussion has as its prime aim the provision of an antidote to this currently pervasive tendency of thought.

[32] Wheeler writes:

The discoveries of the future will outnumber those of the past, we can believe, because of the pace of today's science, the tools, and the pressure, but will they be greater? Nothing so much encourages an affirmative answer as the mysteries encountered wherever we turn. (John Archibald Wheeler, "The Universe as Home for Man," *American Scientist*, vol. 62 [1974], p. 685.)

[33] It is only fair to say that this is not the whole story—there is currently no monochromatic consensus on the future of science. Thus, David Bohm and Jean-Paul Vigier (whose views will be examined in the next chapter) see its progress as unendingly probing more and more fundamental depths of nature. Above all, among communist theoreticians a view of unending scientific progress—along the lines of Vannevar Busch's endless frontier theory—is virtually dogma. (Compare Section 5 of Chapter VII on pp. 123–131 below.)

III

The Potential Limitlessness of Science

Lex posterior derogat priori *("The later law abrogates the earlier.")*

ROMAN LEGAL PRECEPT

Die durchschnittliche Lebensdauer einer physiologischen Wahrheit ist drei bis vier Jahre *("The average lifespan of a physiological truth is three or four years.")*

RUDOLPH LOTZE

1. THE DISPENSABILITY OF COSMIC LIMITLESSNESS

What assumptions are needed to establish a thesis of *potentially unending progress* for science along the lines envisioned in the preceding chapters? What view of nature—and of inquiry into it—will entail limitless horizons for scientific discovery? Let us begin by critically canvassing some current thought on this issue.

To underwrite the prospect of endless scientific progress some theorists have felt compelled to stipulate an intrinsic infinitude in the structural make-up of nature itself.[1] They have presupposed the quantitative or the qualitative infinity of nature by postulating either a principle of unending intricacy or of unending orders of spatio-structural nesting.

This approach takes various forms. The most usual of these proceeds via the suggestion that the range of natural laws is inexhaustible because of an unending ramification of levels in the physico-spatial structure of the world. Such a theory of limitless intricacy inclines towards the

---

[1] Marxist theoreticians take this view very literally—in the manner of Lenin's idea of the "inexhaustibility" of matter in *Materialism and Empirico-Criticism*. Purporting to inherit from Spinoza a thesis of the infinity of nature, they construe this to mean that any cosmology which denies the infinite spatial extension of the universe must be wrong.

musings of Pascal that nature might be an endless nest of Chinese boxes, with microscopic worlds within ever more minute microcosms—an infinite contraction towards the small. On such a Pascalian view, the endless progress of science is assured by the unending prospect of unlocking one world within another.[2]

Sometimes this view of a downwards-moving scaling sequence towards the submicroscopic small is replaced by an upwards-moving scaling sequence towards the transtelescopic large. Consider, for example, the following train of ideas:

> Even within the purely physical realm there are natural properties that are significant on one level of organization but then disappear on another. Nuclear forces, for example, which are all-important between the protons and neutrons that make up an atomic nucleus, have no role whatsoever over somewhat larger distances, not even, for example, between two neighboring atoms in the crystal lattice of a solid. Gravitation, in contrast, is trivial in intensity within the nucleus, or between the electrons and nucleus of an atom, but becomes a dominating force between masses of many, many billions of atoms. It does not at all seem implausible that in the organization of the highly complex structures of living organisms, new natural properties should appear, properties which cannot be reduced to those present among non-animate systems of atoms or

---

[2] The French physicist Jean-Paul Vigier, for example, has revived this idea of Pascal's along Hegelian lines, arguing as follows:

We would prefer to say that at all levels of Nature you have a mixture of causal and statistical laws (which come from deeper or external processes). As you progress from one level to another you get new qualitative laws. Causal laws at one level can result from averages of statistical behaviour at a deeper level, which in turn can be explained by deeper causal behaviour, and so on *ad infinitum*. If you then admit that Nature is infinitely complex and that in consequence no final state of knowledge can be reached, you see that at any stage of scientific knowledge causal and probability laws are necessary to describe the behaviour of any phenomenon, and that any phenomenon is a combination of causal and random properties inextricably woven with one another. All things in Nature then appear as a dialectical synthesis of the infinitely complex motions of matter out of which they surge and grow and into which they finally are bound to disappear. ("The Concept of Probability in the Frame of the Probabilistic and the Causal Interpretation of Quantum Mechanics" in *Observation and Interpretation*, ed. by S. Körner [New York and London, 1957], pp. 71–77; see p. 77.)

The idea of a succession of "layers of depth" in the analysis of nature, each giving rise to its own characteristic body of laws in such a way that each of these law-manifolds is more encompassing than its predecessors and that their successive discovery represents a sequentially deeper penetration of the structure of nature is not peculiar to Vigier. (It was, so far as I know, first mooted in contemporary physics in E. P. Wigner, "The Limits of Science," *Proceedings of the American Philosophical Society*, vol. 94 [1950], pp. 422–27.)

molecules. There might be characteristic forces or modes of organization for systems which are able to reproduce them-selves. . . .[3]

Along this line of thought one might project an ascending sequence: sub-atomic particles, atoms, molecules, organic microorganisms, animals, populations, life-systems, planets, galaxies, etc., each with their own characteristic modes of operation—arranged in a steadily ascending sequence of larger orders of scale, emplacing macroscopic worlds within ever more macroscopic ones. Or again, even if one remains at a fixed level of scale in physical magnitude, one can have rearrangements of items, and rearrangements of rearrangements, and rearrangements of rearrangements of rearrangements, *ad indefinitum*, with emergent lawful characteristics arising at every stage. Think of the examples of letters/words/sentences/paragraphs/books/book-families (novels, reference books, etc.)/libraries/library systems. In such a setting, there are elements, complexes of elements, complexes of complexes of elements, etc.—each level structured giving rise to its own characteristic principles of organization, which are unpredictable from the standpoint of the other levels.[4]

But is it really necessary to maintain the structural infinitude of nature in order to underwrite the prospect of unending scientific progress? The answer is surely negative. After all, the prime task of science lies in discovering the *laws of nature*.[5] And even a mechanism of finitely complex make-up can have endlessly complex laws of operation. The workings of structurally finite and indeed simple system can yet exhibit a finite intricacy in *functional complexity*, exhibiting this limitless complexity at the *operational* or functional—rather than at the spatio-structural or compositional—level. And this sort of operational complexity would be quite enough to underwrite the limitlessness of

[3] Richard Schlegel, *Inquiry into Science* (Garden City, 1972), p. 70.

[4] For an interesting and suggestive analysis of "the architecture of complexity" see Herbert A. Simon, *The Science of the Artificial* (Cambridge, Mass., 1969).

[5] The idea of the "infinite complexity of nature" must in this context be construed with reference to the laws of nature, not its phenomena. For as William Kneale has quite rightly argued:

> If by the "infinite complexity of nature" is meant only the infinite multiplicity of the *phenomena* it contains, there is no bar to final success in theory making, since theories are not concerned with particulars as such. So too, if what is meant is only the infinite variety of natural phenomena . . . that too may be comprehended in a unitary theory." ("Scientific Revolutions for Ever?", *British Journal for the Philosophy of Science*, vol. 19 [1967], pp. 27–42 [see p. 1].)

prospective scientific discovery regarding the behavioral laws of even a system whose physical make-up is extremely simple. (For a useful analogy, think of the theory of chess.) And so structural infinitude becomes irrelevant.

We need not worry ourselves about establishing the structural infinity of nature as a descriptive fact about the ontological make-up of the world in order to warrant the prospect of endless progress in scientific inquiry.

The physicist David Bohm has written:

> The main point of science is not so much to make a summary of the things one knows, but rather to find those laws which are essential and which therefore hold in new domains and predict new facts. . . . Generally speaking, by finding the unity behind the diversity, one will get laws which contain more than the original facts. And here the infinity of nature comes in: the whole scientific method implies that no theory is final. It is always possible there is something that one has missed. At least as a working hypothesis science assumes the infinity of nature; and this assumption fits the facts much better than any other point of view that we know.[6]

But is such a "working hypothesis" of the infinitude of nature really needed to assure the prospect of nonterminating progress in science? Certainly not. Consider the following example:

We shall assume a system two of whose determinative parameters, p and q, are correlated in a functional interrelationship of some sort:

$$f(p) \approx q$$

Let it be that it is in principle impossible to determine q-values directly: one must obtain them obliquely from the relationship f via a prior determination of p. Moreover, the relationship f is to be such that whenever we can determine suitable facets of the comportment of p during time-intervals down to the size d, then this only determines the *average* value of q during these intervals.

---

[6] "Remarks by D. Bohm" in *Observation and Interpretation*, ed. by S. Körner, *op. cit.*, pp. 55–57, see p. 56. For a fuller development of Bohm's views on the "qualitative infinity of nature" see his *Causality and Chance in Modern Physics* (London and New York, 1957).

Thus the system at issue can be very simple indeed; it need contain no complexities apart from those required to assure the preceding assumptions. But endless progress is clearly available. For as *our* capacity to make *p*-determinations down to smaller and smaller values of *d* increases from minutes to seconds to milliseconds to microseconds, etc., we will obtain an increasingly adequate insight into the *modus operandi* of the system and can obtain fuller and fuller information about it. And there is no reason to think that the discoveries to be made as one moves "further down the line" here are of lesser significance than those made early on. Given that the averages at each stage of the example are inferentially independent of one another, the discoveries one makes at each iteration are all major innovations. If the process of data-acquisition is sufficiently complicated, even a simple system can afford the prospect of ongoing discovery.

The crucial fact is that scientific progress hinges not just on the structure of nature but also on the structure of our information about it. But there is no need to assume (as "working hypothesis" or otherwise) that a system is infinitely complex in its physical make-up, as long as we are prepared to envisage an endlessly ongoing prospect of securing fuller information about it. To reiterate: operational not structural complexity is the key.

After all, the "completeness" of science is a function of our interests—a largely homocentric issue.[7] It is a matter of what sorts of things we want to have explained and how our curiosity is oriented. Consider an illustration. One acute analyst of physics has recently written:

> One might be more seriously concerned with the prospect of reaching a stage . . . in which all the basic physics has been learned that is needed to predict the behavior of matter under all the conditions scientists find in the universe or have any reason to create. From chemistry to cosmology, let us suppose, all situations are covered, but one cannot predict with certainty the scattering cross sections for e-neutrinos on μ-neutrinos at 10^{30}eV. Suppose further that the experiments required to explore fully all the physics at 10^{30}eV are inordinately costly and offer no prospect of significantly improving physics below 10^{20}eV, which is already known to be sufficiently reliable. If some such state were reached, one might reasonably expect that research in fundamental physics

[7] Cf. Richard Schlegel, *Inquiry into Science, op. cit.*, esp. Chapter 6.

would be at least brought to an indefinite halt if not closed out entirely. . . .[8]

Actually, it seems very doubtful if physicists would in fact rest content with the situation of physics below 10^{20}eV "well in hand" as long as there was a reasonable chance that new physical principles might manifest themselves at higher energies. With the progress of knowledge there comes about both a *displacement of interest* towards the questions newly opened up that now loom larger in our thoughts, and there is also an *escalation of demands* of the new standards apposite in a more sophisticated knowledge situation.[9] Indeed the very concept of an "achieved understanding" is problematic. It bespeaks a regrettably myopic restrictedness of perspective.[10]

With a mixture of admiration and exasperation, Leibniz wrote of the Electress Sophie of Hanover that "*elle veut toujours savoir la raison de la raison.*" In this regard, the princess typified the spirit of inquiry at its best. We want to know things *in depth*, and, once we do so, seek for yet greater depth. These *epistemological* considerations of themselves virtually assure the prospects of an ongoing scientific enterprise.

There is no adequate basis for the view that the search for greater "depth" in our understanding need ever terminate at a logical rock-bottom.[11] Nor need it ever abort for lack of value or interest. E. P. Wigner has mooted the issue in the following terms:

[8] D. A. Bromley, *et al.*, *Physics in Perspective: Student Edition* (Washington, D.C., 1973; National Research Council/National Academy of Sciences Publication), p. 26.

[9] As the writer of the preceding passage very sagely goes on to remark:

Even if the physicist could reliably and accurately describe any elementary interaction in which a chemist or an astronomer might be interested, the task of physics would not be finished. Man's curiosity would not be satisfied. Some of the most profound questions physics has faced would remain to be answered, if understanding of the pattern of order found in the universe is ever to be achieved. (*Ibid.*, p. 27.)

[10] Stephen Toulmin's strictures are well-deserved:

[T]he claim of some classical physicists, that they had the explanations of everything in principle in their grasp, was peculiarly distasteful. For what was repugnant was not just the fact that the theories advanced were so bare and mechanical but, quite as much, the fact that their idea of what it would be to have explained everything was so much smaller than life. (*The Philosophy of Science* [London and New York 1953], p. 117.)

[11] Compare D. A. Bromley's observation:

Even if physicists could be sure that they had identified all the particles that can exist, some obviously fundamental questions would remain. Why, for instance, does a certain universal ratio in atomic physics have the particular value 137.036 and not some other value? This is an experimental result; the precision of the experiments extends today to these six figures. Among other things, this number relates the extent or size of the electron to the size of the atom, and that in turn to the wavelength of light emitted. From astronomical observation it is

The question now comes up whether science will at least be able to continue the type of shifting growth indefinitely in which the new discipline is deeper than the older one and embraces it at least virtually. The answer is, in my opinion, no, because the shifts in the above sense always involve digging one layer deeper into the "secrets of nature," and involve a longer series of concepts based on the previous ones which are thereby recognized as "mere approximation." Thus . . . first ordinary mechanics had to be replaced by quantum mechanics, thus recognizing the approximate nature and limitation of ordinary mechanics to macroscopic phenomena. Then, ordinary mechanics had to be recognized to be inadequate from another point of view and replaced by field theories. Finally, the approximate nature and limitation to small velocities of all of the above concepts had to be uncovered. Thus, relativistic quantum theory is at least four layers deep; it operates with three successive types of concepts all of which are recognized to be inadequate and are replaced by a more profound one in the fourth step. This is, of course, the charm and beauty of the relativistic quantum theory and of all fundamental research in physics. However, it also shows the limits of this type of development. The recognizing of an inadequacy in the concepts of the tenth layer and the replacing of it with the more refined concepts of the eleventh layer will be much less of an event than the discovery of the theory of relativity was.[12]

The prospect posed here is a perfectly possible one. But it does not bear the weight of interpretation placed upon it. There is no reason whatever for viewing the earlier "layers" of physical theory as more important, more interesting, or more valuable. The discovery of the need to reconstrue the concepts of the nth layer in terms of those of the $(n + 1)$st is surely every bit as significant for large as for small values of n. No preestablished harmony—no metaphysical hidden hand—is at work to assure that the *order of discovery* in our penetration of the secrets of

---

known that this fundamental ratio has the same numerical value for atoms a billion years away in space and time. As yet there is no reason to doubt that other fundamental ratios, such as the ratio of the mass of the proton to that of the electron, are as uniform throughout the universe as is the geometrical ratio $\pi = 3 \cdot 14159$. Could it be that such physical ratios are really, like π, mathematical aspects of some underlying logical structure? If so, physicists are not much better off than people who must resort to wrapping a string around a cylinder to determine the value of π! For theoretical physics thus far sheds hardly a glimmer of light on this question. (Bromley, *op. cit.*, p. 28.)

[12] E. P. Wigner, "The Limits of Science," *Proceedings of the American Philosophical Society*, vol. 94 (1950), pp. 422–427 (see pp. 423–424).

nature replicates their *order of importance*, so that later penetrations of the "deeper" layers are always of lower orders of cognitive significance for the constituting of an adequate picture of nature.

2. THE ROLE OF COGNITIVE LIMITS

Science—the cognitive exploration of the ways of the world—is a matter of the *interaction* of the mind with nature. Now the usual recourse to an infinity-of-nature principle is strictly one-sided—it places the burden of responsibility for the endlessness of science solely on the shoulders of nature itself. On its view, the endlessness of scientific progress presupposes limitlessness on the side of its *objects*, so that the infinitude of nature must be postulated at the structural or the functional levels. But this is a mistake.

Nothing can be clearer than that the progress of science is a matter of mind/nature *interaction*—of the *mind's ability to exploit the data to which it gains access* in order to penetrate the "secrets of nature." Accordingly, the question of the progressiveness of science should not be confined to a consideration of nature alone, since the *modus operandi* of data acquisition and of our mind-originated theoretical perspectives are bound to play a crucial part.[13] Innovation on the side of data can generate new theories; new theories can transform the very nature of the old data. This dialectical process of successive feedback has no inherent limits, and suffices of itself to underwrite a prospect of ongoing innovation. Even a finite nature can—like a typewriter with a limited keyboard—produce a steady stream of *new data* ("new" not necessarily in kind but in their functional interrelationships and thus in their theoretical implications), data on the basis of which our knowledge of its operative laws is continually enhanced and deepened. This example of written text may in fact provide the most helpful analogy for the sort of limitlessness of *conceptual* complexity that is at issue with the potential limitlessness of scientific discovery. For example, knowing the occurrence frequencies of the letters A and T in a certain group of texts yields nothing as to the occurrence-frequency of the word AT. As long

---

[13] The idea that our knowledge about the world plies a two-way street, and represents an *interactive* process to which both the subject of knowledge (the world) and the knowing object (the inquiring mind) make essential and ultimately inseparable contributions, is elaborated in the author's *Conceptual Idealism* (Oxford, 1973).

as we proceed to analyze written text in more and more sophisticated detail we can by casting our net sufficiently widely constantly uncover new laws. Throughout we remain in one basic level—that of text—dealing with one single object from various *perspectives of analysis*. But such a view of the infinity of nature construes this infinitude not so much in terms of spatial extensiveness or physical structure as in *conceptual depth*.

Above all, it is important to realize that in this case such "infinitude" as there is lies on the side of the *conceptual machinery of analysis* and not on that of the *object* being analyzed. The complexity of endless hierarchy-levels need not enter in through the structural make-up of nature itself, but merely in the conceptual apparatus being deployed—at ever greater depths of sophistication—for its description and analysis. The case is much as with that of the geometer, whose hierarchy of definitions, axiomatic facts, lemmas, theorems, etc., does not reside in his materials as such, but in the conceptual taxonomy he chooses—for cognitive reasons—to impose on these materials. Nature herself has no "depths"—they are brought upon the scene only by man the knower and are generated subject to the operation of a cognitive perspective. The endless levels at issue will not be *physical* levels, but *levels of consideration* inherent in the activities of inquiring beings.

From this perspective, *an assumption of the quantitative infinity of the physical extent of the natural universe or of the qualitative infinity of its structural complexity is simply not required to provide for the prospects of ongoing scientific progress.*

3. THE ACCRETIONAL MODEL OF SCIENCE AND ITS FLAWS

A discussion of the future of science must come to grips with the accretional model of scientific progress, as is apparent from many of the passages cited in the preceding chapter. The position at issue has been given a clear and eloquent formulation by Gunther S. Stent:

[T]here are *some* scientific disciplines which, by reason of the phenomena to which they purport to address themselves, are *bounded*. Geography, for instance. . . . And, as I hope to have shown . . . genetics is not only bounded, but its goal of understanding the mechanism of transmission of hereditary information *has*, in fact, been all but reached. Indeed, and here I will probably part company with some who might have granted me the preceding example, even such much more broadly conceived scientific taxa as chemistry and biology are also bounded. For in the last analysis, there is immanent in their aim to understand the behavior of molecules and of "living" molecular aggregates a definite, circumscribed goal. Thus, though the total number of possible chemical molecules is very great and the variety of reactions they can undergo vast, the goal of chemistry of understanding the principles governing the behavior of such molecules is, like the goal of geography, clearly limited. As far as biology is concerned, I [have] tried to show . . . that there now seem to remain only three deep problems yet to be solved: the origin of life, the mechanism of cellular differentiation, and the functional basis of the higher nervous system. . . . [T]here is immanent in the evolution of a bounded scientific discipline a point of diminishing returns; after the great insights have been made and brought the discipline close to its goal, further efforts are necessarily of ever-decreasing significance.[14]

This seemingly plausible analogy of geographic exploration is nevertheless fundamentally mistaken. It views scientific progress as a whole on the basis of one particular (and by no means typical) *sort* of progress, namely the sequential filling-in in greater and greater detail of the positions of certain fixed classificatory pigeon-holes—the working out of more decimal places to lend additional refinement to a fundamentally fixed result. Scientific inquiry is conceived of on analogy with terrestrial exploration, whose results—viz., geography—yield results of continually smaller significance, since what is at issue is the filling-in of ever more minute gaps in our information. It is envisaged that the later problems are always on a smaller and smaller scale, and descend to more and more fine-grained level of detail. We have here an *accretional* view of the progress of science, subject to the idea that each successive accretion inevitably makes a relatively smaller contribution to what has already come to hand. Progress, on this view, consists in driving questions down to a lesser and lesser magnitude, continually decreasing their inherent significance. (This at bottom is the Peircean vision of ultimate convergence in scientific inquiry—and the Kuhnian picture of "normal science.")

[14] *The Coming of the Golden Age* (Garden City, 1969), pp. 111–112.

Such a picture combines two gravely mistaken ideas: (1) that the progress of science proceeds by way of cumulative accretion (like the growth of a coral reef), and (2) that the magnitude of these additions is steadily decreasing. If the former of these collapses so does the position as a whole. And collapse it does. For science progresses not additively but largely subtractively. Today's major discoveries represent an overthrow of yesterday's: the big findings of science, it would appear, inevitably contradict its earlier big findings (in the absence of "saving qualifications"). Significant scientific progress is generally a matter not of adding further facts—on the order of filling in of a crossword puzzle—but of changing the framework itself. Substantial headway is made preeminently by conceptual and theoretical innovation. It will not serve to take the preservationist stance that the old views were acceptable as far as they went and merely need supplementation— significant scientific progress is genuinely revolutionary in that there is a *fundamental change of mind* as to how things happen in the world.

Theorists of scientific method of an older school were deeply committed to the view that science is cumulative, and indeed tended to regard the progressiveness of science in terms of its cumulativeness.[15] But in recent decades this view has come under increasingly sharp attack—and rightly so. The medicine of Pasteur and Lister does not add to that of Galen or of Paracelsus, but *replaces* them. The problems solved by one theory may be left unsolved (nay, even unraisable) by its successors. Relativity brushes aside questions regarding the fine structure of the electromagnetic aether (as investigated by Kelvin, Larmor, and Boltzmann). Descartes' vortex theory explained why planets moved in the same direction, a fact for which the physics of Newton's *Principia* had no explanation, and so on. Science in the main develops not by way of cumulation but by way of substitution and replacement.[16] And its progress lies not in a monotonic accretion of

---

[15] See, for example, George Sarton, *The Study of the History of Science* (Cambridge, Mass., 1936), esp. p. 5, and *History of Science and the New Humanism* (Cambridge Mass., 1937), esp. pp. 10–11. But William Whewell was already an honorable exception to this rule. (See his *Novum Organon Renovatum* [3rd. ed., London, 1858], Bk. II, Chap. IV, Art. 9.)

[16] This shibboleth of the contemporary philosophy of science is not all that new. Already at the turn of the century, Sir Michael Foster wrote:

The path [of progress in science] may not be always a straight line; there may be swerving to this side and to that; ideas may seem to return again and again to the same point of the intellectual compass; but it will always be found that they have reached a higher level—they have moved, not in a circle, but in a spiral. Moreover, science is not fashioned as is a house, by putting brick to brick, that which is once put remaining as it was put to the end. The growth of

more information, but in superior performance in point of prediction and control over nature.[17] It is gravely mistaken to think of scientific progress on the basis of an accretion-model for the matter is one of constantly rebuilding from the very foundations. And there is no reason to think that this process need ever come to a stop.[18]

Peirce to the contrary notwithstanding,[19] ongoing scientific progress is not a matter of increasing accuracy and pushing in the numbers in our descriptions of nature out to a few more decimal places. Theoretical innovation makes our entire earlier picture of natural phenomena look naive—a matter of rough approximation or imperfect understanding. (No recent writer has stressed this aspect of scientific progress more emphatically than K. R. Popper.) Scientific progress, then, is not—or need not be—a matter of increased detail regarding certain *fixed*

---

science is that of a living being. As in the embryo, phase follows phase, and each member or body puts on in succession different appearances, though all the while the same member, so a scientific conception of one age seems to differ from that of a following age.... ("The Growth of Science in the Nineteenth Century," *Annual Report of the Smithsonian Institution For 1899* [Washington, 1901], pp. 163–183 [as reprinted from Foster's 1899 presidential address to the British Association for the Advancement of Science]; see p. 175.)

[17] A detailed exposition and defense of this view is given in the author's *Methodological Pragmatism* (Oxford, 1976).

[18] In this regard the position of E. P. Wigner seems altogether right-minded:

... in order to understand a growing body of phenomena, it will be necessary to introduce deeper and deeper concepts into physics and that this development will not end by the discovery of the final and perfect concepts. I believe that this is true: we have no right to expect that our intellect can formulate perfect concepts for the full understanding of inanimate nature's phenomena (*op. cit.*, p. 424).

[19] "When research is of a quantitative nature, the progress of it is marked by the diminution of the probable Error." (Charles Sanders Peirce, *Collected Papers*, Vol. VII, 7.139.) In this regard, Peirce was prejudiced by his long connection with astronomical observations and geodetic surveys into thinking of scientific progress—once a certain stage of qualitative sophistication had been reached—as largely a matter of quantitative refinement. On the geographic exploration model advance is now a matter of steadily filling in gaps of continually smaller and smaller magnitude. And given the scale-diminution of later findings, they could not possibly match the earlier ones in intrinsic importance:

[A]s the investigation goes on, additions to our knowledge ... are of less and less worth. Thus, when chemistry sprang into being, Dr. Wollaston, with a few test tubes and phials on a tea-tray, was able to make new discoveries of the greatest moment. In our day, a thousand chemists, with the most elaborate appliances, are not able to reach results which are comparable in interest with those early ones. All the sciences exhibit the same phenomenon. ... (*Collected Papers*, vol. VII, 7.144.)

Peirce's espousal of the ultimate-approximation theory of asymptotic development towards a position of final fixity made him the most eloquent and certainly the deepest exponent of the accretion model of scientific knowledge. His theory of knowledge—indeed of truth—in effect carried the implications of the model to their ultimate conclusions.

parameters, but occurs at the much more fundamental level of conceptual novelty and innovation. Its key is the deployment of creative imagination on the theoretical plane in devising new explanatory models to accommodate the data that come to hand.

First-rate findings are not immortal—the later replace the earlier, even as with the passing of human generations. This is a point that cannot be emphasized too strongly. Major scientific findings are not only *made* but *abandoned*. But the historian of science must *count* them even when they have vanished from view never to reappear again—like the past milestones of a journey. Once "in the count," they remain forever. It is in this *numerical* sense only that we shall speak of their accumulation in the course of scientific history: the *cumulation* at issue is numerical, and not in any way *contential*.

Some writers find this prospect of science moving through an endless sequence of fundamental revisions unacceptable. Science being a matter of the pursuit of truth, its progress must—they insist— ultimately tend to some definite result. In this Peircean vein, William Kneale has argued as follows:

> There seems to be no good sense in which nature can be said to be so complex as to require perpetual revolution in science. For if by 'the infinite complexity of nature' is meant ... precisely what Bohm and Vigier state as a consequence of the principle, namely that there cannot be a finally satisfactory theory, there is no point in trying to approach such a theory, either by scientific reforms or by scientific revolution. For if there is no truth, there cannot be any approximation to truth, and the whole enterprise of theory-making is futile. Nor does it help to say that there is indeed a true explanatory theory in some Platonic heaven but that it is infinitely complex and so not to be comprehended by men. For if there can be an infinitely complex proposition, it will certainly not be a single explanatory theory in any ordinary sense of that phrase, but at the best an infinite conjunction of explanatory theories. Perhaps we can produce successive approximations to such a conjunction, if there is nothing else to work for, but in that case our best hope of success will be by steady accumulation of the separate items, rather than by perpetual revolution.[20]

[20] "Scientific Revolutions for Ever?", *British Journal for the Philosophy of Science*, vol. 19 (1967), pp. 27–42. Compare the interesting discussion in Robert F. Almeder, "Science and Idealism," *Philosophy of Science*, vol. 40 (1973), pp. 242–254.

But this argument will not bear close scrutiny. For three fundamental elements must be included in the overall picture:

(1) the way things actually work in nature

(2) the (theoretically laden) data we can secure regarding (1)

(3) the further theories we can project on the basis of (2)

Now however much Kneale's strictures may avail against a cosmic or *ontological* infinitude thesis of the sort advocated by Bohm and Vigier, it will not tell against a cognitive or *epistemological* infinitude approach that takes due heed of (2)—as his passage itself strikingly does not. For in taking a constant-revision view of our knowledge of nature, one need not deny the reality of (1), but can merely hold that the data of (2) come (endlessly) in diversified installments in such a way that the theorizing of (3) must constantly be readjusted. It is not that "the truth" is inherently unformulatable (or formulatable only in an "infinitely complex proposition"), but that we may never realize a body of data fully adequate to its theoretical projection. (It is as though there were nonconvergent oscillations as we progress along successive data levels.) A very small-scale effect—even one that lies very far out along the extremes of a "range exploration" in point of temperature, pressure, velocity, or the like—can force a far-reaching revision and have profound impact by way of major theoretical revision. (Think of special relativity in relation to ether-drift experimentation or general relativity in relation to the perihelion of mercury.)

This view does not question the reality of "the truth" in scientific matters, but—far more tritely—questions the adequacy of our information (at any stage of accumulation) to yield what we can confidently and finally claim to be such, if only by way of approximation.[21]

---

[21] The astute Karl Pearson wrote that "They [i.e., the earlier, ultimately corrected findings of science] are what the mathematician would term 'first approximations,' true when we neglect certain small quantities." (*The Grammar of Science*, ed. by E. Nagel [New York, 1957], p. 97.) But this is seldom true in the face of major advances, when entrenched theories are supplanted by discordant rivals. The chemistry of Priestley was in no way a "first approximation" to that of Lavoisier; nor is steady-state cosmology a "first approximation" to that of the big bang.

4. THE PROBLEM SITUATION

The upshot of these deliberations can be summarized as follows: the possibility of continual progress in science does *not* depend on any problematic supposition of the physical or compositional infinitude of nature. It need not rest one-sidedly with nature at all. Moreover, it is certainly *not* necessary to postulate the infinite extendability of human capabilities. (Indeed, it cannot be argued plausibly that even drastic limitations on the side of inquirers will inevitably bring an end to scientific progress in their wake.) The long and short of it is that one need make no intrinsically implausible suppositions on the side either of nature or of man to secure the prospect of ongoing scientific progress. No philosophically desperate expedients are required to make room for the theoretical prospect of unending discoveries in natural science. All that is needed to assure this prospect is the unending enhancement in our investigative instruments and the techniques of their application. Accordingly, there is no adequate warrant for holding—at the level of "general principles" of the matter—that the theory of endless scientific progress is unacceptable because of its dependence upon inherently implausible presuppositions.

But once this point of principle has been made—and it certainly needs making—it becomes necessary to come down from this somewhat ethereal plane of the abstract theoretical possibilities of the matter and to examine its practicalities at the level of realistic prospects. We must explore the conditions and circumstances for actually enacting the theoretically available scenario of unending progress. It is not just a *theoretical possibility* but a *realistic prospect* that science should swiftly and smoothly move from strength to strength in its exploration of "the endless frontier." It is this problem of the "practical politics" of this issue that will occupy us throughout the remainder of the book.

This problem is topical. As we saw in the preceding chapter, the pendulum of thought on this issue has so swung about that we are once more confronted by a widespread revision of views regarding the future prospects of natural science. Disappointment is abroad that the great promise of the first half of the century is not being kept, and there are many indications that scientists are beginning to move back towards a view of the *fin de siècle* type and to envisage an end to scientific progress. The general public is perhaps even more drastically disillusioned. Science and technology have carried man to the moon, but they have left his condition here on earth to continue in a sorry state. Science has produced numerous and rapid changes in the condition of our lives, but many of them do not seem for the better. Disillusionment all too readily leads to disaffection. A great deal of sentiment is abroad that is anti-scientific and even irrationalistic in orientation. And this bodes ill for that degree of public understanding and support which the enterprise of modern science drastically needs in a democratic context. A realistic and dispassionate reappraisal of the future prospects of science is thus very much in order.

IV

The Historic Acceleration of Science: Adams' Law of Exponential Growth

Knowledge begets knowledge as money bears interest.

—A. CONAN DOYLE, *The Great Keinplatz Experiment*

1. ADAMS' LAW

By the end of the nineteenth century no clear-eyed observer could fail to remark the striking pace of scientific advance. But among the first to detail this phenomenon in exact terms—indeed to give it mathematical formulation—was Henry Brooks Adams (1838–1918), the American scholar, historian, and student of cultural affairs. (He was a grandson of John Adams, George Washington's successor as President.) Noting that scientific work increased at a rate fixed by a constant doubling-time—so that science has an *exponential* growth-rate—Adams characterized this circumstance as a "law of acceleration" governing the progress of science. He wrote:

> Laplace would have found it child's play to fix a ratio in the progression in mathematical science between Descartes, Leibnitz, Newton and himself. ... Pending agreement between ... authorities, theory may assume what it likes—say a fifty or even a five-and-twenty year period of reduplication ... for the period matters little once the acceleration itself is admitted.[1]

[1] *The Education of Henry Adams* (Boston, 1918; privately printed already in 1907), chapter 34 (see p. 491). This chapter was written in 1904. The earliest anticipation of Adams' principle of exponential growth that I know of occurs in an *obiter dictum* in the 1901 Presidential Address to the British Association for the Advancement of Science by William Thomson (Lord Kelvin):

Scientific wealth tends to accumulate according to the law of compound interest. Every

Roughly speaking, Adams envisaged science as doubling in size and content with every succeeding half-century, to produce a picture of progress as in Figure 1 on the next page.[2]

Abstracting from this specific periodization of a 50-year doubling period, the general thesis that science develops under compound-interest conditions with the effect of a continually accelerating—indeed an exponential—growth rate may be designated as *Adams' Law*. It amounts to the claim that the *percentage-rate of the per annum increase in the levels of scientific effort and quantitative productivity remains constant with the passage of time*.[3] Adams characterized this principle as "law of acceleration, definite and constant as any law of mechanics [which] cannot be supposed to relax its energy to suit the convenience of man."[4]

---

addition to knowledge of the properties of matter supplies the naturalist with new instrumental means for discovering and interpreting phenomena of nature, which in their turn afford foundations for fresh generalizations. (Reprinted in G. Basalla, William Coleman, and R. H. Kargon [eds.], *Victorian Science: A Self-Portrait Through the Presidential Addresses of the British Association for the Advancement of Science* [New York, 1970], pp. 101–128 [see p. 114], and compare p. 488.)

The idea occurs in embryonic form in A. Conan Doyle's 1894 short story *The Great Keinplatz Experiment*, in whose opening paragraph the professorial protagonist is described as follows:

As ... the worthy professor's stock of knowledge increased—for knowledge begets knowledge as money bears interest—much which had seemed strange and unaccountable began to take another shape in his eyes. New trains of reasoning became familiar to him, and he perceived connecting links where all had been incomprehensible and startling.

Frederick Engels had entered the field still earlier, with a variant theory of his own as to the (nonexponential) growth of scientific knowledge. (See pp. 123–131 below.) An early development of the idea of the exponential growth of technical knowledge and invention occurs in William F. Ogburn, *Social Change* (New York, 1922; 2nd ed. 1950: see esp. pp. 381–383 of the 1950 edition). Ogburn's ideas are criticized in Jacob Schmookler, *Invention, Growth, and Economic Change* (Cambridge, Mass., 1966; see esp. Chap. III).

[2] Exponential growth has one particularly convenient feature—in substantiating the phenomenon, one need not worry about whether the evidence for it is presented in terms of fresh increments or in terms of cumulative size. An exponential growth in production is correlative with an exponential cumulation of the resulting product. Either way of presenting the evidence substantiates the same phenomenon.

[3] The exponential growth of a quantity—its growth at "compound interest"—is governed by the principle that at any time the rate of growth is proportional to the (then-extant) volume. It produces fixed doubling times (or tripling times, etc.), and sequential fixed-period augmentations that increase in a geometric ratio.

[4] *The Education of Henry Adams, op. cit.,* p. 493. For an interesting discussion of Adams' numerous, complex, and changing ideas regarding scientific and intellectual progress see Ernest Samuels, *Henry Adams: The Major Phase* (Cambridge, Mass., 1964).

Figure 1

HENRY ADAMS' LAW OF ACCELERATION OF PROGRESS

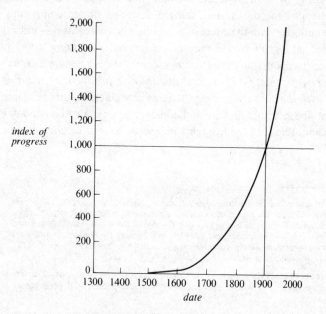

Note If we correlate 1,000 units on the progress scale with the year 1900, and suppose a doubling-time of 50 years (and thus a quadrupling every century) we obtain:

Year	Index of Progress
1600	16
1700	63
1800	250
1900	1,000
2000	4,000

Henry Adams viewed his principle of acceleration as a fundamental discovery regarding the structure of the historical process. Before his mind stood a clear picture of exponential growth in the correlative complex of man's physical power and intellectual potentiality. This view is substantiated by the ever-quickening historical pace of the development of the methodological repertoire of human capacities. For a clearly accelerating sequence of major milestones is encountered here:

locomotion by (erect) walking came about in an era whose temporal distance from us is of the order of magnitude of 10^6 years, that of the introduction of manipulable tools is of the order of 10^5 years, that of the invention of writing is 10^4 years, that of the introduction of mathematics and astronomy is 10^3 years, that of the beginning of serious physics, chemistry and biology is 10^2 years, while that of the harnessing of atomic power is but of 10^1 years. However, these larger aspects of the issue go beyond our present limits, which relate not to human progress at large, but only to progress within the framework of science in particular.

2. DIMENSIONS OF THE PHENOMENON

When Henry Adams enunciated his "law of acceleration," he did so on the basis of shrewd perception, hunch, and insight. Only a few scattered fragments of the statistical basis of information needed to substantiate the reality of this phenomenon were available in his day. However, the situation in this regard is nowadays much improved. The continued data-gathering efforts of statisticians, sociologists, historians of science, science-administrators provide impressive documentation of the phenomenon discerned by Adams.[5] Let us examine some of its dimensions.

A. *Manpower*

In 1875 the American Association for the Advancement of Science had 807 members. Since then its membership has increased as follows:

Year	AAAS Membership
1875	807
1900	1,925
1925	14,263
1950	46,775
1975	118,546

---

[5] The first to take up Adams' thesis on a serious way on the basis of statistical data was F. K. Richtmyer, who on an analysis of the review literature in physics concluded that "since its beginning physics has increased, with each generation, in a geometrical

The register of *American Men of Science* commenced publication in 1903 exhibits a comparable history of growth at a compounding rate of ca. 6% *per annum.*[6] The growth of the scientific community over the past few decades is a particularly striking phenomenon. As regards the numbers of natural scientists working in the U.S. during recent years, Table 1 tells an impressive tale of exponential growth:

---

ratio." ("The Romance of the Next Decimal Place," *Science*, vol. 75 [1932], pp. 1–5 [see pp. 1–2].) In due course, the idea became commonplace:

> The time scale of human progress is certainly not linear. Technical progress grows more rapid as time goes on, and perhaps the best chronological scale for the history of science and technology would be one in which the divisions of the scale were proportional to the logarithms of their distance from the present time. (C. E. K. Mees, *The Path of Science* [New York, 1946], p. 21.)

However, the documentation of Adams' Law improved greatly in the early 1950's. On the side of *outputs* (i.e., scientific papers) a pioneer study was Derek J. Price's "Quantitative Measures of the Development of Science," *Archives Internationales d'Histoire des Sciences*, vol. 14 (1951), pp. 85–93, which maintained that the literature of science has grown with a doubling time of 11 years (a period that seems a bit too small in the light of later studies). On the side of *inputs* the pioneer study was by Raymond H. Ewell of the National Science Foundation, who made a careful study of research and development investments made in the U.S.A. during the period from its inception in 1776 to 1954 (a space of 178 years). Ewell showed in detail that R & D expenditures in the U.S. have grown at 10% *per annum* at least since the first decade of this century, and probably longer. (He also concluded that *half* of the total R & D expenditure of some 40 billion dollars to 1954 had been incurred during the six years 1948–1954.) For a brief description of this work see Raymond H. Ewell, "The Role of Research in Economic Growth," *Chemical and Engineering News*, vol. 33 (1955), pp. 2980–2985. The exponential growth of science (in terms of publications, manpower, findings) also provides one of the basic premises of Pierre Auger's 1960 UNESCO study on *Current Trends in Scientific Research* (Paris and New York, UNESCO publications, 1961; see especially p. 15). Much documentation from the British setting is given in Keith Norris and John Vaizey, *The Economics of Research and Technology* (London, 1973). In the U.S.S.R. the relevant range of ideas was first canvassed in G. E. Vledux, V. V. Nalimov, N. I. Stjazkin, "Scientific and Technical Information as a Task of Cybernetics," *Uspechi fiziceskich nauk*, vol. 69 (1959), pp. 13–56. And see also the fuller treatment in G. M. Dobrov, *Wissenschaftswissenschaft* (Berlin, 1970; first published under the title *Nauka o Nauka* [Moscow, 1966].) But preeminently, Derek J. Price has devoted much further effort to the compilation and depiction of the relevant facts, and the present chapter draws heavily upon his discussion. His initial publication in the area was extended in a later paper on "The Exponential Curve of Science," *Discovery*, vol. 17 (1956), pp. 240–243, but see especially his books *Science Since Babylon* (New Haven, 1961), and *Little Science, Big Science* (New York, 1963). See also Bentley Glass, *The Timely and the Timeless* (New York, 1970).

[6] The older figures are given in S. S. Visher, "Starred Scientists, 1903–1943" in *American Men of Science* (Baltimore, 1947). For further data and discussion of the development of American science see Bernard Barker, *Science and the Social Order* (New York, 1952).

Table 1

NATURAL SCIENTISTS EMPLOYED IN THE UNITED STATES,
BY FIELD: 1950 TO 1970

[In thousands]

Year	Total	Chemists	Mathe- maticians	Physicists	Geologists, geophy- sicists	Other physical scientists	Agricul- tural scientists	Biological scientists	Medical scientists
1950	148·7	51·9	13·6	14·0	13·0	10·2	16·9	19·9	8·8
1955	211·2	73·9	21·5	19·9	17·1	17·4	22·2	27·3	12·3
1960	302·9	99·7	34·2	29·8	20·4	22·1	30·4	44·8	21·5
1961	318·2	102·8	36·3	31·6	20·6	23·8	32·3	46·9	24·1
1962	337·1	106·8	39·8	33·9	21·1	24·2	35·3	49·0	27·2
1963	358·1	110·0	43·6	36·3	22·5	25·3	38·5	51·3	30·5
1964	381·5	115·0	47·2	39·0	23·4	26·3	41·5	54·4	34·6
1965	396·4	116·7	50·3	39·9	25·5	27·1	44·1	55·6	37·2
1966	417·9	119·6	53·9	42·1	26·2	29·1	46·9	56·9	43·2
1967	439·0	122·8	61·9	44·4	28·4	30·2	46·5	62·6	42·0
1968	462·6	127·3	67·1	46·2	29·0	33·6	47·2	65·8	46·4
1969	482·7	131·0	73·0	48·4	29·4	35·0	47·5	67·7	50·7
1970	496·5	132·9	74·3	49·1	30·6	36·2	49·3	71·1	53·0

Data from U.S. Bureau of Labor Statistics, *Employment of Scientists and Engineers in the United States, 1950–1970.*

During most of the present century the number of scientists in the U.S. has been increasing at ca. 6% *per annum* to yield an exponential growth-rate with a doubling time of roughly 12 years. (In the U.K. the comparable figure stands at some $4\frac{1}{2}$%.)[7] A startling consideration— one often but deservedly repeated—is that well over 80% of ever-existing scientists (in even the oldest specialties, e.g., mathematics, physics, and medicine) are alive and active at the present time.[8]

B. *Literature and Information*

It is by now a well-known fact that scientific information has been growing at the (reasonably constant) exponential rate of 6–7% over the past several centuries, so as to produce a veritable flood of scientific

[7] *Statistics of Science and Technology* (London, HMSO, 1970), p. 115.
[8] See, e.g., Derek J. Price, *Little Science, Big Science*, op. cit., p. 11.

literature in our time. The *Physical Review* is now divided into six parts, each of which is larger than the whole journal was a decade or so ago. The total volume of scientific publication is truly staggering. It is reliably estimated that, from the start, about 10 million scientific papers have been published and that currently some 30,000 journals publish some 600,000 new papers each year.

It is readily documented that the number of books, of journals, of journal-papers has been increasing at an exponential rate over the recent period.[9] (See Figure 2.)

To be precise, the printed literature of science has been increasing at some 5% *per annum* throughout the last two centuries, to yield an exponential growth-rate with a doubling time of ca. 15 years—an order-of-magnitude increase roughly every half century.[10]

[9] Cf. Derek J. Price, *Science Since Babylon*, *op. cit.*, see Chap. 5, "Diseases of Science."

[10] To be sure at a more fine-grained level, the situation becomes more complex:

> Even if we ignore those parts of the twentieth-century growth curve that are clearly affected by the World Wars, the remaining parts do not entirely obey an exponential law. Menard [*Science: Its Growth and Change* (Cambridge, Mass., 1971)] has compared the output of periodical literature in chemistry, geology and physics since the beginning of the century and of biology since 1930. These fields show certain overall similarities of development, but are far from having identical growth curves. The annual output of geological papers remained fairly steady all the way through from 1900 to 1945, only going exponential after the Second World War. On the other hand, although the annual physics output was similarly steady before the First World War, it became exponential in the 1920s, continuing so after the interruption of the Second World War. The number of biology papers published annually dropped during the 1930s, and here, too, exponential growth started after the Second World War. Chemistry alone has shown a fairly continuous exponential growth throughout this century. Since the growth curve for all science depends mainly on chemistry and biology (the two numerically predominant sciences), its form for the present century therefore does follow an approximately exponential path, but with considerable deviations. (A. J. Meadows, *Communication in Science* [London, 1974].)

The summary Meadows here gives of Menard's data is not altogether accurate. These data indicate exponential growth at a rate of some 5% per annum for old-line subfields of physics like optics and acoustics, but growth at a far more rapid rate for "hot" subfields like atomic/molecular/particle physics (15% per annum since 1920) or solid state physics (15% per annum since 1945). (Menard, *op. cit.*, p. 51.)

The complexities of the statistics of scientific publication and the occasional local deviations from exponential growth have been particularly studied in the U.S.S.R. For references to the literature see L. N. Beck, "Soviet Discussions of the Exponential Growth of Scientific Publications" in J. B. North (ed.), *The Information Conscious Society: Proceedings of the American Society for Information Science*, vol. 7 (Philadelphia, 1970), pp. 5–16. Jacob Schmookler in examining the contention "that knowledge, in particular technology or invention, tends to grow at an exponential rate" (p. 59 of *Invention and Economic Growth* [Cambridge, Mass., 1966]) suggests that the evidence for the exponential growth of the literature is inconclusive (see especially pp. 60–61). A fuller analysis of the data does not bear out this scepticism. Schmookler's point would be better made by arguing (as we ourselves shall do below) that an exponential growth in the *literature* of science by no means entails an exponential growth in science as a cognitive discipline—i.e., in scientific *knowledge*.

Figure 2

TOTAL NUMBER OF SCIENTIFIC JOURNALS AND ABSTRACT
JOURNALS FOUNDED, AS A FUNCTION OF DATE

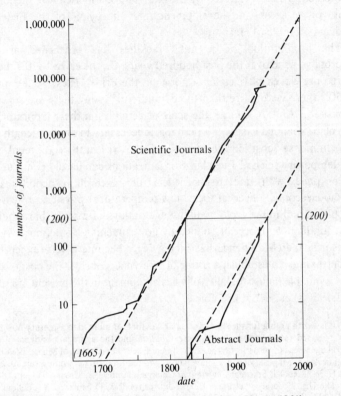

From Derek J. de Solla Price, *Science Since Babylon* (New Haven, 1961).

C. *Facilities and Expenditure*

The historic situation regarding the costs of American science was
carefully delineated in the findings of Raymond Ewell in 1954.[11] His
study of research and development expenditures in the U.S. showed that
growth has been exponential; from 1776 to 1954 we spent close to $40

[11] Raymond Ewell, "The Role of Research in Economic Growth," *op. cit.*

billion, and half of that was spent after 1948. Research and development outlays were found to be increasing at a rate of 10% per year.[12] Projected at this rate, Ewell saw the total as amounting to what he viewed as an astronomical $6·5 billion by 1965—a figure that turned out to be too conservative.[13] By the mid 1960's, America was spending more on research and development than the whole of the Federal budget before Pearl Harbor.

The proliferation of scientific facilities has proceeded at an impressive pace over the past hundred years. (In the early 1870's there were only eleven physics laboratories in the British Isles; by the mid-1930's there were more than three hundred;[14] today there are several thousand.) And, of course, the scale of activities in these laboratories has also expanded vastly. It is perhaps unnecessary to dwell at length on the immense cost in resources of the research equipment of contemporary science. Even large organizations can hardly continue to keep pace with the rising levels of research expenditures.[15] Radiotelescopic observatories, low-temperature physics, research hospitals, and lunar geology all involve outlays of a scale that require the funding support of national governments—sometimes even consortia thereof. Science has increasingly become a very expensive undertaking. To establish a frame of reference, consider the cost of the best-available high-capability physics equipment in the present era (the mid-1970's) as set out in Table 2.

[12] It is worth noting for the sake of comparison that for more than a century now the *total* U.S. federal budget, its *nondefense subtotal*, and the aggregate budgets of all federal agencies concerned with the environmental sciences (Bureau of Mines, Weather Bureau, Army Map Service, etc.) have all grown at a uniform per annum rate of 9%. (See H. W. Menard, *Science: Growth and Change* [Cambridge, Mass., 1971], p. 188.)

[13] The U.S. Federal government's expenditures for R & D came to 13·8 billions in 1965 (60% thereof for Defense, 33% for Space, and the residual 7% for the rest). (The cost implications of the space race was an element with which Ewell did not reckon.) For these data see the NSF biennial series "An Analysis of Federal R & D Funding by Function."

[14] Data from William George, *The Scientist in Action* (New York, 1938).

[15] Du Pont's outlays for research stood at $1 million *per annum* during World War I (1915–1918), $6 million in 1930, $38 million in 1950, and $96 million in 1960. (Data from Fritz Machlup, *The Production and Distribution of Knowledge in the United States* [Princeton, 1962], pp. 158–159; and see pp. 159–160 for the relevant data on a larger scale.) Overall expenditures for scientific research and its technological development (R & D) in the U.S. stood at $.11 × 10^9 in 1920, $.13 × 10^9 in 1930, $.38 × 10^9 in 1940, $2.9 × 10^9 in 1950, $5.1 × 10^9 in 1953–54, $10.0 × 10^9 in 1957–58, $11.1 × 10^9 in 1958–59, and ca. $14.0 × 10^9 in 1960–61 (*ibid.*, pp. 155 and 187). Machlup thinks it a not unreasonable conjecture that no other industry or economic activity in the U.S.A. has grown as fast as R & D (*ibid.*, p. 155).

Table 2

APPROXIMATE CURRENT R & D COSTS OF FRONTIER PHYSICS
TECHNOLOGY

Field	Approximate Cost of Scientific Machinery at the Technological Frontier (in millions of 1970 dollars)
Satellite astronomy (orbital observatories)	1,000
Optical astronomy	10 [1]
Radio astronomy	10 [2]
High-energy physics	300 [3]
Low-energy physics	10
General physics (i.e., most other branches)	2–3
Computers	5–10

Notes (1) Cost of the 200-inch Hale reflector at Mt. Palomar (optics, mounting, and dome only).

(2) Cost of a paraboloid installation with steerable antenna with an aperture diameter of ca. 300 feet.

(3) Cost of the 4-mile 200 GeV proton synchrotron (1972) at the Fermi National Accelerator Laboratory (Batavia, Illinois).

In a prophetic vein, Alvin M. Weinberg (then Director of the Oak Ridge National Laboratory) has written:

When history looks at the 20th century, she will see science and technology as its theme; she will find in the monuments of Big Science—the huge rockets, the high-energy accelerators, the high-flux research reactors—symbols of our time just as surely as she finds in Notre Dame a symbol of the Middle Ages.[16]

3. AN OVERVIEW OF THE EXPONENTIAL GROWTH OF THE SCIENTIFIC ENTERPRISE

A more synoptic view of the over-all structure of the acceleration of

[16] "Impact of Large-Scale Science on the United States," *Science*, vol. 134 (1961; 21 July issue), pp. 161–164 (see p. 161). Weinberg further writes:

The other main contender [apart from space-exploration] for the position of Number One Event in the Scientific Olympics is high-energy physics. It, too, is wonderfully expensive (the Stanford linear accelerator is expected to cost $100 × 10^6$), and we may expect to spend $400 × 10^6$ per year on this area of research by 1970. (*Ibid.*, p. 164.)

scientific effort is presented in the data of Table 3, which affords a vivid overview of the statistical setting of the exponential growth of the scientific enterprise. Its data are best appreciated in the light of the parameters of Table 4.

Two significant considerations thus come to the fore when science is regarded in economic terms as a process with inputs and outputs:

Table 3

SOME DOUBLING TIMES DURING RECENT HISTORY

50 years
    Labor force in the U.S.
    Population in the U.S.
    Number of universities

35 years
    World Population

20 years
    Gross national product in advanced nations
    Real (i.e., inflation-discounted) wages of scientists in the U.S.

15 years
    College graduates in the U.S.
    Membership of scientific institutes
    Number of scientists (worldwide)
    Scientific journals
    Literature in most branches of natural science
    Accuracy of scientific measuring instruments

12 years
    Literature in the more active problem-areas of natural science
    Number of scientists in the U.S.

10 years
    Literature in mathematics
    Number of engineers in the U.S.
    Doctorates earned in science and engineering in the U.S.
    Volumes in university libraries
    World industrial production

 7 years
    Spending on research and development in the U.S.

Data primarily from Derek J. Price, *Little Science, Big Science* (New York, 1963), pp. 6–7.

---

(1) As a sphere of human *effort*, science is a massive undertaking, and one which (throughout recent history) has been rapidly accelerating in scale under the benefit of a vast *input* in terms of manpower, expenditure, and information.

(2) As a *productive* enterprise, science has delivered a massive and (over the recent period) rapidly accelerating *output* in the strictly quantitative terms of the literature which reports its findings and all the other forms of result sharing activities (conferences, international colloquia, etc.)—as well as in an impressive and rapidly growing menu of technological "spin-offs."

Table 4

THE STRUCTURE OF EXPONENTIAL GROWTH

Doubling Times (years)	Ten-Fold (Order-of-Magnitude) Increase Times (years)	% per annum Growth-Rate (at compound interest)
5	16	15
7	24	10
10	34	7
12	40	6
14	47	5
16	52	$4\frac{1}{2}$
20	67	$3\frac{1}{2}$
24	78	3
35	116	2
47	155	$1\frac{1}{2}$
70	231	1

Notes (1) For doubling times: DT × % ≅ 70
(2) For order-of-magnitude increase times: OMT × % ≅ 235

What emerges is a picture of science as an enormous industry. In looking at the matter in this way, one views science in essentially economic terms, as a production process with an input and an output—as a productive enterprise with *costs* (in terms primarily of manpower and resources) and with *returns* (in terms of an output in the first instance of "literature," but more significantly of "findings"). This "science-industry" has a far-flung network of *training* centers (schools, colleges, universities), and of *production* centers (laboratories and research-institutes).

Interestingly enough, the data adduced above indicate that science has been growing exponentially both as to *outputs* (papers), and as to *inputs* (human and material resources). But in the American context, at any rate, input demands have, interestingly enough, been growing faster than output yields (a ca. 10% *per annum* growth for capital requirements—or "material resources"—and a ca. 6% growth in manpower as contrasted with a ca. 5% growth in the yield of published papers).[17] This suggests a phenomenon of rising marginal costs for scientific product, a prospect which must certainly be examined in closer detail.[18]

The data of Table 5 give a clear view of the recent increase of resource investment in science. This picture is particularly impressive, for not only has the gross national product (GNP) of the U.S. grown substantially over the past generations—i.e. at somewhat over 3% *per annum* in constant-dollar terms—but the percentage share of this GNP devoted to science-related research and development has itself been increasing exponentially (at a rate of some 6% *per annum*), from somewhat over one-tenth of one percent in 1920 to almost 3% by 1960.[19] Science has become a big and expensive business—and one whose budgets have increased at an astounding pace.[20] In the recent period, the total expenditure on science per scientist has been doubling

[17] This idea that the economic demands of contemporary science on the side of technology outstrip its demands on the side of manpower is also noted and discussed with respect to Soviet experience in G. M. Dobrov, *Wissenschaftswissenschaft* (op. cit.), especially pp. 98–100.

[18] A particular case of minor intrinsic interest, but useful because of the availability of exact data, concerns the U.S. Geological Survey. For a century now its funding has grown at 9% per annum, its manpower at 5%, its pages of published output at $3\frac{1}{2}$%. The per page cost of the published output of this organization thus increased from ca. $160 in 1880 to $330 in 1935, $1,000 in 1955 and $6,000 in 1965. (See H. W. Menard, *Science: Growth and Change* [Cambridge, Mass., 1971].)

[19] The proportion of the total U.S. Federal expenditure devoted to research and development increased from under one percent in 1940 to nearly 16% in 1965. (Leslie Sklair, *Organized Knowledge* [London, 1973], p. 222.) To be sure, in all these contexts R & D is a complex that conjoins much D with precious little R, so that R & D figures must be used with great caution in relation to science specifically.

[20] No one batted an eyelash when a 1965 National Academy of Sciences study of chemistry research insisted on a need for an increase of 20% *per annum* in U.S. federal expenditure on university chemistry research over the near future. See F. H. Wertheimer *et al.*, *Chemistry: Opportunities and Needs* (Washington, D.C., 1965; National Academy of Sciences/National Research Council), see p. 190.

roughly every ten years, and the population of scientists themselves has been doubling at this same rate, so that the total cost of science has been increasing roughly as the square of the impressively growing number of scientists.[21]

Table 5

SPENDING ON SCIENCE-RELATED RESEARCH AND DEVELOPMENT IN THE U.S.

Year	*Percentage of GNP in the U.S.* *Spent on Research*
1920	·1+
1930	·3
1940	·7
1950	1·3
1960	2·6

Data from Norman Kaplan (ed.), *Science and Society* (Chicago, 1965).

Let us consider this question of the resource inputs of science somewhat more closely. The resources (R) needed for scientific work divide into two predominating categories: (1) *skilled labor* (i.e., professional manpower, trained capability and talent), and (2) *capital* (equipment, machinery, apparatus, fuel, material, and non-human resources).[22] Accordingly, the resources for scientific work are a conjunction of two interlocked components:

$$R = R_L + R_C$$

It should be noted that if R_L and R_C both grow exponentially then R will

---

[21] For fuller details on the recent explosion of research and development expenditures see Leonard S. Silk, *The Research Revolution* (New York, 1960). It is only just, however, to stress that the outlays for science proper—the R part of the complex of science-related R & D—is only a small portion of the whole (perhaps 4% in recent U.S. experience).

[22] Actually we shall also put into the capital-inputs category all strictly routine manpower that is "mechanical" and could in principle be mechanized or computerized. In this context, we shall thus consider it as a somewhat paradoxical but significant aspect of the capital intensiveness of science that there has been an increase in the ratio of scientific workers per scientific author. For striking evidence of this in the U.S.S.R. see Leonard N. Beck, "Soviet Discussions of the Exponential Growth of Scientific Publications," *op. cit.*

grow (roughly) exponentially as well.[23] However, the composite nature of R serves as a reminder that R_L and R_C play a differential role and that one of them may ultimately prove predominant.

From the data of Table 3 we know that: (1) the number of working scientists in the U.S. has been growing at ca. 6% *per annum* (with a doubling time of 12 years), and (2) the real wages of scientists in the U.S. have been growing at ca. $3\frac{1}{2}$% *per annum* (with a doubling time of 20 years). On this basis of a $3\frac{1}{2}$% increase superimposed on a 6% growth, the over-all professional manpower costs of science have been increasing at about $9\frac{1}{2}$% per annum. Given that the over-all *real* expenditures on science in the U.S. have been increasing at a rate of some 10% *per annum*, this suggests that—within the order of accuracy prevailing here—the (real) professional manpower costs of science have been increasing in line with its cost-increase in general. Moreover, the available evidence indicates that investment of resources in science in the non-labor sector have also been increasing at ca. 10% *per annum*.[24]

Given that (as per our analysis) the "capital" resources committed to science have expanded at a substantially more rapid rate (viz., ca. 10%) than its "trained-scientist" requirements (viz., ca. 6%), it does not seem that science as a whole is "neutral" as between capital and labor intensiveness in the recent stages of its development.[25] To be sure, science is a complex mixture of problem areas, and it is possible—nay, probable—that some of them may be one-sidedly labor-intensive or capital-intensive on a transitory or even a permanent basis. But what matters from the standpoint of the previous findings is that—in the aggregate—the investment of physical resources has in recent times

[23] The argument is that when both R_L and R_C grow at compound interest the factor with the larger growth-rate simply predominates to establish its own exponential growth pattern.

[24] Experience in the U.S.S.R. is wholly parallel: "Over the past 22 years (since 1950) the number of scientific workers [in the Academy of Sciences of the Ukrainian SSR] has increased 10-fold, the annual (real) budget 11·3-fold, but the investment in the instrumentalities of research more than 25-fold." (G. M. Dobrov, *Wissenschaft: ihre Analyse und Prognose* [Stuttgart, 1974], p. 87.) This book affords many data from Soviet experience that illustrate the operations and ramifications of Adams' Law.

[25] For example, in the 1954–1964 decade, the number of chemists on the faculties of American universities increased at a rate of ca. 5% *per annum*, but the number of machinists and laboratory technicians (i.e., of those who make and operate the equipment of research) increased at a rate of ca. 12% *per annum*. For details see F. H. Wertheimer *et al.*, *Chemistry: Opportunities and Needs, op. cit.*, see esp. p. 176. On the underlying issues see Harvey Brooks, "Can Science Be Planned," *Problems of Science Policy: Seminar at Jouy-en-Josas on Science Policy* (Paris: OECD, 1967), see p. 20.

played the more strident role in scientific expenditures.[26] To all appearances, the technological demands of modern science render it emphatically capital-intensive,[27] a fact to which any theory of scientific progress will also have to give close scrutiny.

The economic analogy that has figured in this discussion is drawn very deliberately. It is intended literally, and not merely as a figure of speech. Indeed, the economic outlook will in fact permeate the whole of the present discussion: throughout the ensuing deliberations we shall approach the issue of scientific progress from the economists' standpoint of concern with a "production function," viewing science from an economists' perspective as a productive enterprise with inputs and outputs of its own characteristic sort. Science thus represents a growth-industry of impressive proportions—and one whose rapid expansion has been proceeding at an exponential rate. Within the scientific domain, Adams' conjecture of a "law of acceleration" has been amply borne out by the subsequent facts.

4. THE END OF ADAMS' LAW: THE ZERO GROWTH HYPOTHESIS

The cost-escalation of science inexorably raises the question of whether the operation of Adams' Law of exponential growth is a transitory phenomenon or an ongoing condition of things. Is the exponential growth of science itself a "law of nature," as it were, or is it descriptive of the transitory constitution of one particular era? Our present theme of the future prospects of science clearly revolves crucially about the answer to this question.

Since the time of Malthus, every biologist who deals with the development of individuals or populations has realized that exponential growth must come to a halt as one or another factor of the environment

---

[26] The question of the capital vs. labor "neutrality" of *technological change in general production* in modern economics is interestingly discussed in Keith Norris and John Vaizey, *The Economics of Research and Technology* (London, 1973), pp. 138–163. The upshot of the discussion remains indecisive in this case of standard economic production, an indecisiveness that does not, however, seem to afflict the situation in the case of *scientific* production.

[27] Indeed, the decline in the average productivity of scientists seems to be a pervasive phenomenon. (See A. J. Meadows, *Communication in Science* [London, 1974], p. 33.) Such a decline should itself be seen as an aspect of "capital"-intensiveness: it takes more "labor" to run the machinery of science by whose means findings are extracted from nature—more workers extract fewer findings.

becomes limiting. And so, no serious theorist of scientific method and practice—Henry Adams himself included—has been prepared to contemplate the prospect that Adams' Law of the accelerating expansion of scientific work could represent a permanent condition of things.[28] It seems grotesque to suppose an unendingly continued exponential growth of the human and material resources committed to scientific research or of the literature that is its output. As one recent student of scientific affairs has observed:

The present [1960] federal expenditure on research and development [in the U.S.] is 8.4×10^9, which is about 10 percent of the federal budget, and about $1 \cdot 6$ percent of the gross national product. . . . The rate of increase of our research and development budget, averaged over the past ten years, has been 10 percent per year; this corresponds to a doubling time of seven years. Since the

[28] Adams saw an ever more rapidly accelerating succession of historical phases, with the mechanical phase which ended ca. 1900 succeeded by an electrical phase lasting until 1917 followed by a final period of about four years, "bringing thought to the limit of its possibilities in the year 1921." (Quoted from his 1910 essay "A Letter to American Teachers of History" printed in *The Degradation of the Democratic Dogma* [New York, 1919].) In another, somewhat less apocalyptic passage, Adams mooted three possibilities for the development of human potential: a Byzantine stasis for an indefinite period; an uncontrollable runaway expansion of human power, perhaps ending on an explosive paroxism of selfdestruction; a mental breakthrough or jump to a new level producing an administrative elite capable of harnessing the inexhaustible force which a scientific elite has made possible. (See Ernest Samuels, *Henry Adams: The Major Phase* [Cambridge, Mass., 1964], p. 419.)

A more recent theorist of scientific method and practice has pictured the inevitable end to the exponential growth of science in chemical rather than (with Adams) in physical terms:

[T]he growth of science is not only very rapid, but *it is still accelerating*. The production of new science, in fact, is accelerated by the science already produced; and this phenomenon is parallel to that which the chemist knows as an *autocatalytic reaction*.

Autocatalytic reactions are those in which the product of the reaction itself increases the rate at which the reaction proceeds. . . . Any chemical reaction that produces heat will increase autocatalytically if the heat is not conducted away. Such a reaction is interesting to watch. We put the solvent in a vessel, add all the ingredients, and perhaps warm them a little. Then, the reaction starts and generates heat as it proceeds. It goes faster and faster, and the solution may rise in the vessel and froth; and then, as the reaction decreases and the materials are used up, the solution sinks again. If there is not enough room, the vessel will boil over; if there is enough room, it will undergo a complete transformation into a new system. The termination of the reaction is produced by the exhaustion of one of the components, just as the production of plankton in the sea is limited by the supply of mineral salts, principally phosphate, in the water. . . . If the autocatalytic production of science is limited by some factor necessary to it, it will accelerate until that factor becomes exhausted and then settle down to progress at a rate dependent upon the supply of the factor. Up to the present, no such limiting factor for the production of scientific knowledge is apparent. (C. E. K. Mees, *The Path of Science* [New York, 1946], pp. 227–228.)

doubling time of the gross national product is about 20 years, at the present rate we shall be spending *all* of our money on science and technology in about 65 years.[29]

It is clear that if mankind is going to arrive at a condition of zero-growth stability on this planet in population and in the exploitation of resources—as we eventually must[30]—then the total amount of these assets committed to science must also reach a level plateau. In these circumstances, the *per annum* commitment of the scarce resources dedicated to the scientific enterprise each year—trained manpower (real) funding, equipment, hydroelectric power, etc.—will ultimately remain constant. We may thus confidently envision a steady-state situation regarding the availability of resources for scientific work. Let this condition of things be designated as the *Zero-Growth Hypothesis*. It stipulates a level of fixed constancy in the *incremental* availability of new resource-inputs per time-unit (incremental, that is, over and above what has become available in the preceding time-unit).

The accession of a zero-growth condition means that historic situation of investment in science takes on the S-shaped structure indicated in Figure 3.[31]

The course of recent events has made it clear that the idea of a zero-growth world is not a distant prospect that need be envisioned only for an eventual long run. Indeed, as regards the investment of human and material resources in science within the Western world, there is substantial evidence that the transition to such a steady-state situation was already getting under way by the end of the 1960's.[32] The current

[29] Alvin M. Weinberg, "Impact of Large-Scale Science on the United States," *Science*, vol. 134 (1961), pp. 161–164 (see p. 162). In reading this one must, to be sure, recall that it was written before the recent decline in scientific funding due to inflation, economic recession, the end of the space-science boom, etc.

[30] The underlying argument is set out in D. Meadows *et al.*, *The Limits of Growth* (New York, 1972), and holds irrespective of the (sometimes questionable) details of their analysis.

[31] Such sigmoid growth-curves are, of course, familiar from many biological and epidemiological contexts. See the discussion in Alfred J. Lotka, *Elements of Mathematical Biology* (New York, 1956), esp. Chap. 7.

[32] This is documented in detail in the case of physics in D. A. Bromley *et al.*, *Physics in Perspective: Student Edition* (Washington, D.C., 1973; NRC/NAS Publication). For example, spending in the U.S.A. and Western Europe on perhaps the major present-day frontier area in natural science, high-energy physics, had been growing exponentially until ca. 1970, but then abruptly leveled off at roughly 550 millions of U.S. 1974 dollars. See also Nicholas Valery, "The Declining Power of American Technology," *New Scientist*, vol. 71 (1976), pp. 72–73.

Figure 3

THE HISTORICAL GROWTH OF INVESTMENT IN SCIENCE

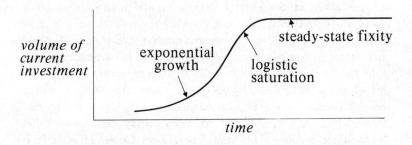

worldwide funding crises of science and the recent decline in
enrollments in science training programs may well be indications that
the juncture of stabilization already lies behind us.

The idea that the normal course of *material* progress in human affairs
is set out by an S-shaped curve of "logistic" growth configuration was
originally maintained by R. A. Lehfeldt in 1916.[33] Our present
discussion postulates that the situation is exactly the same as regards
the development of science *in its material aspect as a* PRODUCTIVE
enterprise. The real problem, however, is to assess what this means for
the development of science *in its intellectual aspect as a* COGNITIVE
enterprise. This problem sets the central issue of the present book.

5. POWER, COMPLEXITY, AND THE INSTALLMENT-PLAN SUPPOSITION

The question of the *total* availability at a given time of resources for
scientific work is readily resolved on the basis of such a Zero-Growth
Hypothesis. The three main categories of resource inputs needed for
scientific work are: trained manpower, material (construed to include
facilities and equipment), and physical energy (electric power, etc.).
While certain of these can in the main be cumulated over time through
storage (in some appropriate form), there remains in each instance an

[33] R. A. Lehfeldt, "The Normal Law of Progress," *Journal of the Royal Statistical
Society*, vol. 79 (1916), pp. 329–332.

element that is not amenable to such cumulation, so that some of the crucial inputs needed for scientific work are of the perishable type whose marginal availability in a zero-growth situation may be supposed to remain in a steady-state condition. Two significant consequences thus follow from the consideration that the incremental availability of newly generated resources proceeds at a *constant* rate under steady-state conditions: (1) after the initiation of the zero-growth limitation, the cumulative sum-total of all resources expended up to any given time increases *linearly*, and moreover (2) the total amount of the specifically *perishable* resources available at any given time remains subject to some fixed upper limit.

Now let us designate as the *Installment-Plan Supposition* the assumption that a scientific problem can in general be factored into smaller parts of a sufficiently reduced size to allow their resolution within the limits of a zero-growth resource-availability (provided only that the problem-solving effort is drawn out over a sufficiently long period of time). This hypothesis amounts to the following contention:

> When the amount of a perishable resource required to solve a scientific problem is greater than Z—the maximum quantity of this resource that can be made available at a given time—then this problem can be factored into components each of which can be resolved within the limits of Z.

This means that in principle the solution to such a scientific problem is affordable—even with a limited resource budget—by simply dedicating to it the storeable resources acquired over a sufficiently long period of time. Because of the problem-factorization envisaged, the perishability of some of the resources requisite for scientific work becomes impotent to *block* progress, but can merely *delay* it. By budgeting the available problem-solving resources over a sufficiently long period of time we can always afford the solution to such a factorable problem provided we are willing to pay the "secondary price" of waiting long enough—of purchasing our desiderata at the cost of time rather than of effort, not only investing physical resources but also expending patience.

To be sure, in actual fact scientific problems can be of two kinds: (1) There are *synthetic* problems which are holistic rather than factorable and have a gestalt unity in virtue of which they do not admit of decomposition but must be resolved all-at-once through the deployment of suitably powerful effort that is marshalled against them in a one-shot manner. (2) There are *analytic* problems which can be factored into pieces admitting of stepwise resolution, so that while a vast total effect may be required for the solution of the problem, this can be expended seriatim in small installments. (A hickory nut can only be cracked by concurrently marshalling a sizable effort; a ball can be rolled to a far-off destination by tiny bits of effort expended successively.) Problems of the former (synthetic) category may be characterized as *power-intensive*, those of the latter as *complexity-intensive*.[34]

The investigation of "fundamental" particles through collisions brought about by high-energy particle-accelerations typifies the category of power-intensive problems. The etiology of cancer and cardiovascular disease affords a prime instance of complexity-intensive research problems, perhaps due to the convoluted functioning of cellular mechanisms. (For example, it is often impossible in the present state of knowledge to predict whether a deliberately induced immune response will stimulate or inhibit the growth of a cancer.) Environmental biology (ecology) with its proliferation of delicately interconnected variables, interlocked in intricate jigsaw-puzzle-like configurations, also exemplifies this case. Or again, molecular biology, with its thousands of investigators painstakingly elucidating step by step the mode of action of the nucleic acids and other cellular constituents typifies the category of complexity-intensive problems.[35]

One vivid illustration of the extent to which the complexity of complexity-intensive problems makes its impact on the conduct of research can be obtained from an analysis of multiple authorship of papers listed in *Chemical Abstracts*. For the number of authors of chemical papers has been increasing at a steady rate of 10% per decade

[34] This dichotomization of problem-areas finds its counterpart in the organization and management of scientific activities. The great national laboratories, institutes and installations that typify "big science" reflect the concentration of effort needed to resolve power-intensive problems; the massive proliferation of other scientific activities among myriad smaller units (universities, industrial laboratories, etc.) reflects the decentralization of effort to which the installment-plan aspect of complexity-intensive problems readily lends itself. For an interesting discussion of the relevant issues see Alvin R. Weinberg, "Institutions and Strategies in the Planning of Research," *Minerva*, vol. 12 (1974), pp. 8–17.

[35] For some interesting theoretical discussions of the concept of complexity and an extensive bibliography of the concept see C. C. Whyle, A. G. Wilson, and D. Wilson (eds.), *Hierarchial Structures* (New York, 1969).

throughout the present century, and at this rate the single-author paper—now accounting for a mere 17% of the literature—may well be virtually extinct in chemistry in a decade or so.[36]

In physics, the difference between power-intensive and complexity-intensive problems is helpfully illustrated in the following passage from a recent A.E.C. study:

> The history of physics . . . shows that progress in the understanding of physics generally comes about in a two-fold manner. On the one hand are the spectacular discoveries which are infrequently made, usually with the help of a new [and more powerful] instrument or machine. Sometimes these discoveries seem to completely change the field overnight, as did the discovery of the neutron. On the other hand, necessary progress is also made by painstaking study and classification lasting over decades, such as the development of quantum mechanics through the study of atomic spectra.[37]

Another way in which the difference between synthetic (power-intensive) and analytical (complexity-intensive) disciplines manifests itself is in the nature of its organizational structure—reflected in the structure of its budgets (rather than their size). The following passage interestingly sets the stage for this point:

> One reason why research expenditures in nuclear particle physics are so highly visible is the concentration of experimental facilities in national and international centers whose budgets form single entities which must be approved by governments year by year. . . . In other fields of scientific research such problems are much less intense. For example, in biological and medical research, where total expenditures are comparable with those in nuclear particle

[36] For a description of the phenomenon of multiple authorship see D. de Solla Price, *Little Science, Big Science* (New York, 1963), pp. 87–90; and also A. J. Meadows, *Communication in Science* (London, 1974), pp. 199–206. An analysis of the complexity-centered rationale of the phenomenon of cooperative research is given in Eugene P. Wigner, "The Limits of Science," *Proceedings of the American Philosophical Society*, vol. 94 (1950), pp. 422–427.

[37] David B. Cline, *et al.*, *The Health of High-Energy Physics*, Report to the Atomic Energy Commission of the Sub-panel of the High Energy Physics Advisory Panel (Washington, D.C., October 1974), pp. 2–3.

physics, the few national laboratories which exist are small in size and run on relatively modest budgets, and international laboratories are only now being considered, for example, for molecular biology in Europe. Furthermore, the size of individual pieces of experimental apparatus is also relatively small and the decision to build them does not usually involve national or international decisions. The research is largely carried out in departments of all the universities in Europe, each of which manages its own modest budget and its own apparatus. Some other fields, however, such as optical and radio astronomy, are beginning to encounter problems similar to those of nuclear particle physics as telescopes reach sizes and costs comparable with accelerating machines. Thus it is nuclear physicists who first encountered the problem of justifying their research publicly, a laborious business which has by no means reached a satisfactory conclusion.[38]

This issue of concentration vs. diversification of facilities clearly reflects the decomposability of complexity-intensive problems in contrast to the holistic nature of power-intensive ones.

Paradigmatically, the power-intensive domain of synthetic inquiry is concerned with the exploration of new *types* of phenomena, while the complexity-intensive domain of analytic inquiry is concerned with the exploration of new *relations* among the already known types of phenomena. In the former case we need more sophisticated *physical* machinery, and so inquiry tends to be capital-intensive. In the latter case we need more sophisticated *conceptual* machinery, and so inquiry here tends to be labor-intensive, or rather talent-intensive. The development of new mathematical formalisms (on the order of group theory, matrix theory, Hilbert spaces, etc.) is called for. The one centers about the *production* of data, the other about their utilization or *processing*. Power is in general required to dig deeper through the strata of the make-up of nature—complexity must be dealt with in unravelling the relationships encountered at a given level.[39] With the

[38] J. B. Adams, "Some Problems of Big Science," *Daedalus*, vol. 102 (1973), pp. 111–124 (see pp. 120–121).

[39] A good example of this demand for enhanced conceptual machinery for complexity-handling is afforded by the following passage:

Consider, for example, man's practically complete ignorance of the evolution of the flat, patchily spiral distribution of gas and stars that he calls his own (Milky Way) galaxy. . . . The

former we must force our way more deeply into the interior of nature, with the latter we must sift more carefully and widely over the areas already traversed. The trademark of the one is the machine for forcing nature's hand in yielding as heretofore unrealized conditions—such as the high-flux reactor—while that of the other is the computer for helping us to exploit relatively familiar data on a larger and more sophisticated scale.

To be sure, the distinction is not hard and fast. Scientific progress is by and large a matter of the interaction and meshing of these two factors, and most significant scientific problems have both a power-aspect and a complexity-aspect.[40] But in a given problem-context, one of these always tends to predominate over the other—*not* to exclude it!—and this is why we speak of the issue in terms of "intensiveness."

However, the Installment-Plan Supposition puts this distinction aside by assumptive fiat. It stipulates that scientific problems are in general of the analytic or factorable sort, where complexity is the paramount factor.

This hypothesis admittedly introduces an element of unrealism. While many scientific problems are certainly amenable to solution on the installment plan, others undoubtedly cannot, having an undecomposable gestalt which allows them only to be solved *in toto* rather than piecemeal. The solution of problems of this latter sort may

---

interaction of molecules, atoms, ions, and fields is now well enough known for this problem, and Newtonian gravitation, on this scale, is unquestionably reliable. With these simple ingredients, why doesn't the problem reduce to a mere mathematical exercise? One good reason—perhaps not the only reason—is that a complete and general theory of turbulence is lacking. It is not just a lack of efficient methods of calculation. There is a gap in man's understanding of physical processes, which remains unclosed, even after the work of many mathematical physicists of great power. This gap is blocking progress on several fronts. When a general theory of turbulence is finally completed, which probably will depend on the work of many physicists and mathematicians, a significant permanent increase in man's understanding will have been achieved.... The solution of these major problems of organized (or partly organized) complexity is absolutely necessary for a full understanding of physical phenomena. Extraordinary insight and originality will surely be needed, as indeed they always have been. The intellectual challenge is as formidable as that faced by Boltzmann and Gibbs in the development of statistical mechanics. (D. A. Bromley *et al.*, *Physics in Perspective*, *op. cit.*, pp. 6–7.)

[40] The experimental techniques of modern physics make enormous demands on the side of power. All the same, the ability to handle complexity is also a requisite:

Computer and special methods had to be developed to perform the many intricate calculations that are needed before the physics can be recognized in the enormous mass of data emerging from an experiment. This task has strained the capabilities of the largest computers. Without such methods, the emergence of hadron spectroscopy, for example, would have been impossible. (D. A. Bromley *et al.*, *Physics in Perspective*, *op. cit.*, p. 53.)

well come to require a deployment of perishable resources greater than the amount which could be marshalled at any given time under the steady state conditions of zero growth. The implications of *this* prospect for our over-all position will be examined in due course (in Chapter XIV). But for the time being this prospect is assumed irrelevant—as it indeed is as long as one is operating in a region where the resource limitations associated with synthetic problems cannot make themselves felt. For the present, then, we may suppose as a working assumption that such an Installment-Plan Supposition is a sufficiently close approximation to the truth to make it sensible to proceed on its basis. This yields the crucial consequence that a budget of resources whose increase is restricted to zero-growth conditions can (in theory) always be effectively applied towards the eventual resolution of major scientific problems, however demanding these problems might become in their over-all resource requirements.

V

Cost-Escalation: Planck's Principle of Increasing Effort

[W]ith every advance [in science] the difficulty of the task is increased.

MAX PLANCK

1. THE BACKGROUND OF THE PROBLEM: PLANCK'S PRINCIPLE

There has been an unquestionably splendid yield on the exponentially increasing investment of human and material resources in scientific work. Nevertheless, there remains the economists' uncompromising question regarding the actual structure of the relationship between resource investment and product output. In particular, the problem arises of whether, as science progresses, a fixed amount of effort continues to yield uniformly significant results, or whether a process of declining yields is operative in this respect. Even greatly increasing resource investments will fail to generate a corresponding increase in output if the unit cost of production is rising.

A great deal of impressionistic and anecdotal evidence certainly points towards the increasing costs of high-level science. Scientists frequently complain that "all the easy researches have been done."[1] The need for increasing specialization and division of labor is but one indication of this. A devotee of scientific biography cannot help noting the disparity between the immense output and diversified fertility in the

---

[1] See William George, *The Scientist in Action* (London, 1936), p. 307. The sentiment is not new. George Gore vainly lambasted it 100 years ago: "Nothing can be more puerile than the complaints sometimes made by certain cultivators of a science, that it is very difficult to make discoveries now that the soil has been exhausted, whereas they were so easily made when the ground was first broken. . . ." *The Art of Scientific Discovery* (London, 1878), p. 21.

productive careers of the scientific collosi of earlier days and the more modest scope of the achievements of their latter-day successors.

It is clearly implausible to interpret this shrinkage as indicating that the days of greatness are over and that our contemporaries are lesser men endowed with less brain-power or with a diminished capacity for hard work. Rather, one is drawn towards the very different conclusion that the work is simply getting harder. This poses the prospect that a stonier soil is being farmed—one where comparable effort simply can no longer yield comparable returns.[2] The successive victories of science —like the battles of Marlborough—are won only at ever-mounting costs.

There are, it would seem, substantial grounds for agreement with Max Planck's appraisal of the situation:

> To be sure, *with every advance [in science] the difficulty of the task is increased*; *ever larger demands are made on the achievements of researchers*, and the need for a suitable division of labor becomes more pressing.[3]

The italicized thesis of this quotation will here be characterized as *Planck's Principle of Increasing Effort*. We shall interpret this as asserting that successive substantial discoveries become more and more expensive over the course of time in terms of the investment of talent, manpower, and material resources—that scientific work is subject to an escalation of costs. Accordingly, we construe this principle of increasing effort in specifically the following sense: As science progresses within any of its established branches, there is a marked increase in the over-all resource-cost of realizing scientific findings of a given level intrinsic significance (by essentially absolutistic standards of importance).[4]

---

[2] This prospect seems borne out also by a phenomenon in whose reality, though it is difficult to substantiate, is nevertheless unquestionable—namely, that there are nowadays not a few authentic scientific geniuses of the first order who never managed to produce first-magnitude results. (For obvious reasons, one is hesitant to cite examples.)

[3] *Vorträge und Erinnerungen*, 5th ed. (Stuttgart, 1949), p. 376; italics added. Shrewd insights seldom go unanticipated, so it is not surprising that other theorists should be able to contest claims to Planck's priority here. C. S. Peirce is particularly noteworthy in this connection. (Cf. footnote 22 on pp. 88–89 below.)

[4] The following passage offers a clear token of the operation of this principle specifically with respect to chemistry:

Over the past ten years the expenditures for basic chemical research in universities have

In the continuing course of scientific progress, the earlier investigations in the various departments of inquiry are able to skim the cream, so to speak: they take the "easy pickings," and later achievements of comparable significance require ever deeper forays into complexity and call for an ever-increasing investment of effort and material resources. And it is important to realize that this cost-increase is not because latter-day workers are doing *better* science, but simply because it is harder to achieve *the same level* of science: one must dig deeper or search wider to find more of the same *kind* of thing as before. (The *intrinsic importance* of really important scientific findings at later stages of the game is certainly neither lesser nor greater than those obtained—or thought to be obtained—earlier on.) And so, if science is to make significant headway in the face of escalating costs, a constantly increasing commitment of talent and effort is inexorably called for. Something approaching Adams' Law becomes inevitable if a thriving pace of scientific progress is to be maintained.

(As Planck rightly saw, this circumstance of increasing costs explains the need for an ongoing division of labor in scientific research. And more than any other factor, it explains a change in the structure of scientific work that has frequently been noted: first-rate results in science nowadays come less and less from the efforts of isolated workers but rather from cooperative efforts in the great laboratories and research institutes.[5] Clearly, if innovative work at a level of high significance requires an ever-increasing effort and input of resources, this provides an immediate and natural account for the organization of large-scale cooperation and the investment of greater resources than the individual worker in a small laboratory could possibly have at hand.)

---

increased at a rate of about 15 per cent per annum; much of the increase has gone for superior instrumentation, [and] for the staff needed to service such instruments. . . . Because of the expansion in research opportunities, the increased cost of the instrumentation required to capitalize on these opportunities, and the more highly skilled supporting personnel needed for the solution of more difficult problems, the cost of each individual research problem in chemistry is rising rapidly. (F. H. Wertheimer *et al.*, *Chemistry: Opportunities and Needs* [Washington, D.C., 1965; National Academy of Sciences/National Research Council], p. 17.)

[5] The talented amateur has virtually been driven out of science. In 1881 the Royal Society included many fellows in this category (with Darwin, Joule, and Spottiswoode among the more distinguished of them). Today there are no amateurs. See D. S. C. Cardwell, "The Professional Society" in Norman Kaplan (ed.), *Science and Society* (Chicago, 1965), pp. 86–91 (see p. 87).

2. COST ESCALATION

When escalating costs are spoken of in the context of scientific discovery, one cannot simply mean that a fixed budget will yield fewer findings as such, but rather fewer findings of a high quality. There is (alas) no point in discussing this phenomenon save in the light of evaluative considerations. Much though one would like to do so, the issue of quality-appraisal thus cannot be avoided.

By a "high-level finding" or "first-rate result" we shall mean a substantial scientific finding of the very first magnitude—one of the sort that establishes its author as one of the collossi of the field—a Gibbs, a Rutherford, a Planck, an Einstein, or a Bohr—a ground-breaking, unforeseeable discovery that can straight-forwardly make its discoverer a person of established reputation with a secure place in the history of the subject.

But it cannot be said too emphatically that no aspect of our present talk of significant discoveries should be construed as a commitment to the coral-reef theory of scientific progress by accumulative accretion. Scientific progress in large measure annihilates rather than enlarges what has gone before—it builds the new on the foundations of the ruins of the old. Scientific theorizing generally moves ahead not by addition and *enlargement* but by demolition and *replacement*. A great part of the contemporary philosophy of science has been devoted to the substantiation and explanation of this fact, and nothing in the present discussion should be construed as being at variance with it. A discovery —of whatever level of importance—is never a claim permanently secured and bound to endure inviolate for all time to come. The significant discoveries of today manifest the deficiencies and untenabilities of the significant discoveries of yesterday. To qualify a finding as first-rate conveys no imputation of irrevocability. (Cf. pp. 48–50.)

With this idea of first-rate discoveries in hand, one can endeavor to clarify the idea of escalating costs by mooting a graph over the course of time of *the number of first-rate results realized per fixed unit of scientific effort* (be it a scientist's working lifetime, a fixed-size expenditure on scientific work, or a given volume of published scientific material). There can be little doubt that the result will be a family of yield/cost curves that yield a picture of uniform decline. For putting the question of the exact shape of this function aside for the moment, there can be little doubt that its slope is uniformly negative. One anecdotal item is indicative. In the 1890's, when the Cavendish Laboratory under J. J. Thomson's headship was just beginning to train research students, Cambridge University contributed £250 [*sic*] a year to the running expenses of the laboratory.[6] Government grants for scientific research at the Cavendish were nonexistent. (From 1882 to 1914 the Royal Society dispensed a research fund of £4,000 per annum made available by a government grant, which had to cover all the sciences in the entire country.[7]) Yet an impressive roster of Nobel laureates in physics did their work in the Cavendish in those penurious days.[8]

More systematic evidence of the escalating costs of scientific progress is provided by reviewing some suggestive statistical facts:[9]

(1) the total (real) expenditure on science per scientist has been increasing at a rate of roughly 4% per year in the U.S.A. during recent decades,[10] while the per-capita productivity of scientists (as measured by contributions to the literature) has declined slightly.

(2) the number of scientists working in the U.S.A. has been increasing at a rate of roughly 6% per year (doubling every 12 years or so), whereas (i) the number of "eminent" men—those selected for listing in the standard biographical handbooks or other registers which select only a limited elite of scientific contributors—has been increasing at a rate of only ca. 3% per year (thus doubling in around 20 years),[11] (ii) the number of relatively significant findings—those cited in the references of synoptic monographs, handbooks, and textbooks—has to all appearances been growing at a merely *linear* rate, and (iii) the

---

[6] In the early 1930's in the regime of Rutherford the budget had grown to around £2500. The great man used to admonish his students: "We have no money to spend, so we shall have to think." Lord Bowden, "Expectations for Science," *The New Scientist*, 30 Sept 1965, pp. 849–853 (see p. 851).

[7] George Thomson, *J. J. Thomson* (London, 1964); see Chapter VI, "The Cavendish Laboratory Under J. J." for the interesting financial details. For the financing of science in the U.K. during the last part of the nineteenth century see Roy M. MacLeod, "The Support of Victorian Science: The Endowment of Research Movement in Great Britain, 1868–1900," *Minerva*, vol. 9 (1971), pp. 197–230; reprinted in P. Mathias (ed.), *Science and Society: 1600–1900* (Cambridge, 1972), pp. 111–166.

[8] On this whole issue of mounting costs and complications compare J. B. Adams, "Some Problems of a Big Science," *Daedalus*, vol. 102 (1973), pp. 111–124.

[9] Data from Derek J. Price, *Little Science, Big Science* (New York, 1963).

[10] *Ibid.*, pp. 92–93.

[11] *Ibid.*, p. 39.

number of scientific papers published in the U.S.A. has increased at some 5% per year (doubling roughly every 15 years).

The rising cost of work in natural science is certainly a well-attested phenomenon. The best current assessment of the situation runs as follows:

Estimates of the escalation in the intrinsic costs of doing scientific research range from 3·5 percent to 7·5 percent per year depending on the exact assumptions made. This figure is quite apart from any consideration of over-all inflation of salary escalation in the research enterprise; it relates only to the increased costs that reflect increased sophistication of the questions addressed and the measurements made.[12]

With the course of scientific progress, nature seemingly exacts an increasingly steep price for revealing her secrets. In Rutherford's day, a physicist could still design an experiment, arrange for a technician to help him build his equipment, and get it put together in a few weeks or months—all at a cost rarely exceeding a hundred pounds. Today the situation is strikingly different, with high-energy physics affording what is no doubt the most dramatic illustration of this process of increasing costs—a field with only a little over a thousand workers in the U.S. whose annual costs now run to some $200 million a year.

Consider some further indications. For one thing, there is ample evidence that the published output of research organizations has not kept pace with the growth of their "fiscal size" over the recent years.[13]

Drs. Ellis A. Johnson and Helen S. Milton of the Operations Research Office of Johns Hopkins University sought to develop a cost-of-research index. Their index was based on the concept of the cost per year of a *technical man*, where "the 'technical man' is the professional scientist or engineer, together with his supporting tech-

---

[12] D. A. Bromley *et al.*, *Physics in Perspective: Student Edition* (Washington, D.C., 1973; National Research Council/National Academy of Sciences Publication), p. 329.

[13] See Kenneth Mellanby, "The Disorganization of Scientific Research," *Minerva*, vol. 12 (1974), pp. 67–82 (see p. 73). See also this author's "A Damp Squib," *The New Scientist*, vol. 33 (1967), pp. 626–627, where he clearly perceives the operation in natural science research of a law of diminishing returns, though his diagnosis of this phenomenon (in terms of the factors of recruitment of scientists and the organization of research) will emerge as an oversimplification in the light of our subsequent analysis.

nical, administrative, and housekeeping staffs, and his machines and equipment, i.e., the man plus his overhead costs." Johnson and Milton secured cost records for the 1920–1960 period, from 17 laboratories, varying in size and divided roughly equally among industry, government, university, and private nonprofit institutions. While the experience of these laboratories varied, a relatively consistent picture emerged. Using 1950 as base year with cost-of-research index of 100, the study showed that during the period 1920–1940 the index hovered within a few points of 50, but it doubled over each of the two decades between 1940 and 1960, increasing at a rate of some 7 percent yearly to reach 191 in 1960. Johnson and Milton found that although the total fixed dollar costs grew by a factor of 4·5 in the decade from 1950 to 1960, the actual output of research and development results only slightly more than doubled, a somewhat more than two-fold increase in the per-project cost over a ten year period. Supposing the intrinsic significance of these projects to be relatively uniform, an escalation of costs is clearly indicated (to be sure, only at the moderate end of the quality-spectrum).[14]

Again, over the five year period from 1966 to 1971, the constant (1966) dollar cost of research projects funded by the National Institutes of Health increased from an average of \$30,400 (for 11,683 projects) to an average of \$34,400 (for 9,170 projects) in 1971, an increase of some 13% for this short period,[15] when there was certainly no comparable escalation in the scientific merit of the researches. All the available data conspire to yield a picture of steadily increasing costs of significant results in terms of the human and material resources committed to scientific work.

The medical area affords a particularly vivid illustration of the extent to which latter-day problems tend to be more intractable than earlier ones and demand for their solution a vastly greater resource-investment. The historical record of the success of modern medicine is doubtless impressive: more than half of the big killer-diseases of 1900 have virtually been eliminated as serious threats. But what is significant from our angle is the greater intractability of the problems that

---

[14] This summary of the Johnson–Milton study is based on the report in Dael Wolfle, "How Much Research for a Dollar," *Science*, vol. 132 (1960), p. 517.
[15] Data from *NIH Research Grant Expenditures: FY 1971* (Washington, 1974; NIH Special Projects and Surveys Section, Special Project Reports, no. 1; January 1974).

remain.[16] Finding a cure for tuberculosis or gastritis or diphtheria is still small potatoes compared with finding a cure for today's big killers.[17] In 1962, a total of $1,032 \times 10^6$ was spent on medical research in the U.S.,[18] distributed as follows:

128×10^6 Cancer

117×10^6 Cardiovascular Disease

787×10^6 Other

The U.S. was spending more money (and effort) on cancer in 1962 than it was spending on *all* of medical research in 1950—and (arguably) more than had been spent on all of medical research in the history of mankind until 1940. Phenomenally, this massive expenditure had more than doubled to $2,277 \times 10^6$ by 1972, and America is currently spending on medical research an amount that is somewhat over 4% of what private consumers spend on medical care.[19] The scale of this research effort is truly impressive. Of course, one tackles the easier problems first—that goes without saying. But the remarkable aspect of this phenomenon is its indication of the *extent* to which the later problems become more difficult and demand ever increasing levels of effort for their resolution—in the bio-medical area exactly as elsewhere in natural science. The operation of a principle of cost-escalation has become strikingly manifest in the contemporary medical research.[20]

A mass of evidence of this general tendency substantiates Planck's contention that scientific progress becomes increasingly more difficult

[16] Compare John Pawles, "On the Limitations of Modern Medicine," *Science, Medicine and Man*, vol. 1 (1973), pp. 1–30.

[17] The basic research that led to the discovery of penicillin did not cost more than $20,000. See Eric Hodgins, "The Strange State of American Research" in The Editors of *Fortune* (eds.), *The Mighty Force of Research op. cit.*, pp. 1–20 (see p. 7).

[18] The data are given in B. S. Cooper, N. L. Worthington and P. A. Piro, "National Health Expenditure: 1929–1973," Social Security Bulletin, February 1974.

[19] B. S. Cooper *et al.*, *ibid.*, Table 4.

[20] See the interesting paper by John Pawles, "On the Limitations of Modern Medicine" in *Science, Medicine and Man*, vol. 1 (1973), pp. 1–30. Its opening sentence reads: "One of the most striking paradoxes facing the student of modern medical culture lies in the contrast between the enthusiasm associated with current developments and the reality of decreasing returns to health for rapidly increasing efforts." Compare also the quote from MacFarlane Burnet in Section 3 of Chapter II and cf. Ivan Illich, *Limits to Medicine* (Harmondsworth, 1977).

and demanding with the passage of time. It would seem that science too is subject to a condition of increasing difficulty whose structure is closely analogous to that which has clearly emerged over the years in the sphere of technological innovation and inventiveness, a phenomenon clearly depicted in Table 1. These data indicate a steady decline in the number of patents per working scientist/engineer in the U.S. over the first two generations of the present century, a decline proceeding at a steady rate of roughly 4·5% *per annum*.[21] An analogous development is apparently underway in natural science as well—a decline in the index of substantial findings per active researcher.

As the available data are pieced together, one is thus driven towards the conclusion that science is subject to a process of cost-escalation when the yield of significant new findings is considered in relation to the investment of effort (talent, manpower, and material resources) needed for their realization. Such considerations may seem somewhat surprising at first sight. Recent history has accustomed one to think of science in terms of swift and sure progress. The striking evidence of massive scientific advance in recent days leaps readily to the forefront of our thinking. But the (certainly correct) impression of the great strides that have been made in science in our time must be tempered by a recognition of the enormously enlarged volume of manpower and resources committed to the enterprise (as indicated in Adams' Law of acceleration). The phenomenon of escalating costs is the portent through which can be discerned—even in an era of great, indeed exponential, growth—the omens of the deceleration that almost certainly lies ahead. For the rapidly—indeed exponentially—increasing pace of effort-investment tends to mask the fact that the volume of high-quality returns per *unit* investment is apparently declining.

---

[21] Experience in the United Kingdom has been essentially parallel. See the data cited in Keith Norris and John Vaizey, *The Economics of Research and Technology* (London, 1973). For an interesting discussion see Fritz Machlup, "The Supply of Inventors and Inventions," *Weltwirtschaftliches Archiv*, vol. 65 (1960), pp. 210–251. See also Edmund L. Van Deusen, "The Inventor in Eclipse" in The Editors of *Fortune* (eds.), *The Mighty Force of Research* (New York, 1953–1956), pp. 74–86. The situation in the areas of invention and technology is, to be sure, significantly unlike that in pure science. The decline of patents is a complex phenomenon, tied—*inter alia*—to the essentially legal issue of the amount of protection patenting actually affords. Nevertheless, a rough suggestive interconnection seems to obtain between patents and technological progress on the one hand and discoveries and scientific progress on the other.

Table 1

NUMBER OF SCIENTISTS AND ENGINEERS COMPARED WITH
NUMBER OF PATENTS ISSUED IN THE U.S.A. 1900–1954

Year	Scientists and Engineers (1)	Index of Growth of Scientists and Engineers (2)	Patents Granted for Inventions (3)	Index of Growth of Patents granted for Inventions (4)	Index of Relative Growth of Patenting in relation to Scientists and Engineers (4) ÷ (2) × 100 (5)
1900	42,000	100	24,660	100	100
1910	86,000	205	35,168	143	65
1920	135,000	321	37,164	151	47
1930	227,000	557	45,243	183	34
1940	310,000	738	42,333	172	23
1950	573,000	1,364	43,072	175	13
1954	691,000	1,645	33,872	137	8

Data from Fritz Machlup, *The Production and Distribution of Knowledge in the United States* [Princeton, 1962], p. 172.

3. CONSTANT RETURNS ON EXPONENTIALLY INCREASING EFFORT

In turning to the key question of the recent rate of scientific progress, a convenient starting point is provided by Adams' Law of Exponential Growth which maintains that the over-all volume of scientific effort (in terms of the investment of human and material resources) has been increasing exponentially in the recent past—specifically at a rate that results in a doubling time of some 15 years in the professional literature of science. But as already indicated, the question of *evaluation* becomes crucial at this juncture. What can be said about the *quality* of this work—its capacity to afford us deepened understanding of the workings of nature?

One sometimes hears that scientific innovation is in a state of decline: that all or most of the really big discoveries have already been made and that newer science is lesser science.[22] But on the other hand, it is

[22] For details see section 5 of Chap. I. The idea that science is not only subject to a principle of escalating costs but to a law of diminishing returns as well is due to the

sometimes held that scientific understanding has been keeping step with the massively increasing volume of scientific effort itself. With respect to this issue we shall opt for the *via media*. The position basic to the present discussion is the thesis that *the substantive level of scientific innovation has remained roughly constant over the last few generations*.

How can one support this seemingly shocking contention that while scientific *efforts* have grown exponentially, the production of really high-level scientific *findings* has remained constant?

One indicator of this constancy in high-quality science is the relative stability of honors (medals, prizes, honorary degrees, membership of scientific academics, etc.). To be sure, in some instances these reflect a fixed-number situation (e.g., Nobel prizes). But if the volume of clearly first-rate scientific work were expanding drastically, there would be mounting pressure for the enlargement of such honorific awards and mounting discontent with the inequity of the present reward-system. There are no signs of this.

Another significant item of evidence relates to citations—citations not in "the literature" at large,[23] but in the synoptic handbooks, monographs and treatises that endeavor to give a rounded picture of "the state of the discipline." The evidence indicates that here, interestingly enough, the number of references cited has in fact grown linearly over the years.[24] Where scientific results of a very high level are

---

nineteenth-century American philosopher of science Charles Sanders Peirce (1839–1914). In his pioneering 1878 essay on "Economy of Research" Peirce put the issue in the following terms:

> We thus see that when an investigation is commenced, after the initial expenses are once paid, at little cost we improve our knowledge, and improvement then is especially valuable; but as the investigation goes on, additions to our knowledge cost more and more, and, at the same time, are of less and less worth. All the sciences exhibit the same phenomenon, and so does the course of life. At first we learn very easily, and the interest of experience is very great; but it becomes harder and harder, and less and less worthwhile. . . . (*Collected Papers*, Vol. VII [Cambridge, Mass., 1958], sect. 7.144.)

[23] Citations are doubtless problematic as a measure of merit. All the same, citation-indices can surely be exploited to yield a fairly good indication of statistical trends. Thus a reasonable indication of a paper's utility would be its citation in a reasonable proportion of papers in its field within a suitable time after its publication. Of course, this utility might be practical/experimental rather than cognitive/theoretical. But ways can always be devised to make allowances for such cases.

[24] An interesting example is given by Joseph Ben-David, *The Scientists Role in Society* (Englewood Cliffs, 1971), who has analyzed the reference-structure of a well-known series of psychological monograph. Over the half-century of its appearance in constantly updated editions, its references to the literature increased at a fairly constant rate of ca. 40 items per annum. And this situation is typical.

at issue, the historic picture seems to present a constant volume of innovation and a linear cumulation (an exponential growth in the scale of effort and activity notwithstanding).[25] Thus while science has been growing exponentially as a productive *enterprise*, its growth as an intellectual *discipline* has—to all appearances—proceeded at a *constant* pace.

This upshot is perhaps not really all that surprising. Consider a cybernetic analogy. A continuing exponential literature-explosion is (from this standpoint) ultimately counter-productive in the peculiar manner of creating circumstances in which the progress of science makes the production of yet further science just difficult enough so that a relatively stable situation is produced even with exponentially increasing effort. (Compare here the crowding phenomenon that curtails the fertility of some animal populations so as to produce a condition of overall stability.) To put it somewhat figuratively, as progress goes ahead, the added information knocking about in the scientific information-system creates just enough "noise" that the level of really significant messages to emerge from the channel remains relatively constant. Various considerations thus conspire to indicate that the conception of a linear rate of advance in first-rate science is by no means frivolous.

4. THE LAW OF LOGARITHMIC RETURNS

The foregoing discussion has adduced evidence of a marked escalation of the cost of significant findings in natural science, as measured in terms of talented manpower and other scarce resources. This constitutes the relatively safe structural thesis that Planck's Principle of increasing effort is operative here. It is merely claimed *that* the resource-cost of substantial results is rising, without any indication of just *how much*. Let us now take the rasher step of devising a more committal, and specifically quantitative picture of the temporal *rate* at which this diminution of returns on fixed-size investment takes place.

The basis of the present analysis is provided by the just-indicated thesis that the production-rate of really significant findings in natural science has in fact remained relatively stable. Consider now the two

---

[25] Recall that in speaking of accumulation here, we have in mind enlargement in the *number* of "significant results" whose *contents* may be in no sense cumulative.

basic parameters of science as a process for "the production of knowledge":

(1) *R*—or better *R(t)*—as a measure of the cumulatively aggregated sum-total of *resources* (human and physical) expended on scientific work up to the time *t* after some suitable origin or starting-point.

And

(2) *F*—or better *F(t)*—as a measure of the cumulative volume of *first-rate scientific findings* (in the previously specified sense) that have resulted from this resource-expenditure (the "yield" on this "investment," so to speak).

Given the fact that *R* has been increasing *exponentially* (as per Adams' Law), while *F* has merely accumulated at a roughly *linear* pace, one can venture a pretty good guess at the production function that links the outputs of scientific inquiry to its inputs. For if the total volume of production-inputs grows exponentially, while yet the output of really first-rate output grows merely linearly, *then we have it that for a (cumulative) total investment (R) the (cumulative) total yield of first-rate products (F) stands merely as the logarithm of R: $F \infty \log R$*.[26] We shall characterize this relationship as the Law of Logarithmic Returns.

The preceding log-proportionality principle is strongly reminiscent of the Weber-Fechner Law in the psychology of sensation, according to which "In order that the intensity of a sensation—the strength of the phenomenological response ϕ—may increase in arithmetical progression, the physical stimulus ψ must increase in geometrical progression." This yields the relationship: $\phi \infty \log \psi$. Only the *logarithm*

---

[26] Throughout the symbol $\propto$ will be used for *strict* proportionality while ∞ is used to indicate *quasi-proportionality* (*q*-proportionality), that is, proportionality-up-to-an-additive-constant. Accordingly, while $y \propto x$ stands for $y = ax$, $y \infty x$ stands for $y = ax + b$. Thus to say that *y* is *q*-proportional to *x* is simply to say that *x* and *y* are linearly related. (Note, however, that *q*-proportionality always reduces to strict proportionality with an appropriate positioning of the origin.) Thus $F \infty \log R$ amounts to $F = a \log R + b = a \log R + a \log c = a (\log R + \log c) = a \log cR$. Hence $F \propto \log cR$ and $F \infty \log R$ are equivalent. With *R* measured in the "right" units, we would simply have $F \propto \log R$. Thus in theoretical discussions we may use $\propto$ to represent log-uniformity relationships, while, when it comes to working with empirically determined numbers (where the choice of units becomes fixed), we must use ∞.

of the volume of the "stimulus" proves cognitively effective in the case of perception. Interestingly enough, in information-oriented cases we now have exactly the same situation with respect to *conception* that the Weber-Fechner relationship stipulates with respect to *perception*.

The mathematics of the situation is such that any two of the relationships

$F \infty \log R$
$F \infty t$ (or equivalently $F^* = \dfrac{dF}{dt} = \text{constant}$)
$R \propto 10^{at}$

will yield the third: the three relations are bound to one another by an iron chain. Thus the very fact that dF/dt remained constant over the exponential-growth past suffices to yield the operation of a Law of Logarithmic Returns during this period.

But one important ramification needs to be stressed. While the relations $F \infty t$ and $R \propto 10^{at}$ are transient truths about a limited historical era (viz., the past period of exponential growth), it is reasonable to suppose that the relationship $F \infty \log R$ which connects them represents a permanent underlying production-relation—one that is reflected in the historical situation, but not confined to it. This Law of Logarithmic Returns reflects (so we suppose) a permanent and general structural situation in scientific production, that can be used to assess the situation beyond the restrictive confines of the exponential-growth history of scientific effort. It indicates *that the exponential growth over recent times in the parameters of scientific EFFORT (manpower, resources) can be viewed as a forced consequence of the desideratum of maintaining the rate of scientific PROGRESS at something like a constant level.*

In this connection, it is worth noting Derek J. Price's suggestion[27] of using the logarithm of a scientist's life-score of papers as a measure of what he calls his *solidness* as a productive scientist.[28] Price goes on to make the following interesting transition:

[27] Derek J. Price, *Little Science, Big Science, op. cit.*, p. 50.

[28] Price remarks that the logarithm of the number of men having at least *s* units of solidness of productivity will (up to a limit) fall off linearly with *s*, noting that the log-normal character of scientific productivity distributions has previously been suggested by William Shockley, "On the Statistics of Individual Variations of Productivity in Research Laboratories," *Proceedings of the Institute of Ratio Engineers*, vol. 45 (1957), pp. 279ff and 1409ff.

If we may take in general the solidness of a body of publications as measured by the logarithm of the number of papers, it has further interesting consequences. Consider the law of exponential growth previously mentioned as a universal condition of freely expanding science. Obviously, the solidness of the field, the logarithm of the number of papers, grows linearly with time. Thus, since it takes about 50 years for the number of men or number of papers in a field to multiply by 10, there is a unit increase of solidness every half-century. This, then, provides a measure that is linear, not exponential. It is the sort of index which might correspond with Nobel Prizes (which come linearly with time because that is how they are organized); possibly also with unexpected, crucial advances.[29]

Our present approach moves in parallel with this line of thought. It takes in all due seriousness the idea that one must not view the output of a branch of science merely in terms of a mass of printed literature but in terms of its "solidity" in such a cognition-oriented sense—a measure of achievement grows with its Nobel-prizeworthy work and its crucial unforeseeable discoveries.[30]

Such, then, is the basic outline of our evaluative posture in the context of increasing costs. It is a position which envisages the progress of science *as an intellectual discipline*—a progress to be adjudged solely in terms of the *really major*, absolutely first-rate achievements of scientific inquiry—to have advanced at a *linear* rate, notwithstanding the *exponential* growth of the scientific enterprise in the scale of the efforts involved and the correlatively exponential production of purely routine results.[31] This position is, however, heavily laden with evaluative

[29] Price, *op. cit.*, pp. 55–56.

[30] However, Price himself does *not* draw from his deliberations regarding this "solidness" the conclusion that, despite the exponential growth of the scientific enterprise itself, the rate of the *progress* of science has been merely linear in recent history. He proposes to evaluate scientific progress in terms of what he calls the *stature* of science, which has also been growing exponentially, albeit at a much slower rate than the literature of science, to which it is related by something approximating to the Rousseau's Law standard (cf. Chap. VI below). There is, says Price, "Reasonable certainty that the stature of science [as assessed 'in terms of its achievements'], however one defines it, grows some two or three times more slowly than any measure of gross size." He estimates the doubling time of this "stature" at ca. 30 years. (*Science Since Babylon* [2nd ed.; New Haven, 1975], p. 188.)

[31] A detailed picture of the analogous phenomenon of a relatively linear pace of major invention in various areas of applied technology (especially railroads, petroleum, agriculture, paper-making) even during periods of history that have seen an exponential expansion of work in the field is drawn in Jacob Schmookler, *Invention and Economic Growth* (Cambridge, Mass, 1966).

commitments as to what constitutes the high-quality findings with reference to which progress in scientific knowledge can be assessed. It is desirable virtually to the point of necessity to examine more closely the implications and ramifications of this evaluative posture.

VI

The Quantity of Quality

"Progress" involves a judgment of value, which is not involved in the conception of history as a genetic process.

J. B. BURY

1. THE PROBLEM OF QUALITY

It is necessary to embark upon some terminological exploration on which infinitely more than "a matter of mere terminology" will hinge. In the setting of present concerns, one must be able in principle *to compare the intrinsic significance of the scientific findings made at different temporal junctures.* If this cannot be done, there can be no valid basis for a claim of escalating costs as opposed to merely increasing outlays. Any application of Planck's idea that work of comparable significance is getting harder calls for being in a position to evaluate—in terms of their *intrinsic* importance—the comparative merits of findings made at different times and places. The data of the preceding discussion of Adams' Law—which relate simply to gross productivity in the published output of scientific literature—cannot of themselves do the needed job. Our concern with progress relates to *net* science not *gross* science—to scientific work that "makes a real contribution to man's understanding of nature." Scientific *progress* is clearly an emphatically nonlinear function of scientific *output*.[1] As Bury

---

[1] In his interesting address "Science: Endless Horizons or Golden Age" (*Science*, vol. 171 [1971], pp. 23–29), Bentley Glass writes:

It is of course dangerous to equate the growth of scientific knowledge with growth in the number of scientists or of their publication of papers. Yet I suppose, although I cannot demonstrate it satisfactorily, that there must be some relatively stable mathematical ratio between the total number of scientific contributions published in a given period and the number among them of highly important, significant "breakthroughs" (p. 25).

Now had Glass written "relationship" here instead of "ratio," there would be little ground for quarrel. But as it stands this thesis could not be more ill-advised. For why should the "breakthroughs"—which, after all, are the highly important and really significant results by more or less *absolute* rather than *relative* standards—form a fixed

rightly stresses, evaluation is an essential element of the very idea of progress. There is thus no way of evading this issue.

The statistical data set out above show that the sum-total of work in natural science as measured in terms of workers (scientists) and output (papers) had been increasing exponentially throughout the recent past at a compound interest of around 5–6% *per annum* (with a doubling time of 12–15 years). But the volume of work that competent judges are prepared to regard as sufficiently substantial to make a significant contribution to the subject[2] has been growing at a much slower rate.[3]

It scarcely needs emphasis that this whole issue of evaluation is a hornet's nest. The difficulties that lie in the way of an objective treatment are doubtless among the main reasons why this theme is so rarely discussed in terms other than those of the grossest generality. All the same, we must somehow cut the Gordian knot. The whole process of assessing the merit of scientific findings may be inexact and "judgmental," but unless we are prepared to abandon the whole topic of scientific progress, we shall have to grasp the nettle of this problematic issue.

2. ROUSSEAU'S LAW

Our evaluative analysis has so far concerned itself only with absolutely

---

percentage of the whole, as the ratio-standard entails? Glass's discussion here commits the serious mis-step of the grave (and uncharacteristic) gaffe of conflating relative with absolute standards. Top percentile results will ever be top percentile results, but there is no reason to think—nay every reason *not* to think—that the top percentile results of one era will be cognitively equi-significant with those of another.

[2] There is a fair amount of evidence to the effect that various currently popular indicators of the quality of scientific workmanship (peer group evaluation, papers published, citation frequencies, Ph.D.'s supervised) stand in fairly good correlation with one another. For some interesting details see S. Cole and J. R. Cole, "Scientific Output and Recognition: A Study in the Operation of the Reward System in Science," *American Sociological Review*, vol. 32 (1967), pp. 377–390, and S. S. Blume and R. Sinclair, *Research Environment and Performance in British University Chemistry* (London, 1973: Science Policy Studies Series of the Department of Education and Science), pp. 20–23.

[3] For example, the physical discoveries registered in Felix Auerbach's *Geschichtstafeln der Physik* have been increasing exponentially since 1500 with a doubling time of roughly 45 years. An analogous situation holds for the far more exhaustive register of Ludwig Darmstaedter, *Handbuch zur Geschicte der Naturwissenschaften und der Technik* (2nd ed.; Berlin, 1908). Compare footnote 11 on p. 102.

first-rate work, scientific findings of a very high order, at—or indeed somewhat above—the level of the discoveries which year by year qualify their authors as candidates for a Nobel Prize. But let us now turn to work of a somewhat lower standard.

There is good reason to think that—in virtually any context where a significant concept of importance is operative—the volume of really "important" production stands as the square root of the total production:

$$\text{Number of "important" results} = \sqrt{\text{total number of results}}$$

This is in fact a rather well-known formula in the study of elites, reflecting the principle that the elite of a group stand as the square root of its size. Such a relationship was initially mooted by Jean Jacques Rousseau, and has accordingly come to be characterized as Rousseau's Law.[4] For example, Galton found that at a time when the adult male population of England stood at some 9,000,000 there were some 3,000 really eminent individuals (persons qualifying as noteworthy by a variety of criteria on the order of featuring in the obituary notices of *The Times*).[5] Also, the square root of the population of a country or profession or other category represents (to within an order of magnitude, at any rate) the number of listings in a *Who's Who* for the population at issue.[6] Or again, there are in the U.S. roughly 1,600 educational institutions that grant a baccalaureate degree, but only some 160 grant higher degrees, with some 40 ($=\sqrt{1,600}$) of them comprising the really "major universities" which among them produce some three-quarters of the Ph.D.'s and are the source of the vast majority of scholarly books and papers.

Applying this idea in the present instance, it eventuates that only the

[4] Thus George K. Zipf writes: "Rousseau curiously enough, argued that the size of the elite (i.e., government) varied with the square root of the population, if I understand correctly. This statement that is so frequently imputed to J. J. Rousseau seems to evade specific reference although its sense is apparent in his *Contrat Social*." (*Human Behaviour and the Principle of Least Effort* [Boston, 1949], p. 452 & n.)

[5] Derek J. de Solla Price, *Little Science, Big Science* (New York, 1963), pp. 33–36, provides a sketch of Galton's findings.

[6] However, the 1974–75 *Who's Who in America* lists 73,000 individuals at a time when the population of the country stands at 211 millions (with a square root of ca. 15,000). This exaggeration by a factor of 3–5 by the Rousseau's law standard is typical of national *Who's Who*. Perhaps the editors of such works are inclined for commercial reasons somewhat to exaggerate who is a who.

square root of the total production of scientific work represents genuinely "important" contributions. Considering that the doubling-time of general activity of science has stood at ca. 15 years, that of "important" work—of high quality science—would by this standard be roughly 30 years: a human generation. On this basis, one arrives at the exponential-growth pattern of duplication with successive generations which, as we have seen, has in fact been mooted by various writers on the subject.[7]

3. THE INTERRELATIONSHIP OF QUANTITY AND QUALITY

As starting-point for the development of a theory of quantity and quality we thus arrive at the idea that, when the total volume of findings of (at least) *routine* quality stands at Q, the volume of (at least) *important* findings stands at $\sqrt{Q} = Q^{\frac{1}{2}}$. This relation may be generalized to obtain the following idea:

> Let the λ-*quality-level* of findings be so construed that when the total volume of (at least routine) findings is Q the volume of findings of this category stands at Q^{λ} (for $0 < \lambda \leqslant 1$).

Accordingly, the "(at least) routine" findings will be those of the quality-level with $\lambda = 1$, and the "(at least) important" findings those of the quality category with $\lambda = \frac{1}{2}$. In general, the lower the index λ, the greater the importance of the findings.

Let us now endeavor to erect a reasonable theory of the quantity/quality relationship upon this foundation, adopting a rather simple five-place scale for measurement of quality, as follows:

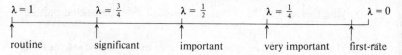

$\lambda = 1$	$\lambda = \frac{3}{4}$	$\lambda = \frac{1}{2}$	$\lambda = \frac{1}{4}$	$\lambda = 0$
routine	significant	important	very important	first-rate

[7] See, for example, Derek J. Price, *Science Since Babylon* (2nd ed.; New Haven, 1975), p. 188, where it is claimed that "The actual *stature* of science, in terms of its achievements appears to double within about one generation (some thirty years). . . ." While Price gives this idea a very different explanation, the following justification seems particularly apt. The growth-rate of the scientific *literature* has long stood at some $6 \pm 1\%$ per annum. The *routine* findings of science follow this by perhaps one percentage point thanks to redundancies (including those in expository and review publications) and duplications, and so grow at $5 \pm 1\%$ per annum. Thus the important findings by the Rousseau's Law (square-root) standard grow at some $2\frac{1}{2} \pm \frac{1}{2}\%$ per annum, corresponding to a doubling time of some 30 years.

Now we know in general that, in an innumerable variety of diverse contexts, one obtains a relationship of the general form depicted in Figure 1,[8] which portrays a log-normal distribution of objects in some evaluative respect. The total number of items of at least the degree of merit m falls off exponentially in m. This logarithmic linearity means

---

Figure 1

VOLUME/MERIT RELATIONSHIPS:
THE GENERIC STRUCTURE

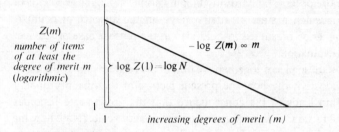

Note: N is the total number of items.

---

that if we partition by successive fractions in terms of decreasing merit (lowest n-th, second lowest n-th, etc.), then the logarithm of the number of items in (at least) the m-th merit group is proportional to $(n+1-m)/n$, so that $\log Z(m) \propto (n+1-m)/n$. Thus in the special case of a four-fold partition $(n=4)$ we have:

bottom merit group:　$\log Z(1) \propto 4/4 \log N = \log N$
next merit group:　　$\log Z(2) \propto 3/4 \log N = \log N^{3/4}$
next merit group:　　$\log Z(3) \propto 2/4 \log N = \log N^{1/2}$
top merit group:　　 $\log Z(4) \propto 1/2 \log N = \log N^{1/4}$

Our picture of the λ-quality-levels thus dovetails perfectly into the Figure 1 relationship.

Note that the size of the group of successively decreasing merit stands at $N^{\frac{1}{4}k}, N^{\frac{1}{2}k}, N^{\frac{3}{4}k}$, and N^{k}, respectively. Accordingly, the successive merit

[8] See George K. Zipf, *Human Behavior and the Principle of Least Effort, op. cit.*, esp. pp. 130–131, and compare A. Rappoport in the *Encyclopedia of the Social Sciences,* art. "Zipf's Law."

groups increase in size as multiples of $N^{\frac{1}{2}k}$—that is, they increase as the successive powers of a constant.[9]

And this can also be approached from a rather different perspective. As "degree of merit" take simply the *logarithm* of some size/frequency/amount parameter of things of a particular sort. And note that the "number of items of at least a certain degree of merit" is simply the rank-order of the item at issue within a group. From this angle then, Figure 1 reflects simply a rank/size correlation. It is known from virtually innumerable cases of the most diverse sort that these situations yield a linear configuration of negative steps when plotted on log-log paper.[10] (See for instance the picture of Figure 2.) Since this is for the more or less standard situation in various analogous contexts of evaluation, such a state of affairs may—in the absence of counter-indications—be presumed to hold also in the present case of science-oriented evaluation.

Putting these pieces together, we obtain the relationship of Figure 3, which shows vividly how the present picture of the quantity/quality relationship leads to the consequence that the growth-rate becomes increasingly slow as one moves up on the quality-scale. (Note how the Rousseau Law relationship dovetails neatly into this framework, obtaining at exactly the middle level of quality—as was foreshadowed by characterizing the findings of this quality-level as "important.")

Supposing that Q grows exponentially with a doubling time of n, the volume of the findings at the various λ-index quality levels will accordingly also grow exponentially, but with a doubling time of n/λ. This gives rise to an historical picture of the following sort. The volume of *new* (incremental) production at the routine level of scientific findings has been increasing exponentially. As one ascends the quality-scale there is still exponential growth, but it becomes increasingly slow. (But at the very top of the quality scale, when F-level findings are at issue, there is merely *constant* incremental output.) We arrive at the general situation whose specific instance is depicted in Table 1. Its Findings-

---

[9] On this phenomenology of an exponential decay of numbers with "merit" in the specific sense of productivity (in publications, patents, or the like) see William Shockley, "On the Statistics of Individual Variations of Productivity in Research Laboratories," *Proceedings of the Institute of Radio Engineers*, vol. 45 (1957), pp. 279–290.

[10] The relevant facts have been painstakingly assembled in George K. Zipf, *Human Behavior and the Principle of Least Effort, op. cit.*

Figure 2

RANK-ORDERING OF THE HUNDRED LARGEST U.S. CITIES, 1940

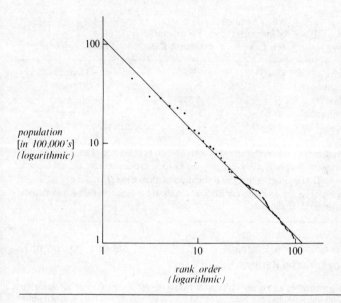

population
[in 100,000's]
(logarithmic)

rank order
(logarithmic)

Figure 3

THE QUANTITY OF QUALITY

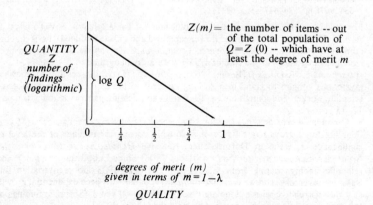

QUANTITY
Z
number of
findings
(logarithmic)

log Q

$Z(m)=$ the number of items -- out of the total population of $Q = Z(0)$ -- which have at least the degree of merit m

degrees of merit (m)
given in terms of $m = 1 - \lambda$

QUALITY

Table 1

THE RATE OF GROWTH AT DIFFERENT QUALITY-LEVELS

Quality-Level	Cumulative No. of Findings of [at least] this Level	Per Annum Growth-Rate	Doubling Time
1. "routine"	$Q = Q^{1.00}$	5%	~15 years
2. "significant"	$Q^{.75}$	3·75%	~20 years
3. "important"	$Q^{.50}$	2·5%	~30 years
4. "very important"	$Q^{.25}$	1·25%	~60 years
5. "first-rate" (F)	$\propto \log Q$	linear growth	

Note The volume of "routine" findings Q is here taken as subject to exponential growth at a rate of 5% per annum (roughly the historic expansion-rate of the scientific literature). Also observe that the F standard (with $F \propto \log Q$) and the Q^λ-standard (with $\log Q^\lambda \propto \log Q$) represent *distinct* evaluative policies, in that F has no fixed place on the λ-continuum.

Quality Coordination Principle $F \propto \log Q$ is yet another version of a Law of Logarithmic Returns.[11]

[11] Perceptive observers have not failed to note that the recent "explosion" of scientific manpower and literature has not been matched by any comparable advance in scientific knowledge:

> Of course there has been a substantial increase in the volume of research publications over the past 30 years. . . . Some of these are valuable, but many seldom contain any papers of importance, and could disappear without much loss to science. . . . I estimate that, in Britain, the number of pages used to communicate the new results of original research has only about doubled between 1936 and 1966. (Kenneth Mellanby, "A Damp Squib," *New Scientist*, vol. 33 (1967), pp. 626–627 [see p. 626].)

For what it is worth, it may be noted regarding line 3 of Table 1 that the Soviet analyst of science G. M. Dobrov has offered the (unexplained and unsubstantiated) thesis that the number of major scientific discoveries (*grundlegende Ergebnisse der Wissenschaft*) have been increasing at the rate of 1·55% with a doubling time of 45 years. (See his *Wissenschaftswissenschaft* [Berlin, 1969], pp. 96–97.) He rightly sees this—somewhat mysterious—figure to stand in a striking contrast to the increase in the number of scientific workers (doubling time ca. 10 years) and scientific papers (doubling time ca. 12–15 years).

Although Dobrov does not explain whence he derives his mysterious 1·55% (45 year doubling time) growth rate figure, it is roughly correct for findings of the level of significance at issue in Darmstaedter's massive *Handbuch zur Geschichte der Naturwissenschaften und der Technik* (Berlin, 1908). Some 13,000 major technical and scientific findings dating from antiquity to the year 1908 are registered in this elaborate inventory, and we find that after ca. 1700 there has been exponential growth at a rate correlative with a doubling time of roughly 40 years. (Scientific findings at *this* level of significance thus stand at roughly the $Q^{.33}$ level.)

Such an account of a differential growth-rate of scientific work at different quality levels is clearly borne out by the historical evidence. Some interesting observations regarding physics were compiled by T. J. Rainoff,[12] who used the data regarding discoveries in physics presented in F. Auerbach's *Geschichtstafeln der Physik*,[13] supplementing them substantially from other sources. The following findings germane to our purposes emerge from these data:

1. With respect to the 500 most substantial physical discoveries made in France during the century and a half from 1750 to 1900 (as registered by Auerbach)—averaging out at some 3 per year—the data indicates a pattern of slow and steady growth from ca. 1 *per annum* in 1750 to ca. 5 *per annum* in 1900, reflecting a doubling time of ca. 70 years.[14]

2. With respect to Rainoff's own enlarged list of 1,592 physical discoveries made in France during 1776–1900—averaging out at 13 per year—the historical data indicate a pattern of exponential growth with a doubling time of ca. 30 years.[15]

3. Finally, with respect to Rainoff's list of 2,863 physical discoveries made in Germany during 1835–1900—averaging out at 44 per year—the historical pattern is one of exponential growth with a doubling time of 15 years.[16]

It is striking that as the numbers of the discoveries at issue decrease—i.e., as the quality-level of those selected for consideration increases—we arrive at a picture of slower and slower exponential growth—a growth which (by extrapolation) becomes essentially linear at the very top of the scale. This is exactly what the preceding analysis of the quantity/quality relationship would lead one to expect. (We would incline to say that in the first case one is dealing with "very important" discoveries, in the second with "important" ones, while with the third massive inventory one has almost descended to the level of "routine" findings.)

---

[12] T. J. Rainoff, "Wave-like Fluctuations of Creative Productivity in the Development of West-European Physics in the Eighteenth and Nineteenth Centuries," *Isis*, vol. 12 (1929), pp. 287–307.

[13] Felix Auerbach, *Geschichtstafeln der Physik* (Leipzig, 1910).

[14] See Figure 1 on p. 293, *ibid.*

[15] See Figure 3 on p. 298, *ibid.*

[16] See Figure 6 on p. 304, *ibid.*

4. THE QUALITY STRUCTURE OF SCIENTIFIC PRODUCTION

Interesting results ensue when one juxtaposes these considerations regarding the quality-levels of findings with "Lotka's Law" of scholarly publication.[17] Lotka remarked that the number $A(n)$ of

Table 2

SCHEMATIC TABLE SHOWING NUMBERS OF AUTHORS
OF VARIOUS DEGREES OF PRODUCTIVITY (IN
PAPERS PER LIFETIME) AND NUMBERS
OF PAPERS SO PRODUCED

Papers/man	Men	Papers	
1	100	100	(The 75 percent of authors who write
2	25	50	only one or two papers produce
3	11·1	33·3	one-quarter of the whole.)
4	6·2	25	
5	4	20	
6	2·8	16·7	
7	2	14·2	
8	1·5	12·5	
9	1·2	11·1	
10	1	10	
10–11·1	1	10+	(10 authors produce more than half
11·1–12·5	1	11·1+	of all papers.)
12·5–14·2	1	12·5+	
14·2–16·7	1	14·2+	
16·7–20	1	16·7+	
20–25	1	20+	
25–33·3	1	25+	
33·3–50	1	33·3+	
50–100	1	50+	(The top two authors produce one-
Over 100	1	100+	quarter of all papers.)
Total	165	586+	

Notes (1) Average papers/author = 586/165 = 3·54
      (2) Table constructed on hypothetical basis of exactly 100 men with a single published paper. Other entries computed from Lotka's Law.

From Derek J. Price, *Little Science, Big Science* (New York, 1963), p. 45.

[17] "The Frequency Distribution of Scientific Productivity," *Journal of the Washington Academy of Sciences*, vol. 16 (1926), pp. 317–323. Cf. Arnold Dresden, "A Report on the Scientific Work of the Chicago Section, 1897–1922," *Bulletin of the American Mathematical Society*, vol. 28 (1922), pp. 303–307.

authors who published exactly n papers is fixed in such a way that the relation $A(n) \propto 1/n^2$ obtains.[18] Exploiting Lotka's ideas, Derek J. Price has observed that, given a total literature of size P, one can calculate the productivity-levels of its contributors on the basis of the data of Table 2.

Coordinating these relationships regarding productivity with those regarding quality implicit in Figure 3, we obtain the sequence of stages depicted in Table 3. Throughout modern history, total science has been moving along the columns of this table at a rate of one order-of-magnitude step around every 50 years, and it currently stands somewhat shy of step IV.

As we have seen, the literatures of physics, chemistry, and biology have all had doubling times of some 15 years in recent years (compare Figure 4), so that these fields too have been moving up the order-of-magnitude productivity ladder at the rate of one step per 50 years. And so, if these fields behave in the indicated manner, they will yield roughly 50 really first-rate contributions every fifty years, given that we have a k value of ca. 50 for these fields. Given that the cumulative number of papers in each of these fields is currently in the order-of-magnitude range of 10^6, these fields will lie in the region of stage II.

The reader will have to judge for himself the acceptability of this over-all economy of productive interrelationships in terms of his intuitive assessment of the situation in physics, biology, and chemistry—recognizing that while biology is a "late bloomer," the development of physics and chemistry reflects something approaching the shift from stage I to stage II over the half-century from 1920 to 1970.

It must be stressed, however, that the considerations of our earlier analysis have generally moved at the global level of science as a whole. Now on first view, this seems to lead to a discrepancy upon application of our stated quality/quantity relationships at the levels of the branches and sub-branches of science. Consider a schematic illustration: If science as a whole were at stage III, but composed of ten stage II branches, this would seem to imply a total quota of 7,000 "important" contributions instead of the mere 2,100 indicated in column III, and

[18] For relevant discussions see: H. T. Davis, *The Theory of Econometrics* (Bloomington, 1941), p. 48; D. J. Price, *op. cit.*, pp. 41–49; Herbert Simon, *Models of Man: Social and National* (New York, 1957), pp. 160ff; Wayne Dennis, "Bibliographies of Eminent Scientists," *The Scientific Monthly*, vol. 79 (1954), pp 180–183. Several writers have observed that for large n ($n > 20$), $1/n^3$ gives a better approximation.

Figure 4

THE CUMULATIVE NUMBER OF ABSTRACTS IN VARIOUS SCIENTIFIC FIELDS
(From the Beginning of the Abstract Service to the Given Date)

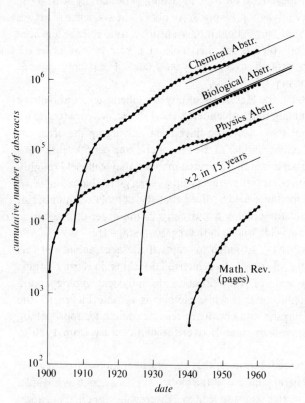

Note After an initial period of rapid expansion to a stable growth rate, the number of
abstracts increases exponentially, doubling in approximately 15 years.
From Derek J. Price, *Little Science, Big Science* (New York, 1963), p. 10.

2,900 first-rate contributions instead of the mere 340 of column III. But
this discrepancy is in fact removed when one takes the view that a shift
in *standard* is entailed by the shift in *focus* to a level lower down on the
taxonomic scale. Not every finding of high importance for *optics* is of
equally high importance for *physics*, let alone for *science* as a whole. As
one moves from one level to another, there is a corresponding shift in

Table 3

THE QUALITY STRUCTURE OF SCIENTIFIC PRODUCTION

	I	II	III	IV
1. No. of Papers (L)	100,000	1,000,000	10,000,000	100,000,000
2. No. of (at Least) Routinely Significant Findings[1] (Q)	56,000	500,000	4,500,000	40,000,000
3. (At Least) Important Findings ($\sqrt{Q}$)	240	700	2,100	6,300
4. First-Rate Findings[2] ($F = k \log Q$)	4·7k (240)	5·7k (290)	6·7k (340)	7·6k (380)
5. No. of Contributing Authors ($A = L/3·5$)	30,000	300,000	3,000,000	30,000,000
6. No. of Prolific Authors[3] ($A/20$)	1,500	15,000	150,000	1,500,000
7. Important Contributors ($\sqrt{A}$)	170	550	1,750	5,500
8. Routinely Significant (i.e., Q-level) Findings per Contributor ($2 \div 5$)	1·9	1·7	1·5	1·3
9. Important Contributions per Important Contributor ($3 \div 7$)	1·4	1·3	1·2	1·1
10. First-Rate as % of Important Findings ($4 \div 3$ in %)	100%	40%	16%	6%

Notes (1) Calculated under the supposition that $Q = L^{\alpha}$ with $\alpha = ·95$ (i.e., that is a certain "drag" separates the expansion of the raw literature from the expansion of actual *findings*). Historically, L has been increasing at roughly 5% *per annum*, and so Q has been increasing at a slightly lesser pace with a doubling time of ca. 15 years, or an OM increase time of some 50 years.

(2) Supposing that at stage I we have $4·7k = 240$ and that $k \cong 50$. This value of k reflects the supposition that row 4 increases by roughly 50 at each stage. (See pp. 82–94 above.) For values of L smaller than those of this Table, the assumptions yield the anomaly that the $\sqrt{Q}$ standard of quality is more rigorous than the F standard, suggesting that the former is an *unduly* rigorous standard at the initial stages of scientific development.

(3) Authors producing a lifetime total of at least 20 papers according to a Lotka's Law distribution of scientific productivity (cf. Table 2).

what is required to qualify as "a really significant member of the league." Results that are substantial by local standards may appear of less value from a more global point of view. The quality-taxonomy structure of Table 3 thus holds *within* each separate level of the variety/species/genus scale, but something of a change of standard is involved in moving from one level to the next—subject to the obvious principle that the standard becomes increasingly rigorous as one moves up the taxonomic scale.[19]

5. QUALITY-DRAG

The relationship $F \propto \log Q$ patently links all of the different Q^λ-sized quality-categories to one another. This relationship, which we have here characterized as the *Findings-Quality Coordination Principle*, correlates production across the various quality levels into lock-step with one another. It is thus built into the structure of our analysis that a definite functional relationship obtains between the high-level findings and the total findings of natural science. An iron chain of mutual relatedness connects the volume of findings at various quality levels. We cannot expand the volume of high-quality information without correlative expansions in the volume of total information. Advances in strictly high-level science inevitably pull the routine rest of science in their wake or rather—inversely—*emerge* from it.

Table 3 above accordingly affords a striking illustration of the phenomenon which the Soviet analyst of science G. M. Dobrov has characterized as "the dilution of the significance-content of scientific information"—namely, that the "significance-content" of the

---

[19] To illustrate, suppose that a field (discipline) of 1,000,000 routine findings is composed of ten 100,000 unit subfields (specialties) each of which is composed of ten 10,000 unit subspecialties. Then by the logarithmic standard of the Findings-Quality Coordination Principle ($F \propto \log Q$) we would have:

Size *(Routine Findings)*	First-Rate Findings *(By the Logarithmic Standard)*
1,000,000	$6k = 6 \cdot 10^0 \cdot k$
$10 \times 100,000$	$10 \cdot 5k = 5 \cdot 10^1 \cdot k$
$100 \times 10,000$	$100 \cdot 4k = 4 \cdot 10^2 \cdot k$

The overall number of first-rate findings *when assessed on the basis of strictly local standards* increases (almost) geometrically as one descends further down the taxonomic scale.

expanding volume of scientific findings Q (construed, say, at the "very important" level of quality, $Q^{.25}$) obviously increases at a much more sedate rate than Q itself, so that "each doubling of the quantity of new [substantial] results in world science in the past years of this century has required an 8 to 10-fold increase in the volume of scientific information. . . ."[20]

This "quality-drag" must, however, be construed as meaning *not* that the expanding literature of science is so much useless verbiage that reflects pointless busy-work, but rather that it represents—on balance and collectively, at any rate—the useful and necessary inputs needed for genuine advances, the indispensable grist, so to speak, for the mill of scientific progress.[21] There is a balance in the economy of science between its various quality-levels. One cannot adequately characterize any exploratory enterprise simply in terms of its successes. While the "big" discoveries are the determinants of *progress* proper, the unsuccessful and less successful efforts are an integral and ineliminable part of the whole venture. We are driven to a holistic view of science which denies the prospect of divorcing the important from the routine. (Compare pp. 164–167 below for other aspects of this model of scientific research in terms of exploration or prospecting.)

Such a correlation relationship between the different quality levels of scientific production is in fact crucial to the cost-escalation principle maintained in the preceding chapter. Consider the hypothetical situation regarding the cost of scientific discoveries stipulated in Table 4. Suppose now an over-all budget of 1,000 resource units. At t this buys (say) a menu of 2 results of magnitude I, 10 of magnitude II, 30 of magnitude III. And at t' it affords us (say) 1 result of magnitude I, 35 of magnitude II, 10 of magnitude III. Now if (so let it be supposed) the "relative weight of importance" of results of the three magnitudes stands in the proportion $100 : 10 : 1$, then at t the significance-weight of

[20] G. Dobrov, *Wissenschaftswissenschaft, op. cit.*, pp. 97–98. Compare G. Dobrov and V. Glushkov in *Izvestia*, May 14, 1968. On the data we have ourselves deployed here, one has the volume of the literature of science L as doubling every 12–15 years, so that $Q (= L^{.95})$ doubles every 14 ± 1.5 years and thus $Q^{.25}$ doubles roughly every 60 years. Now the discrepancy between this figure and Dobrov's doubling time of 45 years (for which see footnote 11 on p. 102 above) may seem large, at the *per annum* growth-level they amount to a small difference ($1\frac{1}{2}$ vs $1\frac{3}{4}$ per cent), one that lies well within the level of accuracy which must—in the present state of our information— prevail throughout this whole discussion.

[21] This position supports José Ortega y Gasset's hypothesis that no cognitive discipline apart from science requires so much work by so many people of routine ability and competence.

Table 4

HYPOTHETICAL CASES OF COST/RETURN RELATIONSHIPS

	Magnitude of Result	Cost of Results (in terms of some suitable resource unit)	
		Time t	Time t' (where $t' > t$)
I.	first-rate discoveries	100	200
II.	important findings	50	20
III.	significant results	10	10

the *average* result is 8 whereas at t' it stands at 10. As this over-simple illustration shows, it is seemingly conceivable—in theory—that the phenomenon of escalating costs at the level of first-rate results might be combined with one of increasing returns on investment as regards the qualitative level of average results. But this, of course, could only happen if (as in the example) it were the case that while first-magnitude results become more expensive, lower-magnitude results (of a still rather high level of significance) become relatively cheap. Clearly such a prospect is totally unrealistic. And it is effectively ruled out by the Findings-Quality Coordination Principle. One must take the stance that: *When a process of cost-escalation obtains, this operates so as to produce a (suitably differentiated) cost-increase at every quality level.*

6. CONCLUSION

The deliberations of this chapter make it clear why the question of the rate of scientific progress is so very tricky. For this whole issue turns delicately on fundamentally *evaluative* considerations. At the crudest—but also most basic—level, where progress is measured simply by the growth of the scientific literature, there has for centuries been astonishingly swift and sure progress: an exponential growth with a doubling time of ca. 15 years. At the more sophisticated, and demanding level of high quality results of a suitably "important" character, there has also been exponential growth, but only at the pace of a far longer doubling time, perhaps 30 years, approximating the reduplication with each successive generation envisaged by Henry Adams. Finally, at the maximally exacting level of the really crucial insights that fundamentally enhance our picture of nature, our theory has it that science has been maintaining a merely constant pace of progress.

As this perspective shows, the seemingly straightforward question of the rate of scientific progress simply has no unequivocal answer. It poses an issue that is intensely sensitive to the resolution of an issue of an enormously intricate and problematic sort—the setting of an evaluative standard.

Our present stance here is blunt and straightforward. *Viewing science as a cognitive discipline,* one whose task is the unfolding of a rational account of the *modus operandi* of nature, we have espoused the most stringent criterion for the progress of SCIENCE as such. The state of science is, on this intellectually oriented view, correlative with its accession of really major discoveries: the "ground-breaking" insights into nature. This perspective points towards that key thesis of our present analysis—that the historical situation has been one of a *constant* progress of science as a *cognitive discipline* notwithstanding its *exponential* growth as a productive *enterprise.* (The Findings-Quality Coordination Principle $F \propto \log Q$ says it all.)

VII

Logarithmic Retardation

It seems to me that what can happen in the future is . . . that the experiments get harder and harder to make, more and more expensive, . . . and it [that is, scientific discovery] gets slower and slower. . . .

RICHARD FEYNMAN

1. THE DECELERATION OF SCIENTIFIC PROGRESS IN A ZERO-GROWTH WORLD

The rising cost of scientific discovery at issue in Planck's Principle combines with the hypothesized onset of a zero-growth condition in the resources available for scientific work to yield *the deceleration of scientific progress* as an immediate consequence. When one's budget remains fixed while the price of commodities increases, one cannot but scale down one's purchases. It is, to be sure, feasible in such a case that the *total number* of items one obtains should remain unchanged or even increased, provided one gets more items in the lower price grades, but it is not possible that the totality of one's purchases should be enhanced in the aggregate.

In the given circumstances, science in its synoptic totality must thus enter upon a phase of deceleration. Progress in point of new discoveries is a continuing prospect—but its realization will have to come at a decreasing pace.

What is at issue now is *not* the question (mooted in Chapter III) of whether the ongoing advance of science is *theoretically* possible in abstract principle. This question, so we suppose, can be resolved in the affirmative. Rather, the present issue concerns the extent to which continued scientific progress is economically possible in a zero-growth world. Subject to Planck's Principle of rising costs, the question takes on the fundamentally *economic* form of whether mankind can so readily *afford the price* in terms of human and material resources for the continued maintenance of scientific progress at the rate to which we have become accustomed in the past.

Various recent students of science have remarked on the saturation ultimately inherent in the exponential growth of scientific effort—in terms of such factors as the number of scientific workers, the number of scientific papers, the volume of funding, etc. The exponential growth-rate of scientific activity over the past generations—considered in its various dimensions (manpower, expenditure, literature, etc.)—results in graphs that soon go off the chart and climb up to the ceiling. And so most commentators envision a "logistic" tapering off in the growth of science into a situation of zero-growth stability. But what contemporary analyses of the structure of science have in general *failed* to remark is the crucial fact that the—readily foreseeable—stabilization of the level of scientific EFFORT inevitably spells a decided deceleration in the rate of scientific PROGRESS because of the rising costs of high-quality production in natural science.[1]

2. LOGARITHMIC RETARDATION IN THE ZERO-GROWTH WORLD

The Zero-Growth Hypothesis leads straightforwardly to a *linear* growth-rate of the further cumulative input of resources (R) with the passage of time: $R(t) \propto t$. Recall now that the cost-relationship of the Law of Logarithmic Returns maintains that the cumulative number of first-rate findings realized (F) in natural science stands as the logarithm of the total volume of resources invested in its pursuit: $F(t) \propto \log R(t)$. We thus arrive at the relationship: $F(t) \propto \log (t + b)$. Given the crucial assumption of a steady-state, zero-growth condition in resources available for scientific work, it follows that *the domain of high-level scientific knowledge grows as the LOGARITHM of a linear transform of the elapsed timespan*, proceeding at a continually decelerating pace even in the face of constant effort. This contention will here be designated as the *Logarithmic Retardation Thesis*.[2]

[1] For example:

Thus . . . we recognize from our discussion so far that saturation is ultimately inevitable . . . [indeed] it may already have arrived . . . [Current conditions] indicate something radically different from the steady growth characteristic of the entire historic past. The new era shows all the familiar syndromes of saturation. This, I must add, is a counsel of hope rather than despair. Saturation seldom implies death, but rather that we have the beginning of new and exciting tactics for science, operating with quite new ground rules. (Derek J. Price, *Little Science, Big Science* [New York, 1963], pp. 31–32.)

[2] A graphic overview of the structure of our line of argumentation in support of this thesis is given in Figure 1 of the Appendix (p. 267).

Historically resource-investments have accumulated exponentially, with $R(t)$ subject to a fixed periodicity in its order-of-magnitude increases. And here F has seemingly increased at a roughly *constant* pace with the passage of time. Progress in science has thus tended historically to run a smooth course—thanks to the exponential growth of the investment of technological and intellectual resources. The principles at issue serve to provide an account why, in the historic situation of the exponential-growth past, we have had to pay exponentially increasing resource costs for effectively linear progress in natural science. But the principles at issue also lead straightaway to the conclusion that the accession of major scientific progress will be subject to logarithmic retardation in the zero-growth future.

A straightforward mathematical argument is operative here. IF (as per our earlier analysis) an exponentially increasing input on resources is requisite to maintain a stable condition of output yield, THEN with a shift to a stable, zero-growth condition of resource-inputs, the output will enter upon a condition of a steady decline (of the inverse time proportionality mode which we shall shortly characterize as quasi-hyperbolic).

If (as one must suppose) the same fundamental production-function of the input-yield relationship holds uniformly over time, then an input history of the form of part A of Figure 1 stands together with an output history of the form of part B. For on the basis of $F(t) \propto \log (t + b)$ we obtain the following relationship as governing the rate of change of F over time:

$$F^* = \text{Current Output} = \frac{\mathrm{d}F}{\mathrm{d}t} \propto \frac{1}{t+b}$$

This mode of decline is *quasi-hyperbolic* in that the basic productivity relationship

[Current output] × [Elapsed time] = constant

yields an equilateral hyperbola for the special case of $b = 0$.[3] The Law of Logarithmic Returns accordingly has the consequence that, in the *stable* situation of a zero-growth world, *the pace of high-level scientific innovation will decrease markedly with the passage of time.* There thus

---

[3] It must be stressed that such *hyperbolic* decay is something very different from *exponential* decay of the form $F^* \propto 10^{-kt}$.

Figure 1

THE EFFECT ON SCIENTIFIC PRODUCTION OF THE TRANSITION FROM EXPONENTIAL GROWTH TO ZERO GROWTH

A. INPUT HISTORY

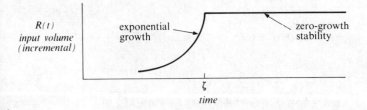

$R(t)$
input volume
(incremental)

B. OUTPUT HISTORY

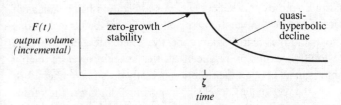

$F(t)$
output volume
(incremental)

Note To be sure, real-life curves are always smooth, and thus a more accurate picture would substitute a gradualistic transition-phase for the transition point ζ.

results the comparative picture of Table 1 to characterize the situation regarding first-rate discoveries.[4]

And so, when the several components of our analysis are put together, a result along the lines of that portrayed in Table 2 ensues. This table is Janus faced. Looking towards the circumstances of the past, it supposes an Adams' Law situation of exponential growth, subject to a doubling time of ca. 15 years or a growth by an order of magnitude every 50 years.[5] As regards the future, it supposes a situation of zero-

[4] The structure of the over-all course of argumentation that underlies this table is summarized in Figure 1 of the Appendix (p. 267).

[5] The starting-date of 1650 reflects the appraisal of E. P. Wigner who wrote as follows:

The most remarkable thing about Science is its youth. The earliest beginning of chemistry, as we now know it, certainly does not antedate Boyle's *Sceptical Chemist* which appeared in

Table 1

FIRST-RATE DISCOVERY IN THE EXPONENTIAL-GROWTH PAST
AND THE ZERO-GROWTH FUTURE

	The Exponential-Growth Past	The Zero-Growth Future
Cumulative Volume of First-Rate Discovery: F	$\infty\, t$	$\infty \log(t+b)$
Current Volume of First-Rate Discovery: F^*	constant	$\propto \dfrac{1}{t+b}$

Notes (1) $F(t) \infty \log R(t)$
(2) $F^* = \dfrac{d}{dt}F(t)$
(3) For the exponential-growth past: $R(t) \propto 10^{\,at}$
(4) For the zero-growth future: $R(t) \infty\, t$

growth stabilization in resource investment after ca. 1950 at the levels of that period. And by this telling, even if stabilization has begun as of the middle of the present century, the effect will not be a marked one until almost another century has gone by. Thereafter, however, the change should become pronounced at the specific level of highly significant results. (Though the situation is really drastic only here. For note that at the $\sqrt{Q}$ quality-level of "important" findings, the model yields a volume of significant productivity in natural science in 2150 that is not drastically divergent from the situation of a couple of generations ago.)[6]

What of the longer run? How does logarithmic deceleration work itself out there?

1661. More probably, one would place the birthyear of chemistry around the years of activity of Lavoisier, between 1770 and 1790, or count its years from Dalton's law in 1808. Physics is somewhat older. Newton's *Principia*, a rather finished work, became available in 1687. Archimedes discovered laws of physics around 250 B.C., but his discoveries hardly can be called the real beginning of physics. On the whole one is probably safe in saying that Science is less than 300 years old. This number has to be compared with the age of Man, which is certainly greater than 100,000 years. ("The Limits of Science," *Proceedings of the American Philosophical Society*, vol. 94 [1950], pp. 422–427 [see p. 422].)

[6] To an eye not finely attuned to the valuation of specifically first-rate findings, the model does not yield the picture of a marked decline of scientific productivity at present or for a long time hence. Such a decline becomes noticeable first and most drastically at the level of the very highest quality production. Hence it will be discerned first by those most keenly scrutinized to quality and inclined to the most rigorous standards of evaluation. It is accordingly not surprising that the Nobel prize-winners should be the first to sound the alarm.

Table 2

THE LOGARITHMIC DECELERATION OF SCIENCE
[See Note (1)]

Date [See Note (1)]	t Elapsed Time (In years since the base-year 1650) [See Note (1)]	R Cumulative Resource Investment [See Note (2)]	$\log R$	$\log \sqrt{\bar{Q}}$ [See Note (3)]	$\sqrt{\bar{Q}}$ Important Findings (Cumulative)	$\Delta\sqrt{\bar{Q}}$	F First-Rate Findings ($F = k \log R + c$)	ΔF	ΔF (With $k=50$)	F First-Rate Findings (cumulative) (With $k=50$)
1850	200	10^3	3	2.38	240	—	$3k+c$	k	50	240
1900	250	10^4	4	2.85	700	460	$4k+c$	k	50	290
1950	300|0|	10^5	5	3.32	2,100	1,400	$5k+c$	k	50	340
2000	|50|	$1\times(2\times10^5)+10^5=3\times10^5$	5.48	3.55	3,500	1,400	$5.48k+c$	$.48k$	24	364
2050	|100|	$2\times(2\times10^5)+10^5=5\times10^5$	5.70	3.65	4,400	900	$5.70k+c$	$.22k$	11	375
2100	|150|	$3\times(2\times10^5)+10^5=7\times10^5$	5.85	3.72	5,200	800	$5.85k+c$	$.15k$	8	383
2150	|200|	$4\times(2\times10^5)+10^5=9\times10^5$	5.95	3.77	5,800	600	$5.95k+c$	$.10k$	5	388

Notes (1) This tabulation somewhat arbitrarily takes 1950 to be the year of switch-over from logarithmic growth to a steady state zero-growth condition. (The actual switch-over point ζ may well fall some 15–25 years later.)

(2) The present calculation assigns the arbitrary index value of 1,000 to 1850 and supposes a steady-state growth at roughly 2×10^5 index units after 1950.

(3) Since $\log Q \propto \log R$, we have $\log \sqrt{\bar{Q}} = a \log R + b$. Letting it be supposed that in 1850 $\sqrt{\bar{Q}}$ was roughly 240 (cf. Table 3 on p. 107) and that this had grown to 700 by 1900, we fix a at ca. 0·47 and b at ca. 0·97. Accordingly we have: $\log \sqrt{\bar{Q}} = 47 \log R + 97$.

The answer is implicit in the previous findings that $F^*(t) \propto 1/(t+b)$. For this relationship ensures the ongoing decline of current production. But observe that $F^*(t)$ will always be some positive quantity, no matter how large t gets to be. Major discoveries never come to a stop. However, the waiting-time for a fixed, constant quantity of significant innovations grows longer with the passage of time. For $F(t) \propto \log(t+b)$ leads to the result that $F(t') = 2F(t)$ only if $t' + b = (t+b)^2$. If the temporal origin is adjusted so as to take b out of the picture, we see that under conditions of logarithmic retardation, the doubling-time of scientific progress increases as the *square* of the elapsed time. And in general, the increase will be m-fold after a waiting time of t^m. The increase in equal-amount steps proceeds in a geometric series: the total growth in the first Y years will be reiterated in the next Y^2 and again in the next Y^3, etc. This geometric elongation vividly delineates the workings of logarithmic retardation.

It would be seriously misleading to think of the logarithmic deceleration of scientific progress on analogy with someone mining an infinite vein of ore where each day he can dig out (say) half of what he extracted the day before. This implies that there are parts of the seam that cannot ever possibly be reached. Our argument does *not* produce a result of this structure. The more appropriate analogy is that of the man who enters a Borgesian infinite library,[7] but has a card that only entitles him to take out one book for the first week, one for the next two, and so on with increasingly long periods of delay. There is no topic about which he cannot inform himself more and more fully—if only he is patient enough. But still, his ever-expanding knowledge grows at an ever-diminishing pace.

3. FURTHER ASPECTS OF LOGARITHMIC DECELERATION

The preceding deliberations have addressed themselves primarily to the development of science at the highest quality-level—that which we have characterized as "first rate" and whose nature is fixed by the principle that the volume of specifically first-rate science is proportional to $\log R$,

---

[7] Jorge Luis Borges, *Labyrinths: Selected Stories and Other Writings*, ed. by D. A. Yates and J. E. Irby (Harmondsworth, 1964).

where R represents the *total* cumulative resource-expenditure on scientific work. It will not do, however, to put all of our eggs into the basket of first-rate findings. Let us examine the situation at various Q^λ- quality levels of submaximal quality.

To begin with, note that $F \propto \log Q$, the Findings-Quality Principle of Chapter VI, together with the Law of Logarithmic Returns, $F \infty \log R$, at once yields $\log Q \infty \log R$ and thus $Q \propto R^h$ (with $h < 1$). As R expands under zero-growth conditions, with $R \infty t$, the proportionality relationship $Q \propto (t + b)^h$ follows.[8] And so we have it that:

$$Q^\lambda \propto (t + b)^{h\lambda}$$

$$(Q^\lambda)^* = \frac{\mathrm{d}}{\mathrm{d}t}\, Q^\lambda \propto (t + b)^{h\lambda - 1}$$

This relationship leads to the situation of Figure 2. With first rate findings the situation is one of *hyperbolic* decay, with findings of successively lesser quality levels it is one of continual, but increasingly less rapid decline.

For anyone minded to regard our adoption of a very high (F-oriented) standard of scientific progress as exaggeratedly demanding and perhaps unrealistic, these considerations indicate that the situation of retardation in the zero-growth future will differ in no more than degree from that of our "preferred" case when some more relaxed standard of findings-qualities is substituted. At the lesser quality levels, the impact of retardation is not altered in any *fundamental* respect, but only somewhat mitigated. Wherever one may choose to set the quality level for one's preferred construction of "significant science," the substance of the present analysis will carry over in its fundamentals. If one lowers one's sights regarding quality-standards below the somewhat exalted level of what we have characterized as "first-rate" science, the retardation of progress in zero-growth conditions becomes less rapid, but it is no less sure and steady.

---

[8] This relationship can also be obtained by another route. For we have $\log Q = kF$. But we have already found that $F \infty \log (t + b)$ in the zero-growth era. Accordingly:

$$\log Q = h \log (t + b) + \log c$$
$$\log Q = \log [c(t + b)^h]$$
$$Q = c(t + b)^h$$
$$Q \propto (t + b)^h$$

Figure 2

THE VOLUME OF CURRENT SCIENTIFIC PRODUCTION
(AT DIFFERENT QUALITY-LEVELS) UNDER
ZERO-GROWTH CONDITIONS

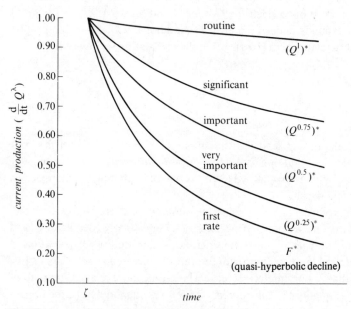

Note The juncture ζ marks the onset of zero-growth.

4. THE ECONOMIC ASPECT OF DECELERATION

The impressive scope of recent advances in science has tended to obscure the fact that this progress has been achieved at an increasingly high cost in manpower, talent, and resources devoted to scientific work. The sheer volume of progress has masked the circumstance that the actual rate of return in terms of high-quality results per unit investment has been decreasing over time. Thus if anything like the present analysis of the matter is correct, the leveling off of the availability of scientific resources into a condition of zero-growth stability does not imply a *leveling off* in the rate at which significant scientific discoveries occur, but rather a very marked *decrease* in this rate. On such an interpretation of the issues, a leveling off in the volume of scientific *effort* (as must be envisaged under zero-growth conditions) implies—over the long run—a substantial retardation of the rate at which really significant *progress* occurs.

One can think of science in two ways: either as an *intellectual discipline*, a body of knowledge defined in terms of its findings, or as an *enterprise*, a human activity defined in terms of the talent, energies, and resources committed to its pursuit. The difference is decisive for present purposes. For in the *latter* sense "science" will (*ex hypothesi*) go on at wholly undiminished strength under zero-growth condition, whereas in the *former* sense "science" will—if our perspective is correct—enter upon a state of substantial deceleration.[9]

If the general picture we have been developing is even approximately correct, the half-millennium beginning around 1650 is bound to appear in ultimate retrospect as a really golden age of scientific progress. The ending of this period does *not* spell the end of scientific discovery—by no means so. The change at issue is merely one of degree and emphatically not one of kind. Our model of logarithmic retardation not only allows but demands the prospect of open horizons for endless potential progress in natural science. But it does mean a *slowing* of the rate of scientific progress—establishing a pace so different in its quantitative aspect from what has gone before as to constitute a new situation and eventually usher in what is in effect, a qualitatively new era.

Our deceleration-thesis rests neither on the claim that the well of undiscovered significant findings is running dry, nor on the claim that the limits of man's capacities for inquiry are being exhausted. The slowing it anticipates is not *theoretically inevitable* for any such absolutistic reason, but rather is *practically unavoidable* for the merely *economic* reason that it is getting more and more expensive to run the increasingly complex machinery of scientific innovation.

---

[9] Consider Mill's claim that:

> It is scarcely necessary to remark that a stationary condition of capital and population implies no stationary state of human improvement. There would be as much scope as ever for all kinds of mental culture and . . . progress. . . . (J. S. Mill, *Principles of Political Economy*, ed. by A. T. Hadley [after the 6th ed. of 1865; New York, 1900], vol. 2, pp. 264–265.)

While this may be true for certain other forms of intellectual progress, our present deliberations suggest that it requires serious qualification as regards progress in the natural sciences.

It cannot be stressed too emphatically how sharply the presently envisaged position of logarithmic retardation differs from the saturation model of the *fin de siècle* school, according to which the domain of attainable knowledge is being *exhausted* totally or asymptotically—at any rate as regards the really first-order issues of physical science. On the *fin de siècle* view, natural science was entering upon its final phase because its ultimate and completed state was being approached. To use a political analogy, the era of scientific revolutions is seen as coming to an end because science is on the verge of entering into its stabilized millennium.[10]

This eschatological aspect is altogether absent from the present position. Its perspective most emphatically does *not* deny that further "revolutions" (=discoveries of the very first importance) lie ahead—quite to the contrary, it decidedly maintains that they do, and indeed do so in endless numbers. Rather, the present theory has it that such revolutions will become less and less frequent, insisting that this is so not because we are approaching utopia, but purely and simply because revolutions are becoming increasingly expensive to mount. The theory admits no intrinsic limit to the quantity of potential discoveries, but merely holds that the *cost* of their successive realization keeps on increasing, a circumstance bound to eventuate in eventual deceleration as the resources we can dedicate to scientific inquiry reach saturation levels.

Thus while the present view agrees with the *fin de siècle* view in also mooting a drastic decrease in the rate of high-voltage innovation in science, it emphatically rejects (for the reasons put forward in the opening chapters) the position that an eventual situation of saturation or fixity in regard to fundamentals in scientific knowledge must be reached. Stabilization in the scientific enterprise betokens a continual decline in the advance of science as an intellectual discipline, but a decline that is without a fall. What it envisages is not a *stoppage* in substantial scientific progress, but merely a *slowing*. (We may accordingly reproach the recent spate of *fin de siècle* theorists with somewhat naively mistaking the latter for the former.)

Only one theorist of science seems to have mooted a deceleration

---

[10] And this is exactly the picture of the latter-day *fin de siècle* theorists. Compare the *locus classicus* of this position in Gunther Stent, *The Coming of the Golden Age* (Garden City, 1969).

theory of the sort at issue in our discussion—Richard Feynman, who in a brilliant side-remark offers a conjecture along the following lines:

> It seems to me that what can happen in the future is either that all the laws become known—that is, if you had enough laws you could compute consequences and they would always agree with experiment, which would be the end of the line—or it may happen that the experiments get harder and harder to make, more and more expensive, so you get 99·9 per cent of the phenomena, but there is always some phenomenon which has just been discovered, which is very hard to measure, and which disagrees; and as soon as you have the explanation of that one there is always another one, and it gets slower and slower and more and more uninteresting. That is another way it may end. But I think it has to end in one way or another.[11]

Feynman's second alternative (the first being simply a *fin de siècle* exhaustion of nature) comes very close to the present theory of logarithmic deceleration.[12] His error is to think of this as an ending.

5. FREDERICK ENGELS AND THE COMMUNIST THEORY OF SCIENTIFIC PROGRESS

It will help to clarify the present theory of scientific progress and its decleration to contrast it with a significant alternative which enjoys a great vogue in Marxist circles. In developing this alternative, let us begin with the ideas of Frederick Engels. In the notes he prepared for the *Dialectics of Nature* during 1873–1882, Engels wrote:

> What Luther's burning of the papal bull was in the religious field, in

---

[11] Richard Feynman, *The Character of Physical Law* (Cambridge, Mass., 1965), p. 172.

[12] One aspect of Feynman's account is puzzlingly unexplained. Why should the fact that progress becomes slower, more difficult, and more expensive be taken to mean that it is "more and more uninteresting"? Or, as Feynman put it a few lines earlier: "This thing [physics] cannot keep going so that we are always going to discover more and more new laws. If we do, it will become boring that there are so many levels one underneath the other." Just why should such slow, difficult, and stratified progress be *boring*—especially in contrast with the infinite ennui of a stoppage-situation of the sort mooted earlier in Feynman's discussion? This aspect of his remarks is not only unsupported but indeed baffling.

the field of natural science was the great work of Copernicus. . . . But from then on the development of science went forward with giant strides, increasing, so to speak, proportionately to the square of the distance in time from its point of departure, as if it wanted to show the world that for the motion of the highest product of organic matter, the human mind, the law of inverse squares holds good, as it does for the motion of inorganic matter.[13]

Apart from the flourish of the Newtonian analogy,[14] Engels does not support and explain these ideas, leaving them in a lamentably undeveloped state.

On the somewhat slender foundations of Engels' *Dialectics of Nature*, latter-day Marxists have built up a formidable edifice of theory regarding scientific progress. Soviet writers tend to reject the idea that there are any limits or limitations to scientific progress. For it is felt that a limit on science entails a limit to technological progress, which in turn implies a limit to the benefits a communist order can bestow on its subjects—a result that is theoretically unacceptable to them.[15] The idea of a saturation or retardation of science is anathema in the U.S.S.R.,

[13] Frederick Engels, *Dialectics of Nature*, tr. by C. Dutt (New York, 1940), p. 184. The corresponding passage in the text itself reads "The Revolutionary act by which natural science declared its independence and, as it were, repeated Luther's burning of the Papal Bull was the publication of the immortal work [of Copernicus]. . . . Thenceforward, however, the development of the sciences proceeded with giant strides, and, it might be said, gained in force in proportion to the square of the distance (in time) from its point of departure. It was as if the world were to be shown that henceforth the reciprocal law of motion would be as valid for the highest product of organic matter, the human mind, as for inorganic substance." (*Ibid.*, p. 4.) In an earlier publication Engels had taken a different line, writing:

Scientific knowledge, however, increases at least as the population, which increases in proportion to the numbers of the previous generation. Thus science advances in proportion to the body of knowledge left by the preceding generation. (*Umrisse zu einer Kritik der Nationalökonomie* in Marx/Engels, *Werke*, Vol. I [Berlin, 1956], p. 521.)

The seemingly implied standard that $dS/dt \propto S(t)$ would entail an *exponential* (rather than *parabolic*) mode of increase in scientific knowledge. In this respect, the early Engels would clearly qualify as a precursor of Henry Adams and Co. in the anticipation of Adams' Law. But Engels was not a mathematician, and so, perhaps, we are entitled to construe his "in proportion to" not literally and technically, but rather more flexibly as "stands in a fixed positive correlation to."

[14] Engels seems to have taken this very seriously, thinking of himself as advancing the understanding of intellectual phenomena in the manner of Newton's advance of our understanding of physical phenomena.

[15] One acute commentator depicts the issue in the following terms:

"[I]n the Soviet Union . . . it is generally accepted that a close relationship exists between scientific research and national productivity. There, a limit on science implies a limit on

and so Soviet writers on scientific growth almost unanimously dismiss the picture of a "logistic" development of science often favored in the West.[16]

Interestingly enough, just this issue of the future of science is the main ideological or doctrinal issue that divides Western scientists from their Communist-bloc colleagues. For while scientists within the two camps nowadays largely agree on issues *within* natural science, they seem to differ radically in the tendency of their thinking *about* science. As we saw in Chapter I, the predominant consensus of thought in the contemporary West is that the potential of science is limited and scientific progress subject to logistic saturation. But in the Communist orbit a very different view of the future of science prevails. Here, theoreticians are seemingly committed to a view of unfettered progress by the doctrine that the destiny of the historic process calls for the ultimate victory of communism. It would be too ironic for doctrinal comfort if this eventuation transpired after the crest of the wave of scientific progress had already passed by during the premillennial era. Thus Marxist theoreticians are given to speaking in an unqualifiedly confident tone of voice when discussing the future of science, offering such statements as: "What we know of science tells us that there can be no end to discovery and hence to the extension of man's control over

---

national productivity, and this is theoretically unacceptable." (A. J. Meadows, *Communications in Science* [London, 1974], p. 33.)

It is viewed as mandatory for a "materialist" to hold a scientific world-view that hinges economic production on science-based technology. Soviet theorists adopt a trickle-down theory: science makes massive advances, some substantial fraction of these redound to the benefit of technology, and technological progress in turn partially spills over into enhanced production. Throughout, the relationship

$$dS/dt > dT/dt > dP/dt$$

obtains, and indeed the growth of the first factor of the Science-Technology-Production triad determines that of the other two. (These ideas, which are now orthodoxy in the U.S.S.R., were initially formulated in Vledux, Nalimov, and Stjazkin, "Scientific and Technical Information as a Task of Cybernetics," *Uspechi fiziceskich nauk*, vol. 69 (1959), pp. 13–56.) In placing cognition into the driver's seat over production, this view stands the orthodox Marxist line on its head, a fact that seems to trouble Soviet theoreticians not at all, particularly as Marx somewhere predicted the conversion of science into a "direct force of production."

[16] See L. N. Beck, "Soviet Discussion of the Exponential Growth of Scientific Publications" in J. B. North (ed.), *The Information Conscious Society: Proceedings of the American Society of Information Science*, vol. 7 (1970), pp. 5–16. The present discussion of Soviet thinking on the future of science is much indebted to this article.

nature."[17] (It is not easy to see just how this claim is to be coordinated with Engels' dictum in the *Dialectics of Nature* that nature always exacts her revenge for man's vaunted "triumphs over nature.")

Perhaps the most detailed discussion of the future of science by a Soviet theoretician is G. M. Dobrov's *Wissenschaftswissenschaft*.[18] Dobrov rejects the idea of insuperable limits to progress, citing five main grounds: (1) Automation and mechanization as a means for overcoming limitations in man's ability to retain and retrieve data. (2) The development of border-sciences and interdisciplinary problem-areas to overcome narrower and narrower specialization in potentially sterile intra-disciplinary specialties, and—more generally—the promise for progress in more effective organization and astutely coordinated direction of scientific work as made possible by the scientific study of science. (3) Improved and streamlined methods of instruction and information-dissemination. (4) Development in cybernetics and computer theory as a means for overcoming limitations of man's ability to process data and to carry out complex calculations and inferences. (5) Deepening insight into the nature of the world and the structure of problems in natural science to show that there is no prospect of "running out of problems" in a science whose development is controlled by an adequate science of science.

Dobrov accepts the picture of the past exponential growth of science,[19] and he admits the claims of the saturation-thesis that such growth cannot be unmodified *ad indefinitum*, and must give way to a "logistic" decline. But—doubtless inspired by the theory of the "inexhaustibility" of matter of Lenin's *Materialism and Empirico-Criticism*—he sees this decline as a merely temporary phenomenon which will give way to further periods of exponential resurgence in future phases of development, in such a manner as to result ultimately in an over-all pattern of cumulatively linear progress as illustrated in Figure 3.

[17] Samuel Lilley, *Men, Machines, and History* (New York, 1966), p. 336.

[18] Originally published in Kiev in 1966 under the title *Nauka o Nauke*, but tr. into German by H. Houtmann and published in Berlin in 1970 under the auspices of the (East) German Academy of Sciences. The discussion of the future of science occurs on pp. 237–258 of the German edition. Dobrov updated this work as *Nauka: Jejo Analis i Predwidenija* (Moscow, 1972), which was translated into German (from an unpublished English version) as *Wissenschaft: ihre Analyse und Prognose* by H. Oehrens (Stuttgart, 1974).

[19] As some Soviet theoreticians do not. Compare A. J. Meadows, *Communication in Science* (London, 1974), p. 33.

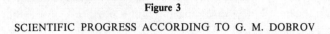

Figure 3

SCIENTIFIC PROGRESS ACCORDING TO G. M. DOBROV

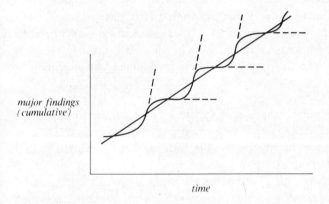

*major findings
(cumulative)*

time

From G. M. Dobrov, *Nauka o Nauke*, tr. into German by H. Houtmann, *Wissenschaftswissenschaft* (Berlin, 1970), pp. 237–258.

There is a certain irony here. Suppose that scientific knowledge were actually *cumulative* (as we have denied at pp. 46–50 above). Then new items of scientific information (Q) would make additions to our current scientific knowledge (K) in inverse proportions with the sum-total of such discoveries already in hand: $\Delta K \propto \Delta Q/Q$. This indicates that $K \propto \log Q$. And then as long as the relationship between the resource-investment (R) committed to scientific inquiry and the information it yields is given by a production-function of a form answering to $\log Q \propto \log R$, we have it that: $K \propto \log R$. With accretional cumulativity and a Q-oriented standard of scientific knowledge (K), we arrive at a law of logarithmic returns. Thus, curiously enough, our own radically variant noncumulativity position, which bases scientific knowledge (K) upon specifically first-rate findings (F), and leads to $F \propto \log R$, produces just this same result. The theory is such that, its abandonment of cumulativity notwithstanding, the situation as regards the cognitive yield of further efforts is precisely similar.

Be this as it may, Dobrov envisages an unimpededly open future for science, espousing a theory of progress which altogether rejects the currently fashionable Western view of science as a fundamentally finite enterprise.[20] And indeed Communist thinkers in general hold to a "the-sky's-the-limit" view regarding the future prospects of scientific and technical progress.[21]

But let us now return to the basic ideas of Engels and endeavour to furnish them with the needed rationale which Engels himself never provided. If the development of science is construed—as it must be construed—in terms of its provision of substantial findings, then it is tempting to construe Engels' Theory as propounding the principle

$$F \infty (t + c)^2$$

which maintains that the aggregate volume of top-level findings increases with the square of the elapsed time (as of some suitable origin).

Interestingly enough, this thesis is readily assimilated into the general framework of our present discussion.

Let us begin with a view of the historic situation. Facing statistical realities of Adams' Law, one confronts the circumstance that scientific *effort* has been increasing exponentially, so that the volume resources committed to scientific inquiry have been growing at an exponential rate, $R(t) \propto 10^{at}$ or (equivalently): $R^*(t) = d/dt R(t) \propto 10^{at}$. Now, to be sure, our present theory of progress has been predicated on the Law of Logarithmic Returns, that is, on the thesis that the yield in first-rate findings (F) of an investment of resources (R) stands as the logarithm thereof: $F \infty \log R$. But suppose that one had applied this productive principle not—as we have done—at the level of the *total* (cumulative) investments and yields, but rather at the level of the *current* (incremental) investment and yields, in the form: $F^* \infty \log R^*$. On the surface of it, this modified version of the principle of logarithmic returns might seem every bit as reasonable as our initial use of it. Why, after all, should one not estimate the volume of first-rate returns on a *current*

[20] Accordingly we find him declaring somewhat melodramatically in a later publication:

> On the basis of a qualitative, historico-logical analysis, as well as by investigating the quantitative parameters of scientific progress, one can establish the ever-quickening rate of its development as a law governing the very life of science. Should this fundamental characteristic ever be lost, then science would cease to be science, for this would mean an end to the accession of new discoveries and would spell the death of science. (*Wissenschaft: ihre Analyse und Prognose* [op. cit.], p. 68.)

[21] See, for example, Samuel Lilley, *Men, Machines, and History*, op. cit., pp. 333–334 for one particularly drastic instance. For a moderate statement of the position see Peter Kapitsa, "The Future Problems of Science" in M. Goldsmith and A. Mackay (eds.), *The Science of Science* (London, 1964), pp. 102–113. Compare also the table given at pp. 52–53 of Dobrov's *Wissenschaft: ihre Analyse und Prognose* (op. cit.).

(i.e., incremental) rather than on a *cumulative* basis—especially since R and R^* keep in exponential step with one another in the historic situation?

Now this change of perspective to $F^*(t) \infty \log R^*(t)$ produces a very different picture of the productive situation. For given the fact of exponential growth, with $R(t) \propto 10^{at}$, we have $R^*(t) \propto 10^{at}$ and thus obtain that $\log R^*(t) = at + k$. And so we arrive at: $F^*(t) \infty t$. This leads at once to:

$$F(t) = \int F^*(t)dt \infty \int (gt + b)dt \infty (t + c)^2$$

Thus Engels' quadratic law of progress is in fact an immediate consequence of our general theory, provided that one makes the shift of applying the logarithmic determination of first-rate findings at the *incremental level of current production* rather than at the *cumulative level of total production*.

All this does not, of course, mean that Engels "had in mind" such a line of reasoning—given his sparse indications it is impossible to say what his reasoning was. But the suggested approach does provide a natural rationale that yields a reasonable basis for Engels' view. By eponymy we may designate the general theory erected on this basis as the *Engels' Theory*. Let us examine its wider implications, beginning with the data set out in Table 3. Note, above all, that in the zero-growth future, when R^* and thus $\log R^*$ remain constant, the basic relation

---

Table 3

TWO ALTERNATIVE VIEWS OF THE VOLUMES AND RATES OF
SCIENTIFIC PRODUCTION

	THE EXPONENTIAL-GROWTH PAST $R(t) \propto 10^{kt}$		THE ZERO-GROWTH FUTURE $R(t) \infty t$	
	The Present Theory	*The Engels' Theory*	*The Present Theory*	*The Engels' Theory*
F (cumulative)	∞t	$\infty (t + c)^2$	$\infty \log (t + b)$	∞t
F^* (incremental)	constant	∞t	$\propto 1/(t + b)$	constant
Q (cumulative)	$\propto 10^{at}$	$\infty 10^{at}$	$\infty (t + b)^h$	∞t
Q^* (incremental)	$\propto 10^{at}$	$\propto 10^{at}$	$\propto (t + b)^{h-1}$	constant

Note For our theory, $F \infty \log R$ and $Q \propto R^h$, while for the Engels Theory, $F^* \infty \log R^*$ and $Q^* \propto R^{*h}$.

$F^* \varpropto \log R^*$ assures the constancy of scientific progress, exactly as the Soviet theoreticians maintain.

It is important (and interesting) to observe how well the structure of this theory in fact dovetails with the general communist view of science. It accepts with empirical realism the statistical realities of the exponential-growth past. It yields exactly the picture of the Engels Theory with respect to the historical growth of science. And, in the setting of a zero-growth future, it provides for the steady and unimpeded flow of scientific progress dear to Soviet theoreticians. It seems admirably attuned at all points to serve as a Marxist theory of scientific progress alternative to that of the preceding discussion.

How is the acceptability of these rival theories to be tested? Seemingly the simplest way would be to proceed to an adjudication on the basis of the behavior of F^* in the exponential-growth past: Have first-rate findings been coming along at a quadratically increasing pace, or has their rate of realization remained constant? Put thus, the issue sounds simple and straightforward. But misleadingly so. For this approach enmeshes us in the almost hopeless difficulty of assessing case by case whether a specified finding is or is not really first-rate.[22] And, as we have seen, this matter of appraising the quality of findings is a very delicate and potentially controversial issue.

Fortunately, one can obtain a clearer vision of the situation by proceeding not with respect to the exponential past, but with respect to the zero growth future. For where the Engels Theory envisages an unimpeded future of constant progress (even in zero-growth conditions), our own theory sees—not (to be sure) a *stoppage*, but—a continual *deceleration*.

Its capacity to come to terms with the Engels Theory may be regarded as a touchstone of our own. Both are based on the same building blocks: the historic structure of exponential expansion and the Law of Logarithmic Returns are a common basis. Moreover—and this is crucial—both alike reject the widely popular conception of science as an inherently finite and self-terminating enterprise. But despite this common basis, they diverge sharply from one another in painting

---

[22] Perhaps one fairly clearcut historical fact favoring the present theory over that of Engels is this. It follows from Engels' standard that the advance of science in either of the quarter centuries 1850–1875 or 1875–1900 equals in scope the whole course of scientific progress from the day of Copernicus to that of Newton—a period including Galileo, Descartes, Harvey, Boerhaave, Stahl, Boyle, Leibniz, and Newton himself. This consequence seems difficult to accept.

radically different pictures of the future prospects of scientific progress. And this brings to the fore the key question: Would it really be reasonable to anticipate a constant augmentation of F in the circumstances one can envisage of the zero-growth future? This question immediately leads back to Planck's Principle of Increasing Effort. For our whole line of reasoning hinges crucially on a cost-escalation principle of a need for continually increasing resource-inputs for significant findings. Given Planck's Principle, the prospect of a constant return on constant investment vanishes. To be sure, such cost-escalation might be seen as a rather accidental, transitory feature of the present period—perhaps owing to the sorts of investigations currently in fashion—rather than being an inescapably fundamental feature of the situation in natural science. This supposition is mistaken. The remainder of the book will seek for an explanatory account capable of yielding a deepened understanding of this fundamental phenomenon of the rising costs of high-level scientific innovation, and will endeavor to provide a rationale of plausibility for its substantiation.

VIII

The Technological Dependency of Science

Nec manus nuda, nec intellectus sibi permissus, multum valet; instrumentis et auxiliis res perficitur; quibus opus est, non minus ad intellectum, quam ad manum. Atque ut instrumenta manus motum aut cient aut regunt; ita et instrumenta mentis intellectu aut suggerunt aut cavent. (*"Neither the naked hand nor the intellect left to itself can effect much. It is by instruments and helps that work is accomplished, which are as much needed by the intellect as by the hand. And as the instruments of the hand either impel or guide its motion, so the instruments of the mind either encourage or admonish the intellect."*)

FRANCIS BACON, *Novum Organon*, Bk. I, sect. ii

Science owes more to the steam engine that the steam engine owes to science.

J. B. CONANT, *Science and Common Sense* (New Haven, 1961)

1. METHODOLOGICAL PRELIMINARIES

The preceding discussion has maintained the eventual deceleration in scientific progress on the essentially economic ground of *an escalation in the resource-input costs of high-level scientific innovation* (Planck's Principle). But, although empirical evidence was adduced to substantiate the *reality* of this phenomenon, it was left hanging in the air as a bare fact, unexplained and unaccounted for. The question remains: Just *why* should the resource-cost of significant scientific discoveries increase so substantially with the progress of science? Until this has been resolved, one really cannot say whether this cost-increase represents a transitory and short-term phenomenon or a permanent structural fact deep-rooted in the very nature of the enterprise of scientific inquiry. Our whole position stands on insecure ground as long as no rationale is developed for this crucial premise on which the deceleration argument rests. This problem sets the stage for the next several chapters, which seek to provide an explanation for the phenomena of cost-escalation and logarithmic retardation, an explanation which turns pivotally about the relationship between science and technology.

Some qualifications and disclaimers are necessary at the outset. We shall attempt to construct a theoretical account of the "production function" of science—its characteristic relationship between the incommensurable factors of resource inputs and cognitive outputs. This account will take the form of a theoretical model to which a precise mathematical articulation will be given. The precision of such a mathematical account is misleading in two respects. For one thing, it conveys an exactness and detail that suggests *finality*. This is emphatically unwarranted, for the account is highly speculative. The meager data at our disposal warrant at best the claim of a tentative, plausible first step at providing a rationale. Secondly, the mathematically formulated model is deceptive in its suggestion of *simplicity*. It portrays as relatively straightforward connections which in reality are doubtless more complex and convoluted; in being relatively simple, it is undoubtedly *oversimple*.

Given these limitations—why offer such an account at all? The answer is that a grosser picture of the general phenomenology at the *qualitative* level underlies the admittedly over-refined *quantitative* picture that is to be presented. And this grosser, less finely drawn picture has far more solid claims to correctness. No doubt, the account given here is an oversimplification drawn in too bold lines—a caricature. But like a good caricature it also conveys the gross features of its object; in short, it is a rough likeness. The reader must thus view the mathematical detail not as accompanied by the claim "This is just exactly how it is" but merely by the claim "The real truth lies in this general direction: this is how the matter lies . . . within an imperfect first approximation."

It is also crucial to see the speculative aspect of the discussion in the proper light. There is speculation and speculation—wild speculation and responsible speculation. In the interests of responsibility, the various explanatory principles of our account must certainly "fit the facts" insofar as they can be discerned. And they must also fit one another. A certain amount of mathematical detail is unavoidable in testing this second kind of fit. An account along the lines to be developed requires the explicit deployment of certain basic assumptions about the nature of scientific work. Unless they are set out with reasonable precision, there is no way of testing the compatibility and consonance of these assumptions. The mathematical detail is necessary to show that the various pieces that must be deployed in the framework of our general approach can in fact be made to fit with one another in such a way as actually to yield the requisite conclusions.

The rationale for science-deceleration to be developed here is admittedly a "tissue of speculations"—in the circumstances of the data at hand it could hardly be anything else. But it is a tissue that is held together at all points by a fabric of plausibility. It is—or, at any rate, is intended to be—a *responsible* speculation, one which endeavors to provide a reasonable approximation to "the real truth" of the matter.

2. THE CONCEPTION OF A TECHNOLOGY OF INQUIRY AND THE TECHNOLOGICAL DEPENDENCY THESIS

It is by now almost a commonplace that technology is a "spin-off" of science, and that scientific progress pulls technological innovation along in its wake. After all, is not technology merely "applied science"? But sagacious minds since Bacon's day have realized that there is much to be said for the converse contention that (under modern conditions at any rate) scientific progress is crucially dependent upon technology.[1] It is, in fact, no exaggeration to say that laboratory science as we know it is an adjunct of the Industrial Revolution—a fruit of its technological harvest. This thesis of the technological dependency of science will prove critical for present purposes and will provide the basis of the line of argument to be developed.

When one speaks of "technology" in the present context, the word must be construed appropriately, for what is relevant for present purposes is *the technology of data-generation and of information acquisition and processing*—in short, the technology of scientific *inquiry* itself.[2] One acute observer has put the matter in the following terms:

[1] [E]xperimental physics heavily depends on some very advanced technology. The research physicist is not only at home with it, he has often helped to develop it, adapt it, and debug it. He is part engineer by necessity—and often by taste as well. An experimental physicist who is totally unmoved by a piece of excellent engineering has probably chosen the wrong career. . . . Currently, in fields such as plasma physics and thermonuclear research, there are many theoretical physicists, with a broad range of interest and expertise, some with a background in elementary-particle physics, intimately concerned with engineering questions. (D. A. Bromley, *et al.*, *Physics in Perspective: Student Edition* [Washington, D.C., 1973; National Academy of Sciences/National Research Council Publication], p. 22.)

[2] The knowledge-facilitating power of his instruments is apt to engender in the experimental/observational scientist an exultation in his instrument that is not

Just as scientific knowledge and methods are entering technology, scientific research is in turn determined by technology. Thus the assimilation of technology to science has its counterpart in the dependence of science on technology. Two main ways can be distinguished in which technology exercises an influence on science: firstly it provides instruments and apparatus for scientific investigations, and, secondly, technological development throws up new fundamental problems that stimulate the course of scientific research. . . . Indeed, many objects of scientific research, such as, for instance, the transuranic elements, many isotopes and elementary particles, and most organic compounds are only created at all through the use of technical aids.[3]

It is not difficult to discern the basis on which a thesis of the technological dependency of natural science rests. As an army marches on its "stomach" (i.e., its logistical support), so science depends upon its "eyes"—it is crucially dependent on the technological instrumentalities which constitute the sources of its data.

This point is—or should be—trite and uncontroversial. Natural science is fundamentally *empirical*, and its advance is critically dependent not on human ingenuity alone, but on the phenomena to which we can only gain access through interactions with nature.[4] And

---

unworthy of a lover. Thus Galileo: "O telescope, instrument of much knowledge, more precious than any sceptic! Is not he who holds.thee in his hand made king and lord of the works of God." (Quoted in A. E. Bell, *Christiaan Huyghens and the Development of Science in the Seventeenth Century* [London, 1947], p. 111.)

[3] Friedrich Rapp, "Technology and Natural Science—A Methodological investigation" in F. Rapp (ed.), *Contributions to a Philosophy of Technology* (Dordrecht, 1974), pp. 93–114 (see p. 99). This passage by one philosophical commentator has many counterparts in the recent discussions of students of scientific method and science-policy theorists. The key point was already quite clear to Lord Kelvin:

. . . the new province of electrical science . . . has grown up, largely in virtue of the great modern improvements in practical methods for exhausting air from glass vessels, culminating in Sprengel's mercury-shower pump, by which we now have "vacuum tubes" and bulbs containing less than 1/190,000 of the air which would be left in them by all that could be done in the way of exhausting (supposed to be down to 1 mm. of mercury) by the best air-pump of fifty years ago. (Presidential Address to the Royal Society of London, Nov. 30, 1893, *Proceedings*, vol. 54 [1893], pp. 382–389 [see p. 387].)

[4] This dependence of theoretical advance on the goading of experimental results is clearly indicated in Max Planck's statement:

. . . it was the facts learned from experiments that shook and finally overthrew the classical theory. Each new idea and each new step were suggested to investigators—where it was not

the days are long past when useful scientific data can be gathered by unaided sensory observation of the ordinary course of nature. *Artifice* has become an indispensable route to the acquisition and processing of scientifically useful data: the sorts of data on which the scientific discovery depends can usually be generated by technological means.

Science has accordingly come to outstrip industry in rivaling military weaponry in its concern for technological sophistication:

> [F]undamental research in physics is crucially dependent on advanced technology, and is becoming more so. Historical examples are overwhelmingly numerous. The postwar resurgence in low-temperature physics depended on the commercial production of the Collins liquefier, a technological achievement that also helped to launch an era of cryogenic engineering. And today, superconducting magnets for a giant bubble chamber are available only because of the strenuous industrial effort that followed the discovery of hard superconductors. In experimental nuclear physics, high-energy physics, and astronomy—in fact, wherever photons are counted, which includes much of fundamental physics—photomultiplier technology has often paced experimental progress. The multidirectional impact of semiconductor technology on experimental physics is obvious. In several branches of fundamental physics it extends from the particle detector through nanosecond circuitry to the computer output of analyzed data. Most critical experiments planned today, if they had to be constrained within the technology of even ten years ago, would be seriously compromised.[5]

As Bacon rightly saw, nature is taciturn, nay virtually mute. She does not declare herself freely, but only speaks when spoken to, or rather, she only answers when questioned in a certain way—she must be "put to the test" through appropriate sorts of interactions; interactions which can only be brought about by the deployment of technology. The

---

actually thrust upon them—as the result of measurements. (Max Planck, *The Universe in the Light of Modern Physics* [New York, 1949], p. 139.)

To say all this is not, of course, to deny that human ingenuity is an important part of the story. We need not gainsay the important Kuhnian point that "the phenomena" are conceptualized and theory-laden—that they are not "just there" but are, so to speak, invisible save from an appropriate theoretical perspective.

[5] D. A. Bromley *et al.*, *Physics in Perspective: Student Edition* (Washington, D.C., 1973; NRC/NAS Publication), p. 23.

creative scientist must have a "nose for problems"—a sensitivity for just where the really crucial big questions are situated—but he must also have a well-developed *sense of the possible* as to the issues which, in the existing state of research technology, one can hope to tackle effectively with the instruments in hand.[6]

For a particularly vivid picture of this technological dependency, consider the situation in nuclear physics, described in the following quotation from UNESCO-sponsored survey of modern physics:

[T]he main trends of investigation in fundamental nuclear physics in the last few years have been the search for new particles, with a view to determining the constituents of our world, and the study of the interactions between the various "elementary" particles, with a view to learning more about the forces involved.

It should be stressed here that the creation and transformation of elementary particles involves energies of at least a hundred million electron-volts (10^8 eV). That is why the development of elementary particle physics has gradually brought about the creation of a special field, "high energy particle physics," which is to some extent separate from other fields of nuclear physics and uses its own special methods and equipment.[7]

---

[6] Thus, "For example, as soon as the high-flux isotope reactor became available, questions in the phonon distribution in solids that had plagued solid-state physicists became answerable." Alvin M. Weinberg, "Socio-technical Institutes and the Future of Team Research" in *Scientific Institutions of the Future*, ed. by P. C. Ritterbusch (Washington, 1972), pp. 113–133 (see p. 126). Science, as Sir Peter Medawar has said, is the "art of the soluble." (See his book of this title published in London in 1967.)

[7] Pierre Auger, *Current Trends in Scientific Research* (Paris, 1961; UNESCO Survey). This entire survey of recent work in natural science and its prospects for the near future reads like an equipment catalogue designed to show the power and promise of the contemporary technology of scientific inquiry. The author proceeds to describe the situation in greater detail:

Our knowledge of the structure of atomic nuclei and of elementary particles has been derived mainly from the study of reactions between colliding particles. The method used is to bombard a "target" with a stream of particles and study the particles resulting from this interaction. The simplest type of reaction is elastic scattering in which the colliding particles simply deflect each other without undergoing any other change. In this case the closest distance of approach which can be explored depends on the initial energy. In inelastic reactions, on the other hand, one or both of the colliding particles may undergo changes, and in addition new particles and quanta of electromagnetic radiation (gamma rays) may be created. The creation of new particles or quanta can occur only if the necessary energy is available in the kinetic energy of the colliding particles. Consequently, in both cases kinetic energy is a determining factor for the phenomena to be observed. . . . The high energy particles (energy greater than 10^8 eV) occur in nature (cosmic rays) or as a result of the interaction of particles artificially accelerated in special equipment—accelerators. Such accelerators have already made available particles of energy exceeding $2 \cdot 5 + 10^{10}$ eV. Particles in a higher range of energies (up to 10^{18} eV) are accessible only through experiments with cosmic rays.

To create pi-mesons, a total energy of somewhat more than 10^8 eV must be imparted to the

The case in nuclear physics in this regard typifies in a particularly emphatic fashion the situation that prevails nowadays throughout the natural sciences in general.[8]

The call of science on technology is indeed so demanding, that the engineering of scientific instrumentation is very likely the most technically advanced and sophisticated mode of engineering:

> This dependence of high-energy physics on technology and engineering frequently stretches the capabilities of existing technology to the utmost, requiring innovations and extrapolations that go well beyond any present state of the art. Because the resulting technological developments have implications much broader than their use in particle physics, all technology benefits from the opportunity to respond to this pressure. New technical developments occur sooner—sometimes much earlier—than they would in the absence of such pressure, and they often present new engineering opportunities, unrelated to high-energy physics, that can be exploited immediately. Examples of such engineering

---

bombarding particles alone; but an energy as high as 6×10^9 eV is needed to produce a pair of hyperons. It seems certain that further discoveries will reinforce this trend towards the development of increasingly powerful accelerators, and that these in turn will pave the way to even larger accelerators. (p. 40.)

Or consider another illustration of this process through which scientific advance waits on progress in the cognitive technology of inquiry:

[Many] problems in basic acoustics still wait to be solved. Among these problems are those that involve the interactions of high-frequency sound radiation with matter in its various phases; but the more purely technological problem of the extension of the practical-frequency limit of ultrasonic radiation must be solved first. The limit in 1967 was about 10^{10} cycles per second. If frequencies of the order of 10^{11} to 10^{14} cycles per second could be realized, our understanding of the nature of the solid, liquid, and gaseous states would be much enhanced. (R. B. Lindsay, *The Nature of Physics* [Providence, 1968], p. 187.)

[8] Consider a case in point from a very different sector of natural science:

Chemistry is undergoing a renaissance. This is a new science. It is, perhaps, oldest of the laboratory sciences but it had fallen into the doldrums about the time of World War II; even the chemists found chemistry rather dull. Just after World War II the situation wasn't much improved. What has changed chemistry again has been the availability of a new set of tools. They have names which you may have read or heard of in one place or another: Nuclear magnetic resonance, spectrophotometry, very careful spectroscopy, electron diffraction, electron paramagnetic resonance spectrometry, instruments for measuring circular dichroism, mass spectrometry, and a few others combine to give the chemists a completely new set of handles on that aspect of the world for which they are responsible. This has permitted the chemists to understand the structure of molecules in a way no chemist understood them before. Instead of vague, two-dimensional chicken tracks written on paper, chemists now have a very clear understanding of the three-dimensional structure and electronic configuration of a large number of molecules as well as of chemical reaction on mechanisms. (Statement by Philip Handler, testimony before Daddario Committee, 1970 NSF Authorization Hearings, vol. 1 of transcript, p. 10.)

developments are manifold: large volume, very-high-vacuum systems; sources of enormous radio-frequency power; cryogenic systems; large-scale static superconducting magnets; variable-current superconducting systems; pattern-recognition devices; very fast electronic circuits; and on-line computer techniques. In this sense, elementary-particle physics has had a major impact on technology, but the effect has been an indirect one resulting from the urgency of the research requirements rather than the results of the research.[9]

The progress of modern science would evidently be impossible without a conjoint progress in its data-oriented technology.

These considerations indicate how technological limits lie at the basis of the operation of a principle of diminishing returns. Writing in the context of invention (*technological* discovery) Fritz Machlup has said:

> The possibility of diminishing returns in the invention industry may seem puzzling on first thought. The phenomenon of diminishing returns is always attributable to the presence of one or more "fixed factors," factors necessary in the production but not present in increased quantities when the input of "variable factors" is increased. The variable factors, in the case before us, are inventive labor plus the required facilities for research and experimentation (laboratory space, instruments and machines, materials, energy, administrative and clerical help). What are "fixed factors" in the production of inventions? In order to answer this we must inquire a little into the technology of the production of technological inventions. . . . Once the multiple role of technology in the inventive process is understood, it will not appear paradoxical if the existing stock of scientific knowledge and of the industrial arts at any moment of time is named as a fixed factor in the process of producing new inventions.[10]

As Machlup sees it, fixed factors that impose diminishing returns so as ultimately to impede technical progress lie largely on the side of "the existing stock of scientific knowledge." In regard to science, however, a

[9] D. A. Bromley *et al.*, *Physics in Perspective: Student Edition*, *op. cit.*, see pp. 55–56. And indeed the dominance of technology in scientific research is so complete that the recent periodization of experimental science is most readily accomplished in terms of its dominant devices.

[10] Fritz Machlup, "The Supply of Inventors and Inventions," *Weltwirtschaftliches Archiv*, vol. 85 (1960), pp. 210–252 (see pp. 238–239).

similar situation seems to hold exactly in reverse. The basis for diminishing returns for scientific progress lies primarily on the side of technology, which remorselessly imposes "the limits of the possible" in the given state of the technological art.[11] In the face of the limits imposed by a *fixed* technology of inquiry, further investment in the research effort becomes increasingly unproductive.

There is no escaping the fact that—natural science being, as it is, an inescapably *empirical* enterprise—remorseless limitations are imposed upon the prospects of effective theorizing at any given stage in its development by this dependency on the available data. To say this is not to sell human ingenuity short; it is simply a matter of facing a very fundamental fact of scientific life. Failure to acknowledge this fact of technological dependency spells a resort to the most arrant rationalism (more extreme than that of any 17th century philosopher) to the effect that the theorizing intellect unaided by any sort of interactions with nature can furnish a satisfactory account of "the ways of the world."

3. DATA AND DATA-TECHNOLOGY

The data requisite for scientific discovery exhibit primarily three distinct albeit connected aspects: (i) new *qualitative sorts* of data (data that are new as to "subject matter"—as, for example, mass differs from temperature, as it were), (ii) new *quantitative degrees of magnitude* in data in point of, for example, size, duration, velocity, etc., and (iii) new *combinatory relationships* for data—i.e., new contextual settings for "old" data, endowing them with a novel significance (through new statistical comparison techniques, mathematical representations, models, etc.). We shall designate these three aspects as *type*, *scope*, and *structure*, respectively. The technology of inquiry corresponding accordingly embraces three principal categories: devices for producing new conditions for experimental observation and testing that nature itself does not conveniently place at our disposal, devices for augmenting the range of observational and discriminative capabilities of the human sense, and devices for the processing and interpretation of

---

[11] To say this is not to deny the reality of the "dialectical interplay" in science between advances on the side of theory and technology—maintaining the relationship between these parameters, it casts the former in the role of generally dependent and the latter in the role of generally independent variables.

data. In a first rudimentary approximation, the taxonomy of this technological domain has the structure shown in Table 1.

Table 1

THE TECHNOLOGY OF INQUIRY: SPECIES OF DATA-TECHNOLOGY

I. *Condition-Producing Equipment for the Realization of Phenomena*
    Equipment for producing low and high temperatures, Particle-accelerators, Power-generators

II. *Instruments of Observation for the Detection of Phenomena*
    A. *Detection Instruments*
        Telescopes, Microscopes, Cloud Chambers
    B. *Measuring Instruments*
        Chronometers, Calipers, Calorimeters, Voltmeters, Geiger Counters

III. *Mechanisms for Processing and Interpreting Data*
    Computers, Statistical Methods, Techniques (mathematical or material) for analyzing interrelationships and building interactional models.[12]

On this tripartite division we have to do with the *production* and the *determination* (detection, measurement) of phenomena, and with the *processing* of the resultant findings.[13] The first two have to do with the *synthesis* of data, the third with their *analysis*. The technology of Category I relates primarily the creation of physical circumstances and situations that nature does not conveniently provide "free of charge."[14] With the technology of Category II we augment the capacity of the senses to extract data from nature. And with the technology of Category III we operate in the cognitive sphere of data-manipulation and exploitation. Categories I and II relate to the crucial aspect of *interaction* with nature without which no *empirical* science is possible. Inquiry in a developed branch of natural science calls for the deployment of the technology of inquiry at all three of these levels. (These

[12] This commits us to a rather broad view of "technology"—one that includes not physical equipment alone but also analytical techniques.

[13] The theoretical taxonomy of scientific instrumentation is a virtually untouched field. For present purposes the crude picture of Table 1 is sufficient. But compare also F. V. Lazarev and M. K. Trifonova, "The Role of Apparatus in Cognition and Its Classification" in F. Rapp (ed.), *Contributions to a Philosophy of Technology* (Dordrecht, 1974), pp. 197–209.

[14] Natural science, after all, is in large measure an *experimental* enterprise in the traditional, Galilean manner of experimentation revolving about the production (or reproduction) of natural phenomena under conveniently selected artificial conditions, ones which are readily observed, conveniently manipulated, and readily screened off from "extraneous" influences.

categories are not disjoint even as regards particular pieces of equipment; complex instrumentation such as process-control devices can operate on all three levels at once.)

Under currently operative conditions, the advance of natural science is crucially reliant upon such data-oriented technology—that scientific progress presupposes technological progress in this area of the inquiry-related mechanisms. All significant improvements in scientific theorizing and in the substantiation of its products demand improvements in the data-base, and thus demand an enhanced technology of data-acquisition and/or processing. The technological means for the acquisition and processing of information provide an infrastructure upon which human ingenuity can proceed to erect the superstructure of scientific theorizing. We are thus led to the articulation of a Technological Dependency Thesis: *Progress in the theoretical superstructure of natural science hinges crucially upon improvements in the technological basis of data-acquisition and processing.*[15]

A vivid illustration of the delicate interplay of technology and discovery in modern science is afforded by contemporary microbiology, a field made possible by the combination of electron microscopy and X-ray diffraction:

> The use of electron microscopy, in particular for the study of cell sections of a thickness of the order of 100 Ångströms, has produced a remarkable crop of observations on ultra-microscopic cell structures. Recent achievements in this field include the discovery of the ultra-structures of organelles such as chondriosomes, the Golgi apparatus, ergastoplasm and centrosomes. It has also been shown that, in addition to the well-known plasma and nuclear membranes, there are many other membranous structures in the cytoplasm, including a wide variety of vesicles bounded by membranes. These membranes almost invariably have a thickness of the order of 11 Ångströms, and the

[15] In his interesting book on *The Scientist's Role in Society* (Englewood Cliffs, 1971), Joseph Ben-David argues forcibly against the theory "that scientific ideas are *determined* by economic interests either directly or through the mediation of technology" (p. 13). This is surely correct as regards the *content* of our scientific findings, which is—presumably—conditioned by the nature of "the real world" (as well as by the state of our theoretical sophistication). But the *access* to the relevant phenomena—and thus the rate, direction, and sequencing of scientific findings—will surely in large measure hinge on economico-technological considerations.

more complex structures such as chloroplasts are frequently composed of many such membranes superimposed. The transport of solutes into and out of cells and of substances across complex membranes such as blood capillary walls have been shown to involve invagination and vesicle formation by the plasma membrane. At present, the results of many of these studies made by electron microscopy cannot be interpreted. This arises from our inability either to assess artifact formation during the preparation of specimens or to identify chemically substances seen in the electron microscope. Much research is therefore being undertaken with a view to remedying these deficiencies and the discoveries which have been made as a result include the recognition that all living 'matter' possesses a unity of structure, that cell organelles appear to be universal, a discovery that confirms the evolutionary thesis that all the living organisms which inhabit our planet derive from a common stock.[16]

And in general, modern natural science is in large measure a matter of the physics of extreme conditions and *could not exist* if the increasingly complex and sophisticated machinery for the production, examination, and analysis of these conditions were not available.

4. THE CENTRALITY OF DATA: SOME REASONS WHY

The preceding section has generated a straightforward syllogism:

1. First-rate discoveries in science require the available data-base to be augmented (the data must be enlarged in quantity, enhanced in quality, amplified as to type, reoriented in point of complexity, or the like).
2. Any substantial enhancement in the data-base calls for improvements in the information-technology of data-acquisition or processing.

Therefore, significant scientific progress hinges upon improvements in data-providing technology.

The second premiss is relatively uncontroversial, but it seems

[16] Auger, *op. cit.*, pp. 76–77.

worthwhile to scrutinize the first more closely and to consider just how improved data based on enhanced interactions with nature provide the motive power that turns the wheels of scientific progress.[17]

The really major advances in natural science involve the opening up of a new point of view, a new conceptual perspective—a new problem area or a wholly new way of posing old problems. But while major developments do involve conceptual innovations, they are, in natural science, never *purely* conceptual and matters of a merely ideational dialectic: they are a response to new facts correlative with new data.

One of the key governing conceptions of contemporary work in science is the idea of "new phenomena," phenomena whose discovery (like Lavoisier's discovery of the behavior of weight in oxydation processes or Röntgen's discovery of X-rays) falls upon the scientific community of the day like a bolt from the blue. This idea is handily developed in a passage by the eminent Russian physicist Peter Kapitsa:

> I would like to define a "new phenomenon" as a natural phenomenon that can neither be foreseen nor explained on the basis of existing theoretical concepts. To clarify the definition, I will name those new phenomena which, in my opinion, were discovered in the past 150 years.
>
> The first discovery I would like to mention is the discovery of Galvani's electric current in 1789. This discovery in no way flowed from the theoretical conceptions of that period. (Volta only half finished this discovery, if you like.) Another discovery worthy of note, in my opinion, was Oersted's discovery in 1820 of the influence of electric current on a magnetic needle. I do not consider Faraday's discovery of electromagnetic induction as a new one, since it is nothing more than the converse discovery to that made by Oersted, which it was already possible to foresee. Oersted's discovery led to Maxwell's equations, and all others were but an elaboration of this discovery. To foresee Oersted's discovery theoretically was impossible.
>
> A further example of a new phenomenon is Hertz's discovery of external photo-effect (not electromagnetic waves which we all

---

[17] The transition sequence—enhanced capacity → novel data → scientific innovation—was interestingly sketched over a generation ago in F. K. Richtmyer, "The Romance of the Next Decimal Place," *Science*, vol. 75 (1932), pp. 1–5. His point is that the pursuit of "mere" increases in accuracy virtually never remains at the level of mereness, offering the injunction: "Look after the next decimal place and physical theories will take care of themselves."

know) which thirty or forty years later led to Einstein's equations, which were impossible to foresee theoretically. The principles of indeterminacy and the quantum theory were contained in the discovery of the photo-effect—all the others were just a further elaboration. Then I would include Becquerel's discovery of radioactivity—this also was an unforeseeable phenomenon. On the other hand, the discovery of the electron cannot be counted as an independent discovery. Next, I would note the Michelson and Morley experiment, the result of which was impossible to foresee. Then Hertau's discovery of cosmic rays, which was also unforeseeable. It also appears to me that the discovery of uranium fission by Lise Meitner and Otto Hahn should be noted.[18]

This idea of "new phenomena" is the talisman of contemporary experimental physics. Workers in this domain do not nowadays talk of increased precision or accuracy of measurement in their own right—it is all a matter of the search for new phenomena. And the development of new data-technology is virtually mandatory for the discerning of new phenomena. The reason is simple enough. Inquiry proceeds on such a broad front nowadays that the range of phenomena to which the old data-technology gives access is soon exhausted. And the same is generally true with respect to the range of theory testing and confirmation that the old phenomena can underwrite.[19]

When such limitations in the data-base occur, they produce correlative imperfections in our theoretical understanding. A homely fishing analogy of Eddington's is useful here.[20] He saw the experimentalist as a "trawler"—that is, as one who trawls nature with the "net" of his equipment for detection and observation. Now suppose (says Eddington) that fisherman trawls the seas using a fish-net of two-

---

[18] Peter Kapitsa, "The Future Problems of Science" in M. Goldsmith and A. Mackay (eds.), *The Science of Science* (London, 1964), pp. 102–113 (see pp. 104–105).

[19] Use of the term "phenomena" and insistence upon their primacy in scientific inquiry goes back to the ancient idea of "saving the phenomena" (see Pierre Duhem, *To Save the Phenomena*, tr. by E. Doland and C. Maschler [Chicago, 1969], and Jürgen Mittelstrass, *Die Rettung der Phänomene* [Berlin, 1962]). It finds its modern articulation in Newton's *Principia*. The key point presently at issue was clearly perceived by Karl Pearson at the turn of the century:

The progress of science lies in the continual discovery of more and more comprehensive [i.e., *comprehensively applicable*] formulae by and of which we can clarify the relationships and sequences of *more and more extensive groups of phenomena*. (*The Grammar of Science*, ed. by E. Nagel [New York, 1957], pp. 96–97; italics supplied.)

[20] See A. S. Eddington, *The Nature of the Physical World* (New York, 1928).

inch mesh. Then fish of a smaller size will simply go uncaught. And the theorists who analyze the experimentalist's catch will have an incomplete and distorted view of aquatic life. Only by improving our observational means for "trawling" nature can such imperfections be mitigated.

A look at the history of major scientific innovation indicates that this is generally not a matter of spontaneous generation but rather a provoked response to three sorts of challenges that crop up uninvited and often unwelcome. We standardly encounter here situations in which the equilibrium of "established" theory and "familiar" fact is upset by the accession of new facts, creating a situation in which *new data-sources* are at issue because existing theories can presumably—and usually—accommodate the old data (this, after all, being the basis on which they *are* the "existing" theories).[21] The new data or data-complexes create a disturbance of the cognitive equilibrium in the general coherence of the over-all constellation of data-cum-theory. A setting is thus created—a novel problem-situation—in which scientific innovation (i.e., readjustment on the side of the accepted scientific theories) becomes a situational imperative.

This circumstance above all accounts for the fact that in the case of virtually every significant modern innovation in science (be it pure or applied), the innovation at issue was either (1) arrived at independently through the concurrent efforts of two or more workers,[22] or was (2) arrived at by one worker (or team of workers) narrowly beating another to a common finish line.[23] The crucial point is that new data derive from new data-technology, and that once this technology becomes available

[21] Compare T. S. Kuhn, "Historical Structure of Scientific Discovery," *Science*, vol. 136 (1962), pp. 760–764.

[22] See the pioneering study by W. F. Ogburn and D. Thomas, "Are Inventions Inevitable? A Note on Social Evolution," *Political Science Quarterly*, vol. 37 (1922), pp. 83–98. Here some 150 cases of independent but redundant major discoveries are considered. (I wish space permitted a reprinting of this list—the cumulative impact of its perusal is a powerful stimulus to thought.) For a brief bibliography of multiple independent discovery in science see Donald T. Campbell, "Evolutionary Epistemology" in P. A. Schilpp (ed.), *The Philosophy of Karl Popper* (2 vols.; La Salle, 1967), pp. 413–463 (see p. 460). Some additions to this listing are: R. K. Merton, "Resistance to the Systematic Study of Multiple Discoveries in Science," *European Journal of Sociology*, vol. 4 (1963), pp. 272–282; F. Reif, "The Competitive World of the Pure Scientist," *Science*, vol. 134 (December 15, 1961), pp. 1957–1962; Thomas S. Kuhn, "Historical Structure of Scientific Discoveries," *Science*, vol. 136 (June 1, 1962), pp. 760–764.

[23] See J. D. Watson, *The Double Helix* (New York, 1968) for a striking case study.

there results a land-office scramble for its exploitation. Nothing more clearly manifests the dependency of scientific progress upon advances in the technology of data-acquisition and coordination which create the conditions requisite for certain scientific innovations than the common phenomenon of a clustering of redundant findings.[24]

Nothing could more emphatically demonstrate the impotence of mere intellect unaided by technological means for the acquisition of empirical data than the fact that nowadays in many areas of natural science, it is virtually impossible that major discoveries (or indeed any original work of real value and interest) should come from some quarter outside the handful of major research groups or institutes that are "on top of the problem" at hand and are privy to the new data generated by the frontier technology of research that represents a special "in-house" information-source: particle-accelerators, research reactors, radio-telescopes, etc. (In this regard we must, regretfully, regard the Einstein of the Geneva patent office as the exception that proves the rule.)

Progress without new data is, of course, possible in various fields of scholarship and research. The example of pure mathematics, for example, shows that discoveries can be made in an area of inquiry that has no empirical datum-content at all. But this hardly represents a feasible prospect for natural science. It is exactly the explicit dependency on data—the *empirical* aspect of the discipline—that sets natural science apart not only from the *formal* sciences (logic and mathematics) but also from the *hermeneutic* which—like the humanities—address themselves ceaselessly to the imaginative reinterpretation of old data from novel conceptual perspectives. Without the influx of new empirical data all one could do is to proceed to an increasingly sophisticated conceptual resystematization and reinterpretation of the same data-base. While this might indeed

---

[24] The process at issue is strongly reminiscent of a biological analogue in evolutionary theory which the psychologist Donald T. Campbell has described as follows:

> The opportunism of science, the rushing in and rapid development following new [technological] breakthroughs, are very like the rapid exploitation of a newly entered ecological niche. Science grows rapidly around laboratories, around discoveries which make the testing of hypotheses easier, which provide sharp and consistent selective systems. Thus the barometer, microscope, telescope, galvanometer, cloud chamber, and chromatograph all have stimulated rapid scientific growth. The necessity for the editing action of the experiment explains why a research tradition working with a trivial topic for which predictions can be checked advances more rapidly than research focused upon a more important problem but lacking a machinery for weeding out hypotheses. ("Evolutionary Epistemology" in P. A. Schilpp [ed.], *The Philosophy of Karl Popper* [2 vols., La Salle, 1974], Vol. 1, pp. 413–463 [see p. 435].)

constitute a progress of sorts, it just is *not* the sort of progress at issue in natural science, and blocks the way to the empirical process of hypothesis-testing-and-elimination on which the progress of science as we know it standardly depends. For while significant innovation in natural science *is* conceptual in nature, it is never simply that—i.e., it is not *purely* conceptual. This sort of reinterpretative innovation can only have major significance in the human sciences where the teleological concept of *meaning* is operative. To be sure, reinterpretation might count as "progress," but *this* sort of progress will not represent a major advance in the area of natural science, where the strictly *hermeneutic* issues of meaning and teleology at best play a minor and peripheral part.

5. DEPENDENCE A PART OF INTERDEPENDENCE

This chapter has so far stressed the contention that scientific progress hinges upon the progress of technology. But the reverse is, of course, equally true—the progress of modern technology hinges crucially upon scientific progress. The dependency at issue is reciprocal; it is simply one half part of a mutual interdependence. While it is true that progress in modern science follows the technology of data acquisition and processing, it is no less true that technology progresses in the footsteps of scientific advance. The relationship of technology to science has long ago become irrevocably symbiotic—it is nowadays not a one-way street, but a thoroughly reciprocal relationship, not a linearly unidirectional process but one that is circular or cyclic.[25] The dependence of science on technology stressed above is but half the story, since it relates to only one half of a feedback loop, with *reciprocal* interplay between innovations at the theoretical/fundamental and at the applied/technological levels.[26] As Stephen Toulmin has acutely

---

[25] On this theme compare Jürgen Habermas, *Theorie und Praxis* (Berlin, 1963; reissued in paperback in Frankfurt a.M. in 1971), see especially pp. 341–342 of the paperback version.

[26] As we have seen, Soviet economists incline towards the trickle-down theory of progress: science (S) → technology (T) → economic production (P) with

$$\frac{dS}{dt} > \frac{dT}{dt} > \frac{dP}{dt}.$$

(See the discussion of Chapter IV above.) Insofar as the present deliberations are right,

observed: "a natural science and an associated technology are partners in a kind of historical gavotte, developing most effectively when their changes are harmoniously synchronized."[27]

No one has depicted this issue of the reciprocal dependence of theoretical science on technology more clearly than the English physicist Hermann Bondi:

> I have spoken earlier of disproof as the essential agent of progress, but why can we disprove today what we couldn't disprove yesterday? The answer is that today we can carry out more accurate experiments relating to matters that were inaccessible yesterday. We can do so because of the progress of technology. And so a progressing technology is an absolutely essential condition for a progressing science. It is a peculiar disease of this country, I think, to feel that science sort of marches in front and that poor, dirty technology follows a long way behind. But the relation of science and technology is the relation of the chicken and the egg; you cannot have the one without the other. It is true that modern technology derives from modern science, but we would not have had any of modern science without modern technology. The enormous stream of discoveries at the end of the nineteenth century that gave us such insight as the discovery of electrons, discovery of X-rays, working with radio-activity, and all that, is entirely due to the fact that the technologists developed decent vacuum pumps; until you have decent vacuum pumps you cannot do any experiments of the kind required. Of course, X-rays are a splendid scientific discovery, but when this is properly used by technologists to make reliable, safe, accurate X-ray equipment, you can employ it to make progress in molecular biology.[28]

The historical development of science thus moves in a dialectic feedback of interchange from the one side to the other of the theoretical/technological divide, doing so at increasing levels of sophistication.

A word of warning for lovers of paradox. One must *not* think that this mutual dependency is immobilizing—that because the range of innovation in technology is limited by the position of present theory and

---

the first part of this relationship cannot be maintained. Science cannot develop faster than the technology that is a presupposition of its advance.

[27] Stephen Toulmin, *Human Understanding*, vol. I (Princeton, 1972), p. 373.

[28] *Assumption and Myth in Physical Theory* (Cambridge, 1967), p. 5.

that of theory is limited by the position of technology, that consequently no innovation whatever can take place. After all, the placement of the left foot is sharply restricted by that of the right—and conversely—but yet this does *not* mean that great distances cannot be traversed by *walking*, that is, by changing the forward position of the two feet *alternatively over short distances*. The present thesis of theory/technology interdependence proceeds in terms of an exactly similar process of "walking" by the *alternation* of relatively restricted advances in the theoretical and technological sectors.

6. TECHNOLOGICAL DEPENDENCY SETS TECHNOLOGICAL LIMITS

Recognition of this cyclic reciprocity between scientific and technological progress does not, however, affect the basic point of the present deliberations. To be sure, technology is largely applied science and technological innovation in some degree reflects new uses of scientific knowledge. But this symbiosis does not displace the crucial consideration that science cannot effectively push its inquiry into nature further than the available mechanisms of informational technology permit. And these limits are not only limitations on one's capacity to test hypotheses that are already in hand (as the ancients could not test hypotheses about mountains on the far side of the moon), but—more crucially—they impose restrictions on one's capacity even to conceptualize certain hypotheses (as the ancients could have no glimmering of the red shift). Progress is insuperably limited at any given stage of scientific history by the implicit barriers set by the available technology of data acquisition and processing. *Technological dependency sets technological limits*—first to data-acquisition and then to theory-projection. One arrives at the crucial fact that the achieved level of sophistication in the technological "state of the art" of information acquisition and processing sets definite limits to the prospects of scientific progress by restricting the range of findings that are going to be realistically accessible.

The ancient Greeks were certainly as intelligent as we are—perhaps, arguably, even more so. But given the information-technology of the day, it is not just *improbable* but actually *inconceivable* that the Greek astronomers should have come up with an explanation for the red shift or the Greek physicians with an account of the bacteriological transmission of some communicable disease. The reason for this is simple—the relevant types of data needed to put such phenomena within the cognitive grasp of man simply lay beyond their reach. Given the data-acquisition technology of the times there *just was no way* for the Greeks (no matter how well-endowed in brain-power) to gain physical or conceptual access to the relevant phenomena. Progress in theorizing in these directions was barred—not permanently, but then and there *for them*—by a technological barrier on the side of data that was as absolute as the then-extant technological barriers in the way of developing the internal combustion engine or the wireless telegraph.

The Danish historian of science A. G. Drachmann closes his excellent book on *The Mechanical Technology of Greek and Roman Antiquity* (Copenhagen and Madison, Wisc., 1963) with the following observation:

> I should prefer not to seek the cause of the failure of an invention in the social conditions till I was quite sure that it was not to be found in the technical possibilities of the time.

The present discussion endorses the idea that the history of *science* as well as that of *technology* is crucially conditioned by the delimitative role of this matter of "the technical possibilities of the time."

IX

The Quantification of Technological Dependency: the Capacity/Findings Relation

Scientia et potentia humana in idem coincidunt. . . . ("*Human knowledge and power are coextensive.*")

BACON, *Novum Organon*, Bk. I, sect. iii

From the beginning . . . man has increasingly implemented himself with power. Had he not done so, he would have had no history. . . . Without power no progress.

CARL BECKER, *Progress and Power* (New York, 1949), p. 24

1. PRELIMINARIES

The preceding chapter developed a key premise for our line of reasoning in maintaining that scientific progress depends crucially upon the available technology of data acquisition and manipulation. This technological dependence must now be put on a quantitative footing. To this end, it is helpful to consider once again the data-taxonomy provided above (see pp. 141–142), which characterized scientific data with respect to three primary aspects, qualitative variety, quantitative extensiveness, and relational complexity—more briefly: *type, scope,* and *structure.* The technological-dependency thesis may correspondingly be construed as maintaining that ongoing significant discovery in a matured branch of natural science—one that has developed to a stage where a constantly enhanced technology of data-acquisition and processing has become established—hinges crucially upon advances in the accession of data in at least one of these three basic respects.[1] This

---

[1] The "off the record" discussions by scientists outside the rigidly professional literature are replete with references to such a need to have theoretical advances await the realization of further technical developments. Consider two cases in point:

leads to the focal question of the present chapter: How is the extent of such advances in data-technology related to that of the progress in scientific knowledge made possible by them?

2. INTRODUCTION TO THE CASE OF SYNTHETIC (POWER-INTENSIVE) PROBLEMS

It is helpful to begin with a closer look at the issue of how improvements in data-technology can be assessed. Consider once again the family of *the characterizing features* of physical processes: particle velocities, wave-frequencies, temperatures, pressures, or the like. In the study of natural processes it is these range-determinative features that are measured and/or controlled. Each of them represents a "dimension" of the physically relevant phenomena of nature. The paradigm example of such a physical dimension is the electromagnetic spectrum as pictured in Figure 1.

Taken together, such parameter-ranges comprise a "parametric space" within which—or within some subspace of which—physical phenomena can be positioned, a sort of natural coordinate-system or location-framework for their placement. Such physical parameter-ranges will be of two types. Some (e.g., distance, density, wave-length, duration, temperature [on the positive side]) are virtually limitless; others (e.g., velocity, temperature [on the negative side]) are physically limited.

We shall suppose that the measurement scale for the former, limitless parameters proceeds in ascending powers of 10, while the measurement scale for the latter, limited parameters proceeds in descending powers of 10 in terms of successive order-of-magnitude steps towards the limit.

Furthermore the W meson, which has been hypothesized as the mediator of the weak interactions (in analogy to mediators of the electromagnetic and strong interactions, the photon and the π, p, ... and K-mesons), has not yet been observed despite various experimental efforts toward its discovery. There are arguments suggesting that its mass should be so large (not less than 37 GeV) that it cannot be produced by existing accelerators or by those now under construction. (Edoardo Amaldi, "The Unity of Physics," *Physics Today*, vol. 261, September 1973, No. 9, pp. 23–29 [see p. 25].)

Or again:

Particle physics is, then, full of life and vitality.... It seems certain, however, that the solution of present problems will again require a considerable increase in our technical resources, such as the 300 GeV accelerator. (C. F. Powell, "The Role of Pure Science in European Civilization," *Physics Today*, vol. 18 [1965], pp. 56–64 [see p. 58].)

Figure 1

THE ELECTROMAGNETIC SPECTRUM

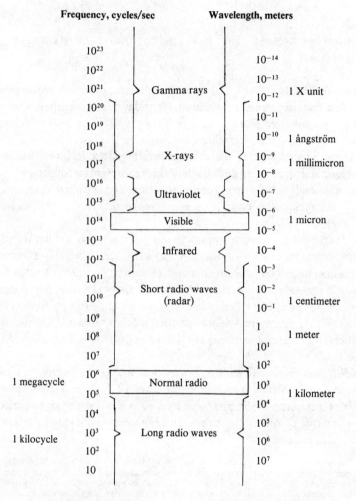

Frequency, cycles/sec   Wavelength, meters

Note The chart shows the waves, of widely differing wavelengths, that make up the electromagnetic spectrum. Those that are visible, which we see as light, constitute only a small portion of the total spectrum. James Clerk Maxwell showed that light consists of electromagnetic waves (jointly oscillating electrical and magnetic fields). These waves all travel in empty space with the "speed of light," 186,000 miles/second or 3×10^8 meters/second.

Thus in the scale of an *unlimited* parameter, a given number of u-steps (i.e., unit steps) on the E-scale will carry us this far forward along the parametric axis at issue. But in the case of a *limited* parameter, n steps on the E-scale will carry us to within a fraction amounting to $(1/10)^{\log n}$ of the way to the limit at issue. The situation is summarized in Table 1.

Table 1

SCALING-RULES FOR MEASURING PHYSICAL PARAMETERS
Distance Covered

E-units	$\log E$	*Unlimited Parameter* (u-unit sized steps)	*Limited Parameter* (proportion of the way left to the limit)
10	1	$10u$	$1/10$
100	2	$10^2 u$	$1/100$
1,000	3	$10^3 u$	$1/1000$
10^n	n	$10^n u$	$(1/10)^n$

$$10^n u \Big\} = 10^{\log E} u \qquad (1/10)^n \Big\} = (1/10)^{\log E}$$

The growth of our knowledge of nature can be viewed—in one of its major aspects—as a matter of the geography-reminiscent *exploration* of the different physical spectra comprising such a parametric space. Thus nowadays the physicist can contemplate (and in large measure explore experimentally):

—a domain of *space* which ranges from 10^{-15} cm (the structure of the proton) to 10^{29} cm (the furthest observable distance of the extragalactic space);

—a domain of *mass* which ranges from the mass of the electron (0.9×10^{-27} g) to the mass of the Universe ($\sim 4 \times 10^{58}$ g);

—a domain of *time* intervals which ranges from the time of a nuclear event (10^{-23} sec) up to the history of the proton ($> 10^{37}$ sec).

The idea of such an exploratory venture is neatly captured in the perspective of the following passage from the UNESCO study of physics by Pierre Auger from which we have already quoted on several occasions:

Present research efforts are not only being extended into space;

science is pushing its investigations into all the newly conquered areas of extreme conditions, which are deviating increasingly from the normal. These are the areas of high and low temperatures, high and low pressures, extreme electric and magnetic fields, zero or very powerful gravitational or acceleration fields, very high and very low energies, ultra-long or ultra-short intervals of time. In each case, these areas have been reached and the necessary measurements made as a result of the discovery and development of new techniques. A few decades ago, the physical universe accessible to the scientist was comparatively limited and conditions in it hardly varied by more than a few powers of ten. Today, the scientist can produce on the spot, in his own laboratories, conditions which occur only in inaccessible regions such as the centre of the stars or the depths of the earth, or which perhaps do not exist anywhere in the universe.[2]

As the range of telescopes, the energy of particle accelerators, the effectiveness of low-temperature instrumentation, the potency of pressurization equipment, the power of vacuum-creating contrivances, and the accuracy of measurement apparatus increases—that is, as our capacity to move about in the parametric space of the physical world (as it were) is enhanced—new phenomena come into our ken, with the result of enlarging the empirical basis of our knowledge of natural processes. The key to the great progress of contemporary physics lies in the enormous strides that have been made in this regard; as one commentator has justly observed: "In almost every observational dimension, short time, small distance, weak signal, and the like, the limits are being pushed beyond what might have been reasonably anticipated."[3]

This idea of scientific progress through the virtually "spectroscopic" exploration of a physical parameter space was envisioned by Alvin M. Weinberg in illuminating terms:

Scientists are naturally much less ready to scrap a 400-MeV proton-synchrocyclotron that costs several million dollars, but

[2] Pierre Auger, *Current Trends in Scientific Research* (Paris, 1961; UNESCO Publication), p. 20.

[3] D. A. Bromley *et al.*, *Physics in Perspective: Student Edition* (Washington, D.C., 1973; NRC/NAS Publication), p. 16.

which no longer can cut at the main edge of high-energy physics, than they are to scrap, say, an optical microscope. The somewhat bureaucratic imperative to exploit expensive machinery circumscribes the direction of scientific growth. The spectroscopic filling in of details tends to crowd out the breakthroughs, simply because the number of breakthroughs possible with a particular machine is very small compared with the practically infinite spectroscopic detail the machine can generate.

It would be foolish to underestimate the importance of spectroscopy in setting the groundwork for important discoveries and conceptual breakthroughs. Quantum mechanics would have been impossible without its underlying detailed optical spectroscopy. Or, more recently, low-energy physics has a strongly spectroscopic flavor. Most experiments seek to measure, in various nuclides, specific properties that already fit into a general theoretical framework. Yet out of this elaborate spectroscopy (conducted, incidentally, by teams) has come a seemingly endless succession of breakthroughs: either in experimental techniques, as in the discovery of the lithium-drifted germanium-detector, or in new insights into nuclear structure, as in the discovery of isobaric analogue states and short-lived isomers.[4]

This discussion clearly indicates the two principal types of present-day empirical/experimental research in natural science: the *power-intensive* surges to extend the explored sectors of the spectrum beyond the frontiers of the previously attained, and the *complexity-intensive* "spectroscopic filling in" of details within the achieved sectors of the spectrum. The crucial feature of this spectroscopic exploration lies in the fact that with the increasingly thorough scrutiny of increasingly remote reaches of parametric space, new phenomena come into view which in turn provide the empirical basis for new substantive findings in theoretical science.

[4] Alvin M. Weinberg, "Sociotechnical Institutes and the Future of Team Research" in P. C. Ritterbusch (ed.), *Scientific Institutions of the Future* (Washington, 1972), pp. 113–133 (see pp. 125–126). See also Weinberg's paper "Scientific Teams and Scientific Laboratories," *Daedalus*, vol. 99 (1970), pp. 1056–1075 (see footnote 2 on p. 1074). While this broadened usage of the idea of spectroscopy is originally due to Alvin Weinberg; the fundamental idea, however, remains that of Eddington's homely fish-trawling analogy. On this enlarged concept of spectroscopy see also J. A. Weisskopf, "The Three Spectroscopies," *Scientific American*, vol. 218 (1968), No. 5, pp. 15–29, as well as D. A. Bromley *et al.*, *Physics in Perspective: Student Edition* (Washington, D.C., 1973), pp. 302–308.

3. THE "POWER"/RANGE RELATION

The ever more widely ranging exploration of the "parametric space" of the spectra associated with different conditions in nature demands continual increases in physical power. To achieve greater velocities, higher frequencies, lower or higher temperatures, greater pressures, larger energy-excitations, greater resolving power,[5] etc., requires ever more powerful equipment capable of continually more enhanced performance. The *sort* of "power" at issue will, of course, vary with the nature of the particular parametric dimension under consideration—be it velocity, frequency, temperature, etc.—but the general principle remains the same.

Our attempt to quantify this phenomenon is based upon the following stipulation:

The "Power"/Range Relation

The "power" requisite for exploration along the dimension of a physical parameter is governed by a definite, fixed relationship between the maximum amount of such "power" (P) available for exploratory probing, and the extent (E)—as measured in the scaling units of Section 1 above—to which this parametric dimension can be explored. This relationship is that *the extent of the accessible parametric range (E) and the available "power" (P) are so related that the logarithms of these quantities are q-proportional*: $\log E \infty \log P$ (or, more specifically, $E \propto P^{\alpha}$ with $0 < \alpha < 1$).

This relationship has it that the ongoing process of exploration in parametric space establishes a drastically increasing demand for "power," since only some suitable root of a P-increase reflects the resulting effect in E-augmentation. The underlying fact is that as we move out from the starting-point of "where we ordinarily are" to explore the physical parameters of nature at more and more remote positions (higher or lower temperatures, greater velocities, further distances of astronomical observation, etc.), the capability

---

[5] The parametric dimension of various modes of "accuracy" correlative with the power of instruments of measurement and detection is one of the most important instances of this general conception.

of operating at this enhanced level demands greater and greater power, and does so at a rate that increases massively with the extent of the remoteness at issue. (A vivid illustration of this phenomenon is afforded by the increasing energy of particle accelerators needed to propel the relevant microprojectiles closer and closer to the speed of light. It is readily shown that the energy requirements here comport themselves in due conformity with the Power/Range Relation.)

4. THE IDEA OF A FINDINGS-DISTRIBUTION ASSUMPTION

This idea of the "exploration" of parametric space provides a basic tool for our present model of the mechanism of scientific innovation in mature science: new technology increases the range of access within the parametric space of physical processes, such increased access brings new phenomena to light, and the detection, scrutiny, and theoretical exploitation of these phenomena is the primary basis for growth in our scientific understanding of nature.[6]

Such a condition of things is vividly illustrated from the monumental report on *Current Trends in Scientific Research* prepared by Pierre Auger for UNESCO in 1961:

> *The extension of physical frontiers.* Present research efforts are not only being extended into space; science is pushing its investigations into all the newly conquered areas of extreme conditions, which are deviating increasingly from the normal. . . . The range of physical conditions has been extended in many cases by several powers of ten and this extension is still continuing. The study of the behaviour of matter and energy under these extreme conditions has proved to be of the greatest importance and has in some cases given rise to immediate applications.

[6] The phenomenon was already clearly recognized by George Gore in 1878: "Every new mode or instrument of observation, and every improvement in scientific approaches is almost invariably quickly followed by new discoveries." (*Op. cit.*, p. 572.) The spirit of the situation is helpfully caught in the following passage from Pierre Auger:

> Improvement in the accuracy of measurement by a few powers of ten automatically opens the way to new discoveries. This is also true of amplification, as is shown, for instance, by the analysis of the structure of viruses, made possible by the linear amplification of the electron microscope. Amplification and accuracy are desirable, provided that corresponding progress is made in the elimination of parisitic effects, commonly known as 'noise', which are amplified simultaneously with the phenomenon to be measured. (Pierre Auger, *Current Trends in Scientific Research* [UNESCO Publication: Paris, 1961], p. 21.)

Another field of physical extension is that opened up by the discovery of new fundamental particles of the class of mesons, hyperons and neutrinos, and the antiprotons. The life-span of some of these particles is extremely short—well below a microsecond —and it is only as a result of the above-mentioned extension of physical measurement to ultra-short time intervals that their observation has become possible.

The perfecting of amplifying devices has enabled phenomena of extremely low energies to be detected and studied. The use of photomultipliers and very high-energy condensing mirrors has made possible the detection of extremely low energies in all fields of electromagnetic radiation from light to radio waves; this is particularly true of radio-astronomy. Amplification also plays a very important part in the study of the life processes, making it possible to detect the production of energy by individual cells and even by certain cell constituents.[7]

A vivid illustration of the growing power demands of progress in modern natural science is furnished by high energy physics. In 1924 the French physicist Louis de Broglie first recognized that in certain fundamental respects the behavior of matter resembles that then already well-known for light waves. His hypothesis—soon amply verified—associated a wavelength with the energy of every particle, smaller wavelengths corresponding to higher energies. Wavelength thus provided a scale for size-specifications of physical entities. And exploring the more minute substructure of matter requires, at each stage, smaller wavelengths and consequently higher energies. Since Rutherford's day the progress of subatomic physics has been marked by the steady succession of ever more powerful probes, with a massive harvest of information regarding the microstructure of matter. For new phenomena that serve to extend our theoretical knowledge swim steadily into ken as we explore along this parametric range. This is vividly illustrated by the following passage from a recent U.S. Atomic Energy Commission Survey:

These two decades of expansion of physical facilities [i.e., the 1950's and 1960's] have seen commensurate developments in the knowledge and understanding of the basic principles underlying high energy physics and in the techniques and devices used in the

<hr>

[7] Auger, *op. cit.*, p. 20.

experimental program. Any selection of significant discoveries and developments is to a considerable extent arbitrary, but the following are some of the most significant and profound physics results obtained in that period:

> The discovery of the pion and the examination of its properties.
>
> The discovery of a large number of short-lived particles and the exploration of their properties (kaon, hyperons, etc.).
>
> The discovery, in electron scattering experiments, that the proton and neutron have a finite size and an internal charge distribution.
>
> The discovery of the anti-proton.
>
> The discovery of the violation of parity conservation in weak interactions.
>
> The discovery of a pattern in the spectrum of elementary particles which was explainable in terms of a mathematical model based on the symmetry group SU(3) and the discovery of the omega-minus particle which confirmed a central prediction of this theory.
>
> The discovery that there were two very similar but not identical neutrinos rather than only one as had long been assumed.
>
> The discovery of the violation of combined charge conjugation and parity conservation.
>
> Formulation of a theory in which most of the elementary particles can be described as made up of combinations of only three different types of "sub-elementary" entities, called quarks.
>
> The experimental observation of a point-like particulate structure within the proton and neutron.[8]

A relatively straightforward chain of dependencies obtain here: new science hinges on access to new phenomena whose production and/or detection hinges on new technology.

To characterize this interconnection between our access to parametric space and the scope of our scientific knowledge we shall suppose:

The Findings-Distribution Assumption
Phenomena of substantial theoretical significance for understand-

---

[8] *Considerations for a Viable and Productive High Energy Physics Program* (Washington, D.C., 1972; U.S. Atomic Energy Commission Publications). The quotation is from pp. 46–47.

ing in a given problem area of natural science are distributed *logarithmically* over the relevant dimensions of parametric space, so that the substantial findings correlated with these phenomena are themselves also so distributed. That is, the number of accessible first-rate findings in a given problem area (F) stands to the range or extent (E) of our exploration of the relevant parametric ranges in the relationship $F \propto \log E$.[9]

On this principle, the significant findings arising through exploration along a given parametric dimension of nature are distributed along this dimension in a continually thinning pattern of infrequency, this thinning-out proceeding in a manner characteristic of the particular problem-area. (In the case of an *unlimited* parametric dimension—like energy or complexity—it means that an order-of-magnitude advance on the relevant E-scale [10 to 100 to 1,000, etc.] is needed to advance F by a fixed-size step. In the case of a limited parameter—like particle velocity—it means that such a fixed size F step occurs with every move towards the appropriate limit that improves on its predecessor by a factor of 1/10th [10% to 1% to ·1%, etc.].) The result is a situation in which a novel cluster of major findings confronts us with each added order-of-magnitude step of effectiveness at E-exploration.[10]

Discovery in the constitutive branches of natural science may thus be envisaged as a correlate of the increasingly comprehensive exploration

[9] The (concealed) constants of this relationship may be supposed to be characteristic of the problem area at issue.

[10] The ideas of F. K. Richtmyer's fascinating piece on "The Romance of the Next Decimal Place" (*Science*, vol. 75 [1932], pp. 1–5) are relevant here. His thesis that "the whole history of physics proves that a new discovery is quite likely lurking at the next decimal place" (p. 3) is virtually a statement of the Findings-Distribution Assumption. I cannot forbear quoting the final paragraph of his discussion:

> In a little over a decade, Thomson's apparatus for studying positive rays evolves into Aston's precision mass-spectrograph, in which the relative masses of atoms can be measured with a precision of the order of one part in 10,000. After observing the "fine structure" of spectral lines the spectroscopist goes on to observe "hyperfine structure." A recently reported critical examination of existing data leads to the conclusion that the most probable value of "e," the charge carried by the electron, is $4\cdot7721 \times 10^{-10}$ as e.s.u. instead of $4\cdot774 \times 10^{-10}$ as previously used. From each such extension of the precision of measurement there results either a significant modification of theory, or not infrequently a new discovery. So frequently has this happened in the history of physics that to sum up what I have said I am disposed to conclude by paraphrasing a famous saying: "Look after the next decimal place and physical theories will take care of themselves." (*Op. cit.*, p. 5.)

For relevant considerations—including the controversies over the relative importance or insignificance of "the next decimal place" see Lawrence Badash, "The Completeness of Nineteenth-Century Science," *Minerva*, vol. 63 (1972), pp. 48–58. (See especially p. 51 for references to the shrewd observations of J. C. Maxwell.)

of the relevant parameter-space. And such exploration furnishes its yields in the manner characteristic of any logarithmic increase (i.e., relatively rapidly at first, but then more and more slowly, yet never coming to a stop—not even asymptotically). Our exploration model contends that no delimited region of the parametric space of physical phenomena will exhaust the realization of results of substantial intrinsic interest for our understanding of the world, while nevertheless phenomena of intrinsic interest are distributed with logarithmic infrequency throughout the increasingly remote reaches of this space.

5. A RATIONALE FOR THE FINDINGS-DISTRIBUTION ASSUMPTION: THE ANALOGY OF EXPLORATION AND PROSPECTING

The Findings-Distribution Assumption can be perhaps best explained by means of a model whose gross structure is as follows.

Let it be supposed that the phenomena conducive to the realization of substantial scientific findings are accessible over the reaches of an (n-dimensional) "parameter space" as our data-gathering efforts move increasingly further outwards along the scale of research-relevant parameters (such as object-sizes, temperatures, energy-levels, pressures, field-strengths, vibrational frequencies, data-volumes, accurate measurements, etc.). For us humans, movement over this spectrum of physical parameters must clearly begin from a position within it that is fixed by the parameter values in "our *physical* neighborhood"—given the position we ourselves occupy *in medias res* within nature. From the egocentric standpoint of our local region we move out to "explore" in the manner of a "prospector" searching for cognitively significant phenomena along the various parametric dimensions. And—so we shall suppose—cognitively utile phenomena thin out more and more as we move increasingly far away from our natural "home base" in the course of this exploration, doing so in the log-uniform manner of the Findings-Distribution Assumption: $F(E) \infty \log E$. (It is crucial, however, that the dimensionality of this parametric phase-space is finite.)

Our picture is clearly not one of *geographical* exploration, but of the *physical* exploration—and subsequent theoretical rationalization—of "phenomena" which are (log-uniformly) distributed over the "space" of the physical parameters spreading out all about us. This exploration-metaphor forms the basis of the conception of scientific *research* as a prospecting-like *search* for the new phenomena needed to furnish the basis for innovative and significant findings.[11]

This principle is crucial for the present analysis, but the point it poses is delicate and liable to misunderstanding. For what is at issue is *not* a somewhat peculiar and strange-seeming fact about nature—viz., that it surrenders easily to our inquiry and affords cognitively significant phenomena comparatively readily at the outset. To put the matter this way is misleading and puts a burden of homocentricity onto the shoulders of nature itself that does not really belong there. A more realistic—and optimistic—way of looking at this principle is as a claim that our power of theoretical triangulation is so great that we can make a disproportionately effective use of the phenomena located in our local parametric neighborhood.

What is at issue is thus not a one-sided thesis about the structure of the physical world itself, but a deeper and two-sided thesis about mind/nature interaction and the structure of our cognition in relation to nature. The pivotal point is that man as inquirer is enormously efficient and effective. We are able to derive less and less cognitive benefit from the later steps in the exploratory process of moving further outward in parameter space precisely because we have been so efficient in the cognitive exploitation of the phenomena that came to hand early.

No doubt, nature is in itself uniform as regards the distribution of its diverse processes across the reaches of parameter space—it does not favor us by clustering them in our parametric vicinity. Significant phenomena do not dry up outside our "neighborhood." But *cognitively* significant phenomena in fact become increasingly sparse because the scientific mind has the capacity to do so much so well early on. This "law of log-uniform distribution of significant phenomena" is thus at bottom as much an epistemological as an ontological thesis.

One caution is necessary to remove a possible misimpression that might—very mistakenly—be drawn from this model of exploring or prospecting. Its use must certainly *not* be construed as suggesting that scientifically significant phenomena and scientifically creative findings

---

[11] The exploration model thus opens up the possibility of applying the techniques of operations research for contriving analogues to the search-strategies developed for fields like prospecting. See in this connection the interesting discussion by Louis B. Slichter, "The Need for a New Philosophy of Prospecting," *Mining Engineering*, vol. 12 (1960), pp. 570–576. Moreover, it would be most interesting to study the statistical structure of the history of science in the light of a systematic theory of search processes.

are somehow "sitting out there" in ready-made completeness, waiting
to be hauled in like fish from the sea as we devise longer and longer
fishing-lines. Our "laws of nature" are in fact the product of mind-
nature *interaction*,[12] and their modes of formulation and conceptu-
alization are certainly man-made. The discoveries or *findings* of
science are thus in significant part *makings*—a matter of conceptual
inventiveness within a contrived framework of explanatory
idealizations. Nothing in the exploratory model should be construed as
negating the fact that scientific discovery is a profound adventure of the
creative spirit working with its characteristic conceptualizing
inventiveness. Nevertheless, to say this is not to deny that our science is
in some measure *the causal result of physical interactions between man
and nature*—interactions on which our "data" are ultimately based and
which thus provide grist to the mill of theorizing inquiry.[13] And such
interaction with an inherently man-independent world is the
indispensable requisite for advances in theorizing in natural science as
an *empirical discipline*.

It is not so much that new phenomena indicate the need for
innovative theorizing—though this is indeed generally the case. But
also, for a new theory to establish itself as duly progressive—as
representing an advance on which in turn yet further steps can and
should be based—this theory must afford some guidance in explaining
hitherto unknown phenomena, phenomena which can only be attained
by a more powerful technology. An equilibrium between the old
phenomena and the old theories was presumably established long
ago—the anomalies that demand theoretical innovation generally come
from the new phenomena afforded by novel technology.[14] Thus as
regards this crucial issue of *substantiation*, the matter can be viewed
from the familiar perspective of the well known model of science as an
enterprise of framing and testing explanatory theories (in Popperian
terms, the model of conjecture and refutation). It is clear that one will

[12] For a further development of this point see the author's *Conceptual Idealism*
(Oxford, 1973).

[13] It is to the immortal credit of Francis Bacon that he was the first to see this point
with total clarity.

[14] Generally, but not inevitably. For example, the main anomaly resolved by general
relativity (the issue of the perihelion of Mercury) had been long familiar. Nevertheless a
good deal of high-power observational work using very sophisticated technology had to
be done before general relativity became "established." The technological imperative
for "new data" in natural science is usually operative on the side of the *genesis* of new
theories, but even more emphatically so on the side of their *validation*.

here soon exhaust the tests available within the familiar sector of the parametric range and must move on to virgin territory to carry out the further tests on which—on this model—theoretical progress is crucially dependent. The cleverness of theoreticians assures that the data attainable over the old physical parameter-range will soon come to be accommodated, and their refutatory prospects exhausted, so that one must press on into heretofore inaccessible regions of power or complexity. For at each stage of scientific inquiry we face the need to reduce live hypotheses to manageable numbers—a need that grows more elaborate with the exponential proliferation of possibilities that lies down the road of sequential conjecture, with iffy hypothesis piled upon iffy hypothesis.

Scientific progress thus depends crucially and unavoidably on our technical capability to push outwards in ever widening circles into the increasingly distant—and increasingly difficult—reaches of the power/complexity spectrum of physical parameters to explore and explain the ever more remote phenomena to be encountered there. It is of the very essence of the enterprise that natural science is forced ever further into the extremes of nature.

The assumptions that underlie the detailed functioning of such a prospecting·model of inquiry in natural science are thus as follows:

(1) The processes of nature hinge on the interconnected operation of certain parameters, each such parameter varying over a range which defines one particular physical dimension of the "phase space" envisaged by natural science. (These parametric ranges are such that in the case of an inherently limited range—e.g., speeds to the velocity of light, temperatures to absolute zero—an "order of magnitude" step along the range carries us yet another 1/10th of the way to the limit, as per the sequence: to within 10% of the limit from "where we started from," to within 1% of it, to within ·1% of it, etc.)

(2) We humans ourselves occupy a certain (for us) natural position within this parametric space—a location within it that is the (for us) natural starting point for its exploration. (For example, our sensory organs respond to radiation in the visible part of the electromagnetic spectrum or in the audible range of vibration frequencies.) In our own environing "parametric neighborhood" we can—thanks to the equipment of our evolutionary heritage of perception—generally make explorations relatively simply—and cheaply.

(3) Moreover, by suitable technical means we can explore regions of

this phase space at locations increasingly remote from the "home base" of our natural starting point. This is an ongoing process, and one which is altogether crucial to scientific progress because the cognitive potential of fixed-distance explorations is soon exhausted. We are forced to move ever further outwards in parametric remoteness or complexity of detail. This requires a rapidly increasing commitment of effort and resources. It is as though we needed to overcome the impedance of a restraining force which pulls us towards home base and—unlike gravitation—makes it increasingly difficult for us to move further away from it. To pursue the metaphor of a voyage of exploration, the further the journey from home base, the larger the vessel we need and the more difficult and complicated is its outfitting.

(4) The phenomena which ground important findings are encountered in sporadic clusters throughout this parametric phase space in such a way that the logarithm of the parametric *distance* covered in the course of exploratory "prospecting" keeps more or less in proportion with the number of phenomena that yield the empirical basis for highly significant findings. A "law of log-uniform distribution significant phenomena" is operative, and functions in such a way that $F(E)$—the number of first-rate findings realized after moving a distance E along a given dimension of parametric space—increases log-uniformly: $F(E) \infty \log E$. The structure of our exploration model accordingly places the Findings-Distribution Assumption in the framework of a rationalizing model of epistemologico/metaphysical orientation.

6. GORE'S LAW AND THE POWER/FINDINGS RELATION

George Gore wrote in 1878:

> By means of great improvements in the power of magneto-electric machines investigators have been enabled to more completely examine and discover new truths respecting the electric light, the electric fusion of metals, etc. In microscopy, spectrum analysis, and other subjects, a whole multitude of discoveries have been made by means of powerful apparatus which could not have been effected without such assistance; and *in every department of science, every increase in power of the apparatus has been quickly followed by new discoveries and an increase of knowledge*, and the

foregoing are only a few instances selected out of the great multitude of new truths which have been discovered by the aid of this method.[15]

We shall characterize the italicized thesis of a generic correlation between increases in the effectiveness of scientific apparatus and the accession of knowledge-augmenting discoveries as *Gore's Law*. To be sure, this principle establishes a connection of a merely qualitative or descriptive sort. We are at present in fact in a position to endow this relationship with a more exact, indeed quantitative, structure.

When one puts together the Power/Range Relation (log $E \propto \log P$) and the Findings-Distribution Assumption ($F \propto \log E$) one immediately arrives at the relationship $F \propto \log P$—the Power/Findings Relation, as we shall call it—which asserts that the number of accessible first-rate findings is q-proportional to the logarithm of the power available for the "exploration" of parametric space.[16] Every order-of-magnitude increase in the available power P is correlated with a constant-unit increase in the volume of findings F. This circumstance clearly provides an explanatory rationale for Gore's Law.

To be sure, the provision of a concrete illustration of the workings of the Power/Findings Relation is not all that straightforward, because "power"—as the idea is used here—is a technical, artificial construct which can be related to more straightforward physical parameters only by introducing special assumptions. But it is certainly safe to suppose that the use of "power"—like all the several resources of scientific work—has been growing exponentially in recent times in such a way as to establish a secular trend that makes for an exponential increase in the power of equipment-families. (We have already seen this in the case of particle accelerators and chronometric instruments.) Given the

---

[15] George Gore, *The Art of Scientific Discovery* (London, 1878), p. 562. (Italics supplied.) Compare the following discussion of a subsequent generation:

Now why should we wish to make measurements with an ever-increasing precision? Having measured the velocity of light to four significant figures, why should one wish to know what the next 'decimal place' is? . . . To these two [familiar] answers I wish to add a third: 'Because the whole history of physics proves that a new discovery is quite likely to be found lurking in the next decimal place'. (F. K. Richtmyer, "The Romance of the Next Decimal Place," *Science*, vol. 75 [1931], pp. 1–5 [see p. 3].)

[16] It might be useful to introduce the idea of *effective power* (π) in such a way that $\pi = \log P$, envisaging a physical analogue of the Fechner/Weber Law in psychology. (The Richter scale for measuring the intensity of earthquakes already embodies this idea.) Since $\pi \propto \log E$ (by the Power/Range Relationship), the "effectiveness" at issue is that of exploring E-space.

Power/Findings Relation, this circumstance yields the upshot that progress in most problem areas of natural science can be gauged as the uniform development of *F* in a manner that is roughly linear over time: $F \propto t$. Figure 2 provides an interesting illustration of this phenomenon.

Figure 2

THE NUMBER OF KNOWN CHEMICAL ELEMENTS
AS A FUNCTION OF DATE

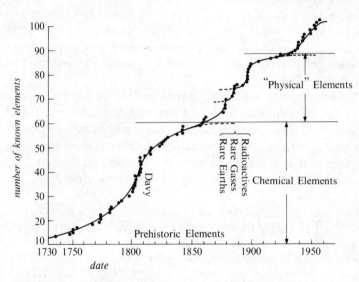

Note After the work of Davy there is a logistic decline followed by a set of escalations corresponding to the discovery of elements by techniques that are predominantly physical. Around 1950 is the latest escalation produced by the manufacture of trans-uranic elements.

From Derek J. Price, *Little Science, Big Science* (New York, 1963), p. 29.

Again it is, on this perspective, a natural aspect of the smooth progress of astronomy throughout the modern period that the accuracies of measuring time and astronomical angular distance have each increased fairly constantly since ca. 1600 at an exponential pace with doubling times of ca. 20 years.[17]

[17] For the data see H. T. Pledge, *Science Since 1500* (New York, 1949), pp. 70, 291.

7. THE CASE OF ANALYTIC (COMPLEXITY-INTENSIVE) PROBLEMS

The discussion has thus far stressed the case of *synthetic* problems whose solution hinges on increases in the availability of "power," problems of the sort typified by the issues of fundamental-particle theory and astrophysical cosmology. The *analytic* sector of complexity-intensive problems—where sheer complexity is determinative—needs closer examination. (For this important distinction between synthetic or power-intensive and analytic or complexity-intensive problems see Sect. 5 of Chapter IV above.) It is necessary to deal also with the case of these *analytic* problems whose solution hinges primarily on augmenting our capacity to deal with "complexity" (problem-areas typified by microbiology, organic chemistry, and meteorology).

Just as with power-intensive problems the "old" physical machinery of earlier technological stages does not help one in the solution of present-day frontier problems, so in the complexity-intensive problems the "old" conceptual and methodological devices will prove unavailing and new analytical expedients are called for. Richard Feynman has succinctly formulated the underlying escalation-principle at issue:

> I am sure that history does not repeat itself in physics, as you can tell from looking at the examples I have given. The reason is this. Any schemes—such as "think of symmetry laws," or "put the information in mathematical form," or "guess equations"—are known to everybody now, and they are all tried all the time. When you are stuck, the answer cannot be one of these, because you will have tried these right away.[18]

In complexity-intensive cases one is thus also caught up in an escalation of levels of difficulty, and increasingly sophisticated conceptual "mechanisms" are needed for the manipulation of the data to extract profitable results.[19]

---

[18] *The Character of Physical Law* (Cambridge, Mass., 1965), p. 167.

[19] For a rough but suggestive picture of the historical situation with respect to complexity-escalation in science and technology, see G. M. Dobrov, *Wissenschaft: ihre Analyse und Prognose* (Stuttgart, 1974), pp. 52–53. The discussion there suggests that the manipulative and cognitive technology of today is able to accommodate systems whose complexity-level is such as to encompass perhaps 10^5 elements, where the

But the situation as regards technological escalation in the complexity-intensive sphere is in fact parallel with that in the case of power-intensive problems. A relationship analogous to $F \infty \log P$ can also be argued with respect to complexity-intensive problem-areas. Our reasoning here will rest on the plausible assumption that the complexity (C) at issue with a body of data suitably relevant to a given scientific issue and the sheer volume of the relevant findings of *routine* importance (Q) that can be attained with regard to it are so related that the logarithms of these quantities are q-proportional:

$\log C \infty \log Q$ or equivalently $C \propto Q^{\beta}$ (with $0 < \beta < 1$).

The relationship has it that the complexity C of a problem area increases as some specifiable root of the overall volume Q of its routine-level findings, so that the more data we need to "get a handle" on the issue, the greater its complexity. One may suppose that this *Complexity-Determination Rule* obtains on virtually definitional grounds in view of the construction of the "complexity" at issue.

At this juncture we may return to the discussion of Chapter VI of the interrelationships of the quantity and quality of findings. Specifically let us apply (now, however, at the problem-area level!) its thesis of the Findings-Quality Coordination Principle which stipulates the coordination relationship $F \propto \log Q$ to obtain between the volume of basic or routine findings, Q, and that of first-rate ones, F. (That is, an order-of-magnitude increase in Q is correlated with a mere constant-unit sized increase in F.) In the presence of the Complexity-Determination Rule $\log Q \infty \log C$, this leads at once to: $F \infty \log C$. One thus arrives—with respect to complexity-intensive issues—at this specified Complexity/Findings Relation (as we shall call it). As one solves the easier problems in the complexity-intensive (analytic) domain, the newly arising problems become increasingly more difficult to resolve. Ongoing progress demands that we must move ever further outwards along the dimension of the complexity parameter.

Accordingly, a situation obtains in the case of "complexity"-intensive findings that is strictly parallel to that for "power"-intensive findings as maintained above. A structurally identical relationship holds

---

exponent has increased at a rate of roughly a unit per century since the rise of modern science in the mid-seventeenth century.

in both cases. Progress hinges upon our ability to push outwards in the power/complexity "phase-space" so as to encounter the new phenomena at issue in new *phenomena* or new *relationships*. A Capacity/Range Relation of the same fundamental form, $\log E \varpropto \log X$, operates in both cases to govern alike the power-oriented and the complexity-oriented dimensions of our parametric space.

8. THE CAPACITY/FINDINGS RELATIONSHIP

The preceding considerations indicate that the two cases of power and complexity are isomorphic. The number F of accessible first-rate findings stands in the following relationships: (i) with power-intensive problems we have $F_p \varpropto \log P$, and (ii) with complexity-intensive problems we have $F_c \varpropto \log C$. These two relationships combine to yield $F \varpropto \log X$, where X represents the "capacity" to dispose of power (P) and/or complexity (C). Both cases have the same fundamental structure, namely that F stands in a q-proportional correlation with $\log X$. On either side—power or complexity—we find isomorphic relationships which can be synthesized in a single pattern: $F \varpropto \log X$. We arrive at a Capacity/Findings Relation according to which an order-of-magnitude increase in "capacity" is required to generate a merely fixed-size unit increase in F-level findings within particular problem-areas.[20]

The sum-total F of the accessible first-rate findings—at any stage of the availability of the "capacity" needed to accommodate the requisite power and/or complexity—is accordingly governed by the correlation relationship of Figure 3, which takes the stance that the problem-resolving effectiveness of improvements in the capacity of the data-technology of natural science is proportional not to the *magnitude* of this improvement in capacity, but merely to its *logarithm*. This principle implements the notion—implicit in our basic model of the exploration of "parameter space"—that it requires an ever more massively potent searchlight for science to penetrate further into the surrounding darkness, to put it somewhat figuratively.

Our theory thus has it that, as science progresses, the realization of

---

[20] A graphic summary of the (somewhat convoluted) course of formal argumentation that has led to this upshot is given in Figure 2 of the Appendix (on p. 268).

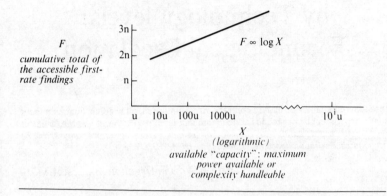

Figure 3

THE CAPACITY/FINDINGS RELATIONSHIP
(FOR FIRST-RATE FINDINGS)

new substantial findings requires that the available data-productive capacity must be increased massively. In particular, to increase F by one single unit, we must increase the capacity X of our data-technology by an entire order of magnitude. This circumstance motivates the idea of a data-technology level correlative with the successive order-of-magnitude stages of effective "capacity," an idea whose ramifications need to be examined more closely.

X

The Stratification of Discoveries by Technology-levels: Technological Escalation

Insanum quiddam esset, et in se contrarium, existimare ea, quae adhuc nunquam facta sunt, fieri posse, nisi per modos adhuc nunquam tentatos. ("It would be the height of folly—and self-defeating—to think that things never heretofore done can be accomplished without means never heretofore tried.")

BACON, *Novum Organon*, Bk. I, sect. vi.

1. T-LEVEL SEQUENCING

The picture of scientific progress as the correlate of a movement through sequential stages of sophistication in data-technology was already clearly discerned by the astute Charles Sanders Peirce around the turn of the century:

> Lamarckian evolution might, for example, take the form of perpetually modifying our opinion in the effort gradually to make that opinion represent the known facts as more and more observations came to be collected. . . . But this is not the way in which science mainly progresses. It advances by leaps; and the impulse for each leap is either some new observational resource, or some novel way of reasoning about the observations. Such novel way of reasoning might, perhaps, be considered as a new observational means, since it draws attention to relations between facts which would previously have been passed by unperceived.[1]

Physicists often remark that the development of our understanding of nature moves through successive layers of *theoretical* sophistication.[2]

---

[1] *Collected Papers*, ed. C. Hartshorne *et al.*, vol. I (Cambridge, Mass., 1931), pp. 44–45 (sects. 108–109), c. 1896.

[2] "Looking back, one has the impression that the historical development of the

But scientific progress is clearly no less dependent on continual improvements in strictly *technical* sophistication:

> Some of the most startling technological advances in our time are closely associated with basic research. As compared with 25 years ago, the highest vacuum readily achievable has improved more than a thousand-fold; materials can be manufactured that are 100 times purer; the submicroscopic world can be seen at 10 times higher magnification; the detection of trace impurities is hundreds of times more sensitive; the identification of molecular species (as in various forms of chromatography) is immeasurably advanced. These examples are only a small sample. . . . [F]undamental research in physics is crucially dependent on advanced technology, and is becoming more so.[3]

Research in natural science nowadays makes great demands on technology and the magnitude of these demands is steadily increasing. This phenomenon, which may be characterized as *technological escalation*, provides the theme of the present chapter.

Let us explore the idea of a "technological level," corresponding—in our context—to a certain *state of the art* in the technology of inquiry (data-generation and processing). These levels reflect the capacity of a technology to set up experiments (to create specified temperatures, pressures, voltages, etc.), to determine the quantities in such situations (to yield exact measurement, sensitive detection, etc.), or to process the data (to deploy mathematical technique, computers, etc.). This technology of inquiry falls into relatively distinct levels or stages in sophistication—correlatively with successively "later generations" of instrumentative and manipulative machinery. Such levels are generally

---

physical description of the world consists of a succession of layers of knowledge of increasing generality and greater depth. Each layer has a well defined field of validity; one has to pass beyond the limits of each to get to the next one, which will be characterized by more general and more encompassing laws and by discoveries constituting a deeper penetration into the structure of the Universe than the layers recognized before." Edoardo Amaldi, "The Unity of Physics," *Physics Today*, vol. 261 (1973), No. 9 (September), pp. 23–29 (see p. 24). See also E. P. Wigner, "The Unreasonable Effectiveness of Mathematics in the Natural Sciences," *Communications on Pure and Applied Mathematics*, vol. 13 (1960), pp. 1–14; "The Limits of Science," *Proceedings of the American Philosophical Society*, vol. 93 (1949), pp. 521–526; and chapter VIII of Henry Margenau, *The Nature of Physical Reality* (New York, 1950).

[3] D. A. Bromley *et al.*, *Physics in Perspective, Student Edition* (Washington, D.C., 1973; National Research Council/National Academy of Science Publication), p. 23.

separated from one another by (roughly) order-of-magnitude improvements in performance in realizing the relevant information-providing parameters (exactness of measurement, detection-sensitivity, high voltages, high or low temperatures, etc.).

We shall thus adopt the idea of *technological levels* (T-levels, for short) in relation to the successive stages in the technological "state of the art" as characterized by the enhanced "capacity" (in point of power or complexity-handling) attained by the data-relevant technology of natural science, subject to the specification that *successive T-levels represent order-of-magnitude improvements in performance as regard "power" or "complexity."*[4]

The sequencing of successive T-levels is neatly illustrated in the development of the technology of particle-accelerators as pictured in Figure 1, where the relevant variable is the (unlimited) parameter of *energy*. This figure indicates a steady evolution of technical developments in this area of energies of acceleration. The linear envelope of the individual curves of accelerator performance at different state-of-the-art stages shows an increase in energy by roughly one order-of-magnitude step every seven years, indicating a steady climb at this rate from one T-level to the next. This sector of experimental physics is a splendid instance of technology triumphant:

A most spectacular example is the steady increase in energy of accelerated particles from the 200-KeV protons, with which Cockcroft and Walton produced the first artificial nuclear disintegrations in 1930, to the 200-GeV protons of the National Accelerator Laboratory—in 40 years a factor of a million! This stupendous advance was achieved not in many small steps but in many large steps, each made possible by remarkable inventions and bold engineering innovations produced by physicists. Although numerical factors of increase do not have the same implications in different technologies, few branches of engineering

---

[4] One must not interpret "order of magnitude" improvements naively in this present context. When increases in limited parameters like particle velocity or temperature are at issue, the limits of the speed of light and of absolute zero temperature must be recognized. Here an order-of-magnitude improvement must (as we saw in the last chapter) be construed in terms of the percentage of *the distance yet remaining to reach the limit*. (Thus in the case of cooling, the first order-of-magnitude step takes us from, say, 300°K to 30°K—i.e., 90% of the way from "where we are" in the absolute zero—the next order-of-magnitude step would carry us down to 3°K or to within 1% of absolute zero, and the next to within ·1% of absolute zero or ·3°K, etc.)

have come close to that record. . . . The acclerator physicists have a remarkable record of practical success as engineers. From the time of the early cyclotrons to the present, no major accelerator in

---

Figure 1

ENERGIES ACHIEVED BY PARTICLE ACCELERATORS
FROM 1932 TO 1968

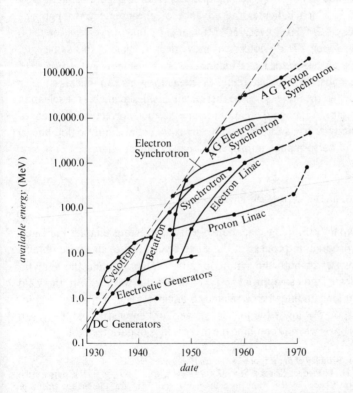

Note The exponential growth of accelerators was first noted by John P. Blewett in an Internal Report of the Cosmotron Department of Brookhaven National Laboratory, dated June 9, 1950. The first public presentation of this material was made by Fermi in his address as retiring President, at the American Physical Society meeting in January, 1954. The Figure is from M. S. Livingston and J. P. Blewett, *Particle Accelerators* (New York, 1962), p. 6.

From M. Stanley Livingston, *Particle Accelerators: A Brief History* (Cambridge, Mass., 1969), p. 111.

this country, however novel, has failed to work; most of them exceeded their promised performance.[5]

The historical tendency in the development of science-relevant technology has in general been to make the transition through successive order-of-magnitude improvements at a *linear* rate over time—i.e., to develop exponentially in performance. This phenomenon is illustrated not only by the example just given in Figure 1, but also by Figure 2, which indicates the advance of chronometry through one technological T-level every 50–60 years. Again, the years after 1600 have also seen a fairly consistent movement at roughly this same rate, through successive order-of-magnitude improvements in the power of microscopes, in the accuracy of measuring astronomical angular distance,[6] in the increase of the thermal intensities available for scientific work,[7] etc. Again and again—in one science-correlative branch of technology after another—such an exponential (and so log-linear) course of performance-improvement can be substantiated.[8]

2. THE STRATIFICATION OF FINDINGS

The Capacity/Findings Relationship of the previous chapter indicated that a production process of the same basic general structure obtains with respect to both the synthetic (power-intensive) and the analytic (complexity-intensive) problem-types in natural science, with the yield (F) of major findings being related to technological "capacity" (X) by the relation $F \infty \log X$ (with X as "power" or "capacity," indifferently). On this basis we may combine the present idea of data-technology levels

[5] D. A. Bromley *et al.*, *Physics in Perspective, op. cit.*, p. 24.

[6] See H. T. Pledge, *Science Since 1500* (New York, 1949), p. 291. Compare the graphs on pages 70 (for time measurement) and 126 (for the measurement of mass—with an OM accuracy-increase period of ca. 120 years). Similar graphs could be prepared in many other cases (e.g., astronomic/optical magnification).

[7] The general phenomenon at issue here was clearly discerned by Henry Adams, who adduced the just-indicated example as an illustration of it. (See Ernest Samuels, *Henry Adams: The Major Phase* [Cambridge, Mass., 1964], p. 393.)

[8] It is interesting in this connection to contemplate Lewis Mumford's warning of a developing crisis because man's technological skills have "multiplied at a geometrical ratio" whereas "social skills and moral controls have increased at an arithmetical ratio." (See Mumford's *Values For Survival* [New York, 1946], p. 203.) The first of these contentions—at any rate—seems well attested. See, for example, the diversified data compiled in *World Facts and Trends*, ed. by J. McHale (London, 1972).

Figure 2

THE RISE IN ACCURACY OF THE MECHANICAL
CLOCK THROUGH THE CENTURIES

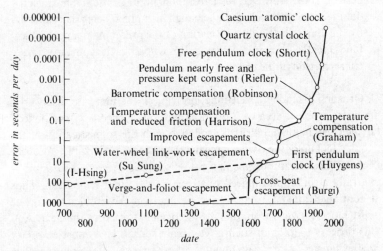

Amplified by J. Needham from the original graph of F. A. B. Ward, with his approval
(after consultation with J. H. Gombridge and H. von Bertele). From Joseph Needham,
The Grand Titration (Toronto, 1969), p. 278.

(T-levels) correlative with fixed-size increases in log X to obtain the
following:

Findings Stratification Principle

In the problem-areas of a developed sector of natural science,
theory is so dependent on data that new findings that make a
substantial contribution at the level of theoretical understanding
cannot be realized without major innovations—somewhere along
the line—in the technological means of obtaining information.
Such massive innovations are correlated with levels of
sophistication in data-technology. They call for advancing to a
higher plateau in the "state of the art," making it possible to
operate at a substantially higher level of data-relevant "capacity"
(X)—each data-level being superior to its predecessor in some
parametric respect by at least an order of magnitude. First-rate
discoveries in the problem-areas of a matured branch of natural

science thus *come in (very roughly uniform-sized) clusters correlated with major and massive improvements in data-technology,* improvements of at least an order-of-magnitude in performance. However, the substantial findings attainable at each data-technology level are rather small in number, being determined by the Capacity/Findings Relation of the preceding chapter—the fundamental principle, $F \propto \log X$, whose tacit constants are characteristic of the problem-area at issue.

On such a model of scientific innovation, the first-rate discoveries in every problem-area of a matured natural science are "positioned" in such technological strata correlative with the sophistication of the inquiry technology by whose means they become realizable. At every technological stratum *some* first-rate discoveries become accessible— but only a *finite* (and indeed relatively small) number of them. Thus if continued major progress is to be made in the problem-area, one must move forward from one technological stratum to the next. And this process unfolds in such a way that the n-th level must be pretty well exhausted in first-rate findings before one can move on to realize those of the $(n + 1)$st. There is a *technological sequencing* of first-rate findings. They are positioned in a sequential order not just by the passage of time itself, but by the successive development of a technological state of the art that enables each sort of result to be achieved in its due turn, as the requisite "capacity" becomes available.[9]

Consider an analogy. The production of metals hinges crucially on the capacity of furnaces. With a furnace-technology in the 800–1,000°C range one can extract copper and smelt bronze, but to make iron one must be able to operate at over 1,500°C. One must thus pass through the less demanding technology enroute to the more demanding one. And so it is only natural that a Bronze Age should have preceded an Iron Age. Even so, the generation of those phenomena on whose availability scientific progress hinges is crucially dependent on

---

[9] Perhaps just one illustration of this process through which scientific advance waits on progress in the correlative technology of inquiry may be in order:

There are, however, many problems in basic acoustics still to be solved. Among these problems are those that involve the interactions of high-frequency sound radiation with matter in its various phases; but the more purely technological problem of the extension of the practical-frequency limit of ultrasonic radiation must be solved first. The limit in 1967 was about 10^{10} cycles per second. If frequencies of the order of 10^{11} to 10^{14} cycles per second could be realized, our understanding of the nature of the solid, liquid, and gaseous states would be much enhanced. (R. B. Lindsay, *The Nature of Physics* [Providence, 1968], p. 187.)

the capacity of the relevant machinery—of what we have characterized as data-technology.[10]

3. DISCOVERY SEQUENCING AND TECHNOLOGICAL ESCALATION

The fundamental idea on which the Stratification Principle rests is that, while findings-productive improvements in data-technology are possible *within* a technological stratum (correlative to a particular "generation" of data-technology), yet further *these* intra-stratum improvements will eventually (and generally rather sooner than later) come to be relatively minor and of limited significance.

The key feature of this principle is that once the major findings accessible at a given data-technology level have been attained, the attainment of further major progress in the problem-area requires ascent to a higher level on the technological scale. We thus espouse the view (or hypothesis) that each individual data/technology level is subject to *discovery-saturation*. The body of highly innovative scientific findings realizable at any such level in a given problem-area of science *is finite* (and indeed not just finite but relatively small). *Within* a given problem area and *relative to a fixed level of data-technology* one thus obtains a localized version of the geographic-exploration theory of progress envisaged by the apple-picking model of discovery, and so one here encounters the situation of discovery-saturation. In consequence, an ascent in the scale of technology levels is periodically required for really substantial progress.

The exhaustion of the first-rate findings of a problem-area accessible at a given level of data-technology does not, of course, mean that progress at this level has been brought to a dead stop here. (Further findings of the lesser magnitudes may yet be available—at least up to a point.) But the crucial fact remains that after the first-rate findings accessible at a given data-technology level have been realized, the

---

[10] This principle of an inherent natural sequencing in scientific development may be credited to Bernard de Fontenelle (1657–1757, long-term Perpetual Secretary to the French Academy and author of innumerable *éloges* of its eminent deceased members). He wrote that "there is an order which regulates our progress. Every science develops after a certain number of preceding sciences have developed, and only then; it has to await its turn to burst its shell." *Préface des élémens de la géometrie de l'infini; Oeuvres*, vol. X (Paris, 1790), p. 40. Quoted in J. B. Bury, *The Idea of Progress* (New York, 1932), p. 110.

realization of further major findings will call for an ascent to the next level of sophistication in data-relevant technology. We shall characterize the phenomenon—inherent in the stratification principle —as the imperative of *technological escalation.*

Once the potential of a given data technology level has been exploited, not all our piety or wit can lure the ongoing frontier back to yield further first-rate returns at this stage. The need for new data becomes one for new *sorts or constellations* of data, and this forces one to look at the situation of more and more remote from man's familiar "home base" in the parametric space of nature. Thus, while we continue to espouse the general thesis (argued in Chapter III) that further scientific progress is in principle always possible—that there are no absolute or intrinsic limits to significant scientific progress—we nevertheless insist that the *realization* of this ongoing prospect demands a continual enhancement in the "state of the art" in data-technology.[11] This is the basis for the phenomenon of technological escalation.

Nature inexorably exacts an *exponentially increasing effort* in enhanced sophistication in data-deployment for revealing her "secrets" and accordingly becomes less and less yielding to the efforts of our inquiry at given fixed levels of information-gathering technique.[12] This accounts for the continual introduction of more and more sophisticated technology into inquiry in natural science and the subsequent

---

[11] It is useful to contrast the present conception of stratification with the idea (mooted in section 1 of Chapter II in connection with the passage from Jean-Paul Vigier) that nature has infinitely many levels of "depth" in point of the complexity of its workings. The two conceptions are quite different. At present we are concerned with the layers of technological effectiveness to be used in the investigative probing of nature, so that the levels at issue lie on the side of the tools available to the investigator. This is perfectly compatible with the idea that nature itself is homogeneous and without "levels" in its own *modus operandi.*

[12] The following passage offers a clear illustration of this phenomenon in chemistry:

A survey of several thousand articles in representative U.S. and foreign journals shows that the use of such instruments for chemistry has increased by more than sixfold in the United States during the past twelve years, and has drastically changed the character of chemical research. Modern instrumentation has made it possible to attack and solve important problems that could not previously have been solved, and some perhaps that could not even have been considered. For example, modern X-ray crystallography made it possible to elucidate the unusual structure of penicillin; special electronic instrumentation permits measurement of the rates of reactions at high temperatures (over 1,000°) and of reaction rates of enzymes with their substrates (reactions that may proceed with the speed of diffusion); vapor-phase chromatography plus mass spectrometry detects harmful contaminants in the atmospheres of submarines and spacecraft, and measures trace residues of pesticides on crops. Electronic digital computers are especially vital to modern research in chemistry. Although their use is just beginning, they are already widely needed for theoretical

increasingly extensive reliance upon it in the conduct of research in natural science, a phenomenon clearly illustrated in Figure 3. This ongoing need for the constant enhancement of data-technology lies at the basis of the enormous cost of modern experimental science.[13]

The sequencing of the accessible findings-clusters across successively more demanding technological strata commits progress in modern natural science to its onerous task of climbing ever upwards from one level of technological sophistication to the next.[14] It is not merely frustrating, but virtually mad to seek to "buck the system" here (as per our motto from Bacon). Purely intellectual processes can sometimes *divine* but never *establish* the ways of nature in heretofore unexplored parametric regions. Creative genius alone cannot outrun the processes of technological evolution. It would be altogether futile to tackle a problem that lies beyond one's technological means (not means-in-hand, for one can, to be sure, improve on these, but *means-that-can-be-got-into-hand*).[15] (In this regard there is merit in Hegel's idea that the really able man is he who is in step with history and makes the most of the opportunities in the situation actually at hand.) The very

---

calculations, for processing the results of X-ray crystallography, and for the solution of many complex problems. (F. H. Wertheimer *et al.*, *Chemistry: Opportunities and Needs* [Washington, D.C., 1965; National Academy of Sciences/National Research Council], p. 9.)

The current proliferation of the use of multi-million volt electron microscopes for research in biology and the materials sciences is another case in point.

[13] It is typified by the following example:

A permanent addition to physicists' knowledge of nature was the recognition, several years ago, that there are two kinds of neutrino. This fact, although compatible with then existing theory, was not predictable *a priori*, nor is the reason understood. The question was put to nature in a fairly elaborate high-energy experiment, at a total monetary cost that reasonable accounting might put at $400,000 (not including beam time on the Alternating Gradient Synchrotron Accelerator). The answer was unequivocal: The electron neutrino and the muon neutrino are not identical particles. (D. A. Bromley *et al.*, *Physics in Perspective, op. cit.*, p. 9.)

[14] The institutional implications of this technological escalation are interestingly discussed in David Z. Robins in "Will the University Decline as a Center for Scientific Research," *Daedalus*, vol. 102 (1973), pp. 101–110. George Gore saw the issues clear-headedly a century ago:

To some of these questions it is possible to obtain answers at the present time, others can only be decided when other parts of science are more developed. All the different branches of knowledge must advance together. A geometric and mechanical basis of physical science cannot be constructed until we know the forms, sizes, and positions of the molecules of substances. (*The Art of Scientific Discovery* [London, 1878], pp. 26–29.)

[15] The synthesis of diamond, for example, can be obtained at enormous static pressures at high temperatures (ca. 1,500°C at pressure of between 80,000 and 120,000 atmospheres). Napoleon for all his power could not have had diamonds made artificially. To gain admission into the phenomenal range, one must pay the entrance fee, which was beyond his technical means.

Figure 3

THE USE-RATE[*] IN CHEMICAL RESEARCH IN
THE UNITED STATES FOR SEVEN OF THE MOST
COMMONLY USED TYPES OF INSTRUMENTS

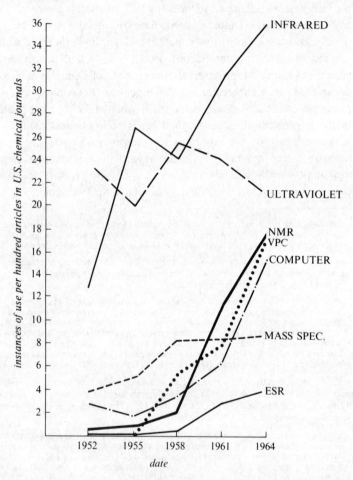

From F. H. Wertheimer *et al.*, *Chemistry: Opportunities and Needs* (Washington, D.C.,
1965; National Academy of Sciences, National Research Council), p. 88.

* The "use rate" is defined as the number of instances of use cited per 100 papers in
selected representative U.S. journals.

structure of scientific inquiry forces us into the situation of an arms-race-reminiscent technological escalation where the frontier-equipment of today's research becomes the museum-piece of tomorrow under the relentless pace of technical obsolescence. One acute observer has rightly remarked: "Most critical experiments [in physics] planned today, if they had to be constrained within the technology of even ten years ago, would be seriously compromised."[16]

At a certain stage we must—if scientific inquiry is to be really productive—"play a whole new ballgame" in technical sophistication.[17] It is this imperative of technological escalation that rushes us, willing-or-not, into the domain of "big science."

Alvin M. Weinberg, formerly Director of the Oak Ridge National Laboratory (and currently Director of the Office of Energy, Research and Development in the Federal Energy Office) is incontestably the prime prophet of this tendency to technological escalation in science. In support of this thesis Weinberg adduces the following example:

Genetics was done with fruit flies, with their large chromosomes, because fruit flies are inexpensive, not because fruit flies are as much like man as are mammals. Those questions that required large protocols of expensive animals were answered poorly or not at all, not because the questions were unimportant, but because to answer them was expensive and required the style of Big Science, which was so foreign to the biologists' tradition. But this is changing, in part at least, because the Big Scientists from neighboring fields have taught the habit of Big Science to the biologists. Perhaps the best-known example of the drastically changed style of some biological research is the large-scale mouse genetics experiment of W. L. Russell at Oak Ridge. For the past sixteen years Russell has been studying the genetic effects of ionizing radiation in a mammal, the mouse. Since mutations even at high dose rates are so rare, Russell uses colonies containing

---

[16] D. A. Bromley et al., *Physics in Perspective: Student Edition* (Washington, D.C., 1973; NRC/NAS Publication), p. 23.

[17] Consider the following example:

Fifteen years ago, it would have been virtually impossible to isolate and identify minute amounts of sex attractants. That it is now possible is owing to the evolution of electronic instruments, and their application in chemical technology. The new tools (such as infrared and ultraviolet spectrometry, mass spectrometry, gas chromatography and nuclear magnetic resonance) enable chemists to work with substances available in milligram or even microgram amounts. (Martin Jacobson and Morton Beroza, "Insect Attractance: With Biographical Sketches," *Scientific American*, vol. 211 (1964), pp. 20–27.

100,000 mice. To perform such experiments takes much money
and many people, and yet it seems impossible to visualize any
other way of obtaining the data. The problem of large protocols
that Russell faced, and the AEC solved (at a cost of a million
dollars per year for this single experiment), is one which arises in
many other situations.[18]

No doubt the very idea of a single biological experiment of such
complexity whose costs run on the order of 10^6 per annum would have
boggled the imagination of biologists a generation ago, when most
elaborate experiments were orders of magnitude less expensive. Such
nevertheless are the technical imperatives of any complexity-intensive
problem-area which—like human genetics—involve statistics on a
grand scale.

One hears on many sides laments about the negative aspects of "big
science" as stressing the public relations aspects of funding needs, and
producing inefficiencies of scale,[19] administrationitis, a dampening of
initiative, etc. For example, a disillusioned young physicist has argued
as follows:

The massive funding for physics in general and high energy
physics in particular has resulted in the construction of
experimental facilities of unprecedented size and cost, together
with an exponential growth in both manpower and publications.
But the amount of real progress we have achieved in the past 30
years in understanding nature seems much less than was achieved
in the first three decades of this century when both quantum
mechanics and relativity theory were developed. . . . Apparatus
used to be whatever you could put together with string and sealing
wax; today a single piece of apparatus, the National Accelerator
Laboratory (NAL), cost $250 million to build and $60 million a
year to run. The Physical Review is now divided into six parts,
each of which is longer than the whole journal was 10 or 15 years
ago. Many people have stopped subscribing simply for lack of shelf
space. Has the stagnation taken place because of, rather than in

[18] Alvin M. Weinberg, *Reflections on Big Science* (Cambridge, Mass. and London,
1967), p. 107.
[19] "There is much to be said for the small group. It can work quite efficiently.
Efficiency does not increase proportionally with numbers. A large group creates
complicated administrative problems, and much effort is spent in organization." (Laura
Fermi, *Atoms in the Family: My Life with Enrico Fermi* [Chicago, 1954], p. 185.)

spite of, these developments? The consequences of "big science" —elitism, competitiveness, "grantsmanship", bureaucratisation, business management mentality, and concentration of economic and decision-making power—have entered the field along with the government money. They have stifled spontaneity, independence, originality, creativity, and even objectivity. The commitment of the majority of available research funds to a few large experimental facilities like the NAL has destroyed the flexibility necessary to deal with unexpected discoveries. . . .[20]

Whatever validity such plaints may have, the *inevitability* of this trend is a fundamental aspect of the whole structure of our analysis of the conditions of scientific progress. From the angle of our deliberations, the thesis of the author of this quotation that "high-energy physics is stagnating because of, rather than in spite of, its massive funding" is simply perverse. To be sure, nobody wants to deny that what's being done might be done in ways that here and there improve on current levels of (in)efficiency. But the crucial fact remains that if significant new phenomena are to be extracted from nature in the problem-area spanned by high-energy physics it must be done in the technology-intensive manner quintessential of latter-day big-science.

It would thus be as futile to follow this author into hankering after the days of "string and sealing-wax" apparatus as it would be to join Talleyrand in lamenting the lost *douceur de la vie* of the old régime. There is no point in blaming human foibles or administrative

[20] Robert J. Yaes, "Physics, Fads, and Finances," *New Scientist*, vol. 71 (22 August 1974), p. 462; see also his essay "Physics from Another Perspective: A Cynical Overview," mimeographed publication of the Department of Physics, Memorial University of Newfoundland (1974). Compare also the views of Sir Karl Popper who, in a recent publication, surveys with dismay the economic involvements of modern science, casting them in the role of hindrances to scientific progress and maintaining that "Big Science may destroy great science." (K. R. Popper in R. Harré [ed.], *Problems of Scientific Revolution* [Oxford, 1975], p. 84.) Our general perspective puts into a very questionable light those increasingly popular proposals along the lines of the late Dr. Jacob Bronowski's suggestion that science should become "disestablished"—that it should dissociate itself from public funding in general and from the apparatus of governmental grants and contracts in particular. (*Encounter*, vol. 37 [1971; July issue], pp. 8–16.) A good deal of thinking of this general tendency—including the widely current anti-science to which big science is nowadays giving rise—is documented in Bernard Dixon's interesting book, *What is Science For?* (London, 1973). If technological escalation is a "fact of life" in natural science—as we maintain—this sort of thinking reflects an unrealistic nostalgia for the simpler days of an irrecoverable past. The Biblical dictum (I Corinthians 13:1) holds good here: science too must (no doubt regretfully) put away the things of its childhood.

arrangements for a circumstance that is built into the very structure of investigation in natural science (realizing, to be sure, that the facts that make bigness a necessary condition of significant progress do not establish it as sufficient). The enormous power or sensitivity or complexity deployed in present-day experimental science has not been sought for its own sake, but rather because the research frontier has moved on into an area where this sophistication is the indispensable requisite of ongoing progress.[21] Once a condition of maturity is reached, technological escalation becomes an inescapable fact of life throughout natural science; the choice now lies between big science and no science. No doubt "small is beautiful," but in natural science big becomes necessary: in science as in war one cannot fight the battles of the present with the armaments of a bygone era.

It might seem on first thought that the apparent exemption of the *formal* sciences, preeminently mathematics, from technological escalation could undermine the whole line of reasoning at issue here. For the absence of technological escalation and rising costs at the level of mathematical foundations might so operate as to exempt the whole sphere of complexity-intensive problems from such escalation. If the cost of developing the machinery of analysis does not escalate, then—so one might reason—the cost of research in the sphere of analysis-intensive problems is also nonescalating. But this plausible-sounding reasoning is mistaken. If the history of science from the invention of the calculus to the blossoming of probability and statistics in twentieth-century science teaches any one lesson, it is that the *applicative deployment* of major advances in analytic devices always entails data-providing interventions in nature on a massively enlarged scale. The analytical devices themselves may come to hand in a relatively cheap and non-escalating way, but its *exploitation* in scientific inquiry will always exhibit the characteristic process of technological escalation. The reason is simple. The *applications* of mathematics require information (data-acquisition), and—as we know from cybernetics—the gathering of information is always a matter of interacting with nature. And increasingly sophisticated mathematics

---

[21] It boggles the mind, for example, that a modern photomultiplier—a photoelectric sensor for measuring gas pressures—can gauge such pressures at less than one millionth of a millionth (10^{-12}) atmospheres. Yet once such a hypersensitive capability is available, experiments are at once contrived to exploit it—and indeed these experiments themselves pretty soon run dry, generating a demand for yet greater capabilities.

makes for ever more complex applications which call for a correspondingly more extensive and elaborate interaction with nature.

4. THE "DIRECTIONALITY" OF SCIENTIFIC PROGRESS AND THE PROBLEM OF CONTINUITY

The historians of science and its other theoretical analysts are occasionally heard to complain about the absence of any clear sense of the direction of development in the structure of modern scientific work. In the words of one such writer:

> The blackest defect in the history of science, the cause of dullest despair for the historian, lies in the virtual absence of any general historical sense of the way science has been working for the last hundred years.[22]

But any such lack of direction at once disappears when we turn from the content of scientific discovery to its tools and their mode of employment—in short, when we turn to the *technological* side of the matter. For all of recent science has a clear thrust of development—using ever more potent instruments to press ever further outwards in the exploration of physical parameter-space, forging more and more powerful physical and conceptual instrumentalities for the identification and analysis of new phenomena.

Some recent writers on the philosophy of science, influenced by the doctrines of Thomas Kuhn's influential book on scientific revolutions,[23] tend to stress the ideational discontinuities produced by innovation in the history of science.[24] Scientific change, they rightly maintain, is not just a matter of marginal revisions of opinion within a fixed and stable framework of concepts. The crucial developments involve a change in the conceptual apparatus itself. And when this happens there is a

---

[22] Derek J. Price, *Science Since Babylon* (New Haven, 1961), p. 137.

[23] *The Structure of Scientific Revolutions* (Chicago, 1962; 2nd ed., 1970). See also I. Lakatos and A. Musgrave (eds), *Criticism and the Growth of Knowledge* (Cambridge, 1970).

[24] The prime exponent here is Paul Feyerabend. See his essays "Explanation, Reduction, and Empiricism" in Herbert Feigl and Grover Maxwell (eds.), *Minnesota Studies in the Philosophy of Science*, Vol. III (Minneapolis, 1962), "Problems of Empiricism" in R. G. Colodny (ed.), *Beyond the Edge of Certainty* (Englewood Cliffs, 1965), pp. 145–260 and "On the 'Meaning' of Scientific Terms," *The Journal of Philosophy*, vol. 62 (1965), pp. 266–274.

replacement of the very *content* of discussion, a shift in "what's being talked about" that renders successive positions "incommensurable." The change from the Newtonian to the Einsteinian concept of time, exemplifies a meaning-shift of just this sort. And these discontinuities of meaning make it impossible (so it is said) to say justifiedly that the latter stages represents a somehow "better treatment of the same subject-matter," since the very subject that is at issue at the later stage has become something different.

Such a theory of a radical discontinuity of meaning-shifts seems to throw the very concept of progress in science into question. For if the later stage of discussion is conceptually disjoint from the earlier, how could one consider the later as constituting an improvement upon the earlier? The replacement of one thing by something else of a totally different sort can hardly qualify as meliorative. (One can improve upon one's car by getting a better car, but cannot improve it by getting a computer or a dish-washing machine.)

To draw this sort of implication from the meaning-shift thesis is, however, to take an unduly literary view of science. For at bottom the progress at issue does not proceed along purely theoretical but rather practical lines. Once one sees the legitimation of science to lie ultimately in the sphere of its applications, the progress of science will be taken to rest on its pragmatic aspect—the increasing success of its applications in problem solving and control, in cognitive and physical mastery over nature.

The traditional theories of scientific progress join in stressing the capacity of the "improved" theories to accommodate new facts. Agreeing with this emphasis on "new facts," we must, however, recognize two distinct routes to this destination: the predictive (via *theory*) and the productive (via *technology*). And it would appear proper to allow *both* of these routes, the predictive and the productive, to count. To correct the overly literary bias of the purely *theoretical* stress of traditional philosophy of science requires a more ample recognition of the role of technology-cum-production. To say this is not, of course, to deny for one moment that the two (theory and technology) stand in a symbiotic and mutually supportive relationship in scientific inquiry. But the crucial fact is that the effectiveness of the technological instrumentalities of praxis can clearly be assessed in the absence of any invocation of the cognitive content of the body of theory brought to bear in their devising.

The introduction upon the stage of consideration of the technological sector as supplementary or complementary to the theoretical has far-reaching ramifications. Since Bacon's day, this idea of control over nature has been recognized as the keynote of scientific progress. The question of *technological* superiority (i.e., our ability at a given state-of-the-art level to obtain desired results—never mind for the moment if they are intrinsically desirable or not) is something far less sophisticated, but also far more manageable than issue of *theoretical* superiority. For the factors determinative of *technical* superiority operate at a grosser and more rough-and-ready level than those of theoretical meaning-content. At the level of praxis we can operate to a relatively large degree with the *lingua franca* of everyday affairs and make our comparisons on this basis—we need not worry about the issue of incommeasurability owing to the inaccessibility of a theory-neutral perspective for appraising "incommeasurable" theories. Just as the merest novice can detect a false note in the musical performance of a master player whose activities he could not begin to emulate, so malfunctioning of a missile or computer can be detected by the relative amateur. Dominance in technological power to produce intended results tends to operate across the board. (The superiority of modern over Galenic medicine requires few if any subtle distinctions of respect.)

This technological dimension endows science with the continuity it may well lack at the contextual level of the theoretical machinery of its ideas and concepts—a continuity that finds its expression in the persistence of problem-solving tasks in the sphere of *praxis*. Despite any *semantic* or *ideational incommensurability* between a scientific theory and its latter-day replacements, there yet remains the factor of the *pragmatic commensurability* of a constellation of problem-solving tasks than can (by and large) be formulated in the ordinary everyday language that antedates scientific sophistication alike in the development of the species and that of its individuals.[25] The fundamentally pragmatic aspect of its applications in problem-solving and control at the level of everyday life manifests those continuities of the scientific enterprise with reference to which the idea of progress can be invoked.[26] And in this way, applicative and technological dimension

[25] Practical problems have a tendency to remain structurally invariant. The sending of messages is just that, whether horse-carried letters or laser beams are used in transmitting the information.

[26] On this approach it is easy to account for the contrast between the growth of consensus in science and the cumulative progressivism of the enterprise on the one

of scientific progress can be assessed comparatively—without any explicit reference to the semantical content of scientific theories or the conceptual framework used in their articulation. When the "external" element of *control over nature* is given its due prominence, the substantiation of imputations of scientific *progress* becomes a more manageable project than it could ever possibly be on an "internal," content-oriented basis. The progressiveness of science appears most strikingly and decisively on its technological side, marked by an ever widening ability to operate at further and further removes in parametric remoteness or complexity of detail, and by an ever expanding predictive and physical control over nature.[27] The old Hobbesian conception of *scientia propter potentiam* provides a perfectly workable basis for taking the expanding horizons of technological capacity as an index of scientific progress.[28]

----

hand, and on the other the endless disagreements regarding most questions of philosophy, ethics, or religion. The difference lies precisely in this, that the latter fields are so little subject to the controls of pragmatic efficacy.

[27] This (essentially Baconian) idea that control over nature is the pivotal determinant of progress—in contrast with purely intellectual criteria (such as growing refinement, complication, precision; let alone cumulation or proliferation)—has been mooted by several writers in response to Kuhn. See, for example, Peter M. Quay, "Progress as a Demarcation Criterion for the Sciences," *Philosophy of Science*, vol. 41 (1974), pp. 154–170 (see especially p. 158). The relevant issues are treated in depth in the author's *Methodological Pragmatism* (Oxford, 1976). See also Friedrich Rapp, "Technological and Scientific Knowledge" in *Logic, Methodology, and Philosophy of Science: Proceedings of the Vth International Congress of DLMPS/IUHPS: London (Ontario) 1975* (Toronto, 1976).

[28] For Hobbes' ideas in this region see Hans Fiebig, *Erkenntnis und technische Erzeugung: Hobbes' operationale Philosophie der Wissenschaft* (Meisenheim am Glan, 1973).

XI

The Economics of
Scientific Technology:
an Arms Race Against Nature

*For which of you, intending to build a tower, sitteth not down first, and counteth the
cost....*

LUKE 14:28

1. THE RAMIFICATIONS OF TECHNOLOGICAL ESCALATION: RISING COSTS

The present theory of scientific inquiry views the availability of first-rate
results as *locally finite* within the limits of a fixed technology of
research, but yet as *globally infinite* thanks to the theoretically limitless
prospects of—increasingly expensive—breakthroughs from one level
of investigative technology to the next. In any problem-area of a
matured branch of natural science, continually greater capabilities in
point of "capacity" are required to realize further first-rate results.
Findings are realized through their "purchase" with a certain
investment in scientific resources—equipment, energy, talent. And this
"purchase"-price of significant new findings constantly increases. Once
all the findings accessible at a given state-of-the art level of investigative
technology have been realized, one must continually move on to a more
expensive level. An ongoing enhancement in the quality and quantity of
the requisite data-input becomes requisite—one requires more accurate
measurements, more extreme temperatures, higher voltages, more
intricate combinations, etc. On such a view, the phenomenon of cost-
escalation is explained through a combination of the finitude of the body
of first-rate results realizable *within a given level* of investigative
technology, together with a continual (geometric) increase in the
resource-costs of pushing from one level to the next.

Commenting on the race for even higher power in nuclear physics
research, Pierre Auger wrote in 1961:

Besides the above-mentioned obstacles to building more powerful accelerators, there are also many others: the greater weights involved, the greater power supply needed, the very strict requirements for the constancy of the magnetic field, etc. In view of the situation just briefly described, it will doubtless prove impossible to obtain marked increases in particle beam intensities and to produce ultra-relativistic particles with energies of the order of 10^{11} eV and more by methods of acceleration used up to now; accordingly, some totally new method will have to be found. One such method might be the use of colliding beam devices.[1]

This passage rightly locates the ground of cost-escalation in the ever-mounting *technical obstacles* that must be overcome in enhancing the capacity of data technology, obstacles which require an ever-growing commitment of resources for their resolution.

One sometimes hears the cost-increase in scientific work accounted for with reference to decreasing efficiency in recruitment, or to increasing personnel costs,[2] or even to boondoggling and projecteering by affluent scientists. From the present perspective, such explanatory recourse to the manpower-management side of the issue seems misguided. For the fundamental thesis to whose substantiation much of our present discussion has been dedicated is that *the primary and predominant reason for the ongoing escalation in the resource cost of significant scientific discovery resides in the increasing technical difficulties in the realization of this objective*, difficulties that are a fundamental—and ineliminable—part of the enterprise itself.

2. THE ECONOMIC BASIS: THE COST/CAPACITY CORRELATION THESIS

But just what is the nature of the correlation between enhanced technological "capacity" and larger resource-cost? Here we must look more deeply into the economics of scientific technology, and, in particular, into the mechanism of the cost-escalation associated with progress in this sphere.

Our present analysis of the economic bases of scientific progress will

[1] Pierre Auger, *Current Trends in Scientific Research* (Paris, 1961; UNESCO Publications), p. 43.
[2] Derek J. de Solla Price, *Little Science, Big Science* (New York, 1963), see pp. 92–93 and 101ff.

hinge upon the thesis of a fixed and definite correlation of costs and returns. Specifically, let X be the "capacity" of the data-technology relevant to inquiry in a problem-area of natural science (be it in terms of *power* (P) or *complexity* (C)), and let R be the resource-cost of achieving this degree of effectiveness. Then we shall have the relationship: $\log X \infty \log R$. This relationship—which we shall here designate as the Cost/Capacity Correlation Thesis—means that *the total resource-cost* demand of a capacity increase in data-technology keeps pace with the magnitude of this increase as a suitable *power* thereof ($R \propto X^{\alpha}$ with $\alpha > 1$). Fixed-size capacity augmentations thus become rapidly more expensive in resource-cost terms.

To clarify this thesis, let us return to the parametric-space exploration model of Chapter IX. Specifically, let us suppose that the (cumulative) *effort* in terms of the resource-expenditure (R) needed to operate outwards to the distance E of the parametric range—and thus to realize the findings that are accessible within this "distance"—does not increase *linearly* in proportion with the extent of the total range covered (namely in proportion with E), but rather increases with some constant ($\beta > 1$) power thereof (E^{β}), so that the cumulative magnitude of this effort increases as a fixed power of the "distance" at issue. Accordingly, one arrives at the relationship: $R(E) \propto E^{\beta}$ (or equivalently: $\log E \infty \log R(E)$. This Exploration-Cost Relation (as we shall call it) provides a vivid view of the cost increases involved in going to greater removes from "home base": the resources required for operating further and further out from such a starting point grow as a fixed power of the "distances" involved.

Now when this present relationship $\log E \infty \log R$ is joined to the Capacity/Range Relation of Chapter IX ($\log E \infty \log X$), the presently envisaged Cost/Capacity Correlation, $\log X \infty \log R$, is an immediate consequence.

This thesis does not, however, stand on the rather tenuous theoretical footing of such abstract principles, but is confirmed empirically across a wide range of data-technology: particle accelerators, optical and radio telescopes, research reactors, computers, etc. The cost of modern particle accelerators affords a striking illustration.[3] Consider for a

---

[3] Data for the major U.S. proton synchrotrons and electron synchrotrons built since 1960 are given in M. Stanley Livingston, *Particle Accelerators: A Brief History* (Cambridge, Mass., 1969). And see also Alvin M. Weinberg, "Socio-technical Institutes and the Future of Team Research" in P. C. Ritterbusch (ed.), *Scientific Institutions of the Future* (Washington, 1972), pp. 113–133.

concrete example the cost of astronomical telescopes which has been studied in detail in a report of the National Academy of Sciences/ National Research Council, yielding the data presented in Figures 1 and 2.

Figure 1

COST OF OPTICAL TELESCOPES

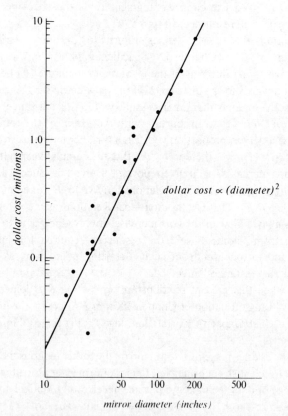

$dollar\ cost \propto (diameter)^2$

mirror diameter (inches)

Note Costs of optical telescopes as a function of aperture, in millions of 1963 dollars, and including optics, mounting, and dome. Land costs, site development, and auxiliary instruments are not included.

From *Ground-Based Astronomy, A Ten Year Program* (Washington, D.C., 1964; National Academy of Sciences/National Research Council Publication).

Figure 2

COST OF RADIO TELESCOPES

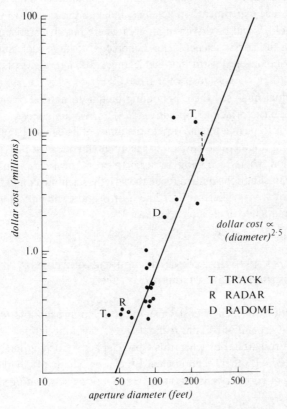

$$dollar\ cost \propto (diameter)^{2.5}$$

T TRACK
R RADAR
D RADOME

aperture diameter (feet)

Note Costs of steerable antennas as a function of diameter, in millions of 1963 dollars. Paraboloids with added construction features not ordinarily needed for radio astronomy are marked with a special symbol.
From *Ground-Based Astronomy, A Ten Year Program* (Washington, D.C., 1964; National Academy of Sciences/National Research Council Publication).

Comparable relationships regarding the costs of science-technology can also be established in other areas—for the pioneering frontiers of computers (hardware and software), for example, or for high-flux reactors.[4] Nor is this phenomenon of cost-escalation confined to the power-intensive area of data-technology in physics. In biology, experiments which aim at detecting delicate statistical relationships, involving the control of large-scale animal populations, such as the "million mouse experiment" in genetics, indicate the lengths to which data-technology will be driven in an area where massive statistics are needed. (In the social sciences, the technology of large-scale surveys affords a comparable illustration—collecting 2,500 interviews of ca. 30 minute length nowadays costs over $100,000.[5])

In the final analysis, there is nothing unique to natural science as regards the basic principles operative here. For we are concerned with an endeavor to push a technology to the limits of its capacity, and one knows from innumerable cases there is an analogous cost-increase in any situation where technology is used to press towards *any* natural limit, even in situations quite outside the strictly scientific context. (See Figure 3 for a vivid illustration.) The cost of increasing effectiveness grows dramatically in all such contexts.

3. COST ESCALATION: THE EXPONENTIALLY INCREASING COST OF A LINEAR PROGRESS THROUGH DATA-TECHNOLOGY LEVELS

The operation of such a cost/capacity correlation accounts for the drastic cost-escalation of the technology of scientific inquiry at the frontiers of research. For when this Cost/Capacity Correlation Thesis is juxtaposed with the Technological Escalation Thesis of Chapter X, the important corollary ensues that: *Every successive ascending step in*

---

[4] The latter indeed affords another vivid illustration of the penetration of modern physics-research into areas of high costs: the Liquid Metal Fast Breeding Reactor (LMFBR). Alvin M. Weinberg has written about this project as follows:

> President Nixon has committed the United States to the construction of an LMFBR by around 1980. Here the goal is definite: a 500-MwE plutonium-fuelled, sodium-cooled reactor which will demonstrate the technical feasibility of breeding. The scientific strategies are also clear. Though some technical questions still remain, few doubt that the project is feasible and that it probably can be achieved by following any of several routes. The reactor is very expensive—about $500 × 10⁶—and even the experiments which must be done in support of the project are not inexpensive. (Alvin M. Weinberg, "Institutions and Strategies in the Planning of Research," *Minerva*, vol. 12 [1974], pp. 8–17 [see p. 10].)

[5] See the interesting discussion of surveys in Peter H. Rossi, "Researchers, Scholars, and Policy-Makers: The Politics of Large-Scale Research," *Daedalus*, vol. 93 (1964), pp. 1142–1161.

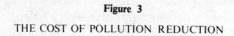

Figure 3

THE COST OF POLLUTION REDUCTION

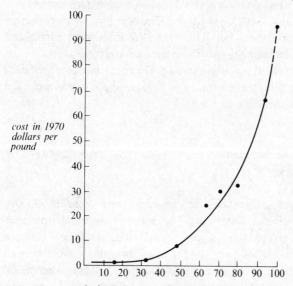

biological oxygen demand reduction (per cent)

Note Incremental cost of reducing organic wastes from a 2,700-ton-per-day beet sugar plant rises steeply as emission standards approach complete purity. Reduction of biological oxygen demand (a measure of the oxygen required to decompose wastes) costs less than $1 a pound up to 30 percent reduction. Reduction beyond 65 percent requires more than $20 for each additional pound removed, and at 95 percent reduction, each pound removed costs $60.

From *Second Annual Report of the Council on Environmental Quality* (Washington, D.C.: Government Printing Office, 1971).

the sequence of the T-levels of data-technology calls for an order-of-magnitude increase in resource-expenditure.[6]

As was noted above for many areas of data-technology species (chronometric instruments, particle accelerators, astronomical

[6] One useful way of conceptualizing this situation is as follows. The thesis of cost-capacity correlation yields a series of steps in ascending data-technology levels the resource-requirements of whose realization grow in a geometric series. Such a series can be conceived through the idea that each member (after the second) is simply a constant times the sum of its two (or more generally *n*) immediate predecessors. On this basis, the step to the *i*-th level of data-technology involves an increase of resource outlays in such a way that its cost *is always a fixed proportion of the sum-total of its n immediate predecessors put together.*

measuring equipment, etc.), the historic course of technical progress
has been such as to maintain an exponential pace in the enhancement of
the "capacity" (X) of scientific technology (its accuracy, power, etc.).
Technological innovation has been such as to maintain a linear pace in
the increase of log X, with log $[X(t)] \propto t$. The operation of a logarithmic
cost-capacity correlation, log $X(t) \propto$ log $R(t)$ accordingly establishes
the need for an exponential growth in resource investments to assure a
merely uniform rate of transition through the successive stages of data
technology. And this circumstance is in fact amply confirmed. (See
Figure 4 for one striking instance.)

4. TECHNOLOGICAL ESCALATION IN SCIENCE: THE UNAVAILABILITY OF
   ECONOMICS OF REPRODUCTION

The preceding considerations set science apart from productive
enterprises of a more ordinary sort. The course of historical experience
in manufacturing industries since the industrial revolution yields a
picture where: (i) the industry has grown exponentially in the over-all
investment of the relevant resources of capital-and-labor, whereas (ii)
the *output* of the industry has grown at an even faster exponential rate.
As a result of this combination, the ratio of investment cost per unit of
output has declined exponentially due to favorable "economies of
scale" throughout the manufacturing industries. However, this
relationship does NOT hold for the *science industry*—the "industry" of
the scientific enterprise itself. To be sure, the analogue of (i) has indeed
been maintained—by Adams' Law. But we have seen that, while the
gross output (at a "routine" quality level) has grown at an exponential
pace roughly equal to that of investment inputs, the growth of *higher
quality output* has grown at a *substantially lesser* exponential
rate—one that steadily diminishes as one raises the quality level of the
output at issue. Accordingly, we have the upshot that *the ratio of
investment per unit of output has increased exponentially in "the
science industry"*—the exact reverse of the more standard case of
industrial production.[7]

---

[7] This latter relationship has been verified for many industries including the
production of fuels, chemicals, metals, etc. See, for example, the data cited in M.
Korach, "The Science of Industry," *The Science of Science*, ed. by M. Goldsmith and
A. Mackey (London, 1964), pp. 179–194.

Figure 4

INCREASES IN THE COST OF NUCLEAR MAGNETIC RESONANCE
EQUIPMENT AT THE TECHNOLOGICAL FRONTIER 1950-1970

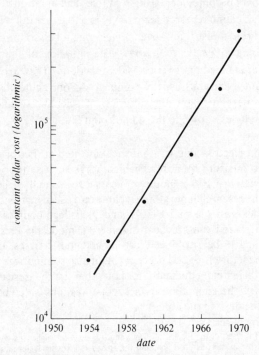

From D. A. Bromley *et al., Physics in Perspective: Student Edition* (Washington, D.C.,
1973; National Research Council/National Academy of Science Publication), p. 278.

The economies of mass production are unavailable in research at the
scientific frontiers. Here the existing *modus operandi* actually in hand is
always of limited utility—its potential is soon wrung dry; the frontiers
keep moving "onwards and upwards." Of course, if it were a matter of
doing an experiment over and over—as in a classroom demon-
stration—then the unit cost could be brought down and the usual
economies of scale would be obtained. The economics of mass
*re*production is altogether different from that in pioneering production.

With mass production costs, it is as though each item made chipped off a bit of the cost of those yet to be made.[8] Here too an exponential relationship obtains, but one of exponential decay. Figure 5 offers a vivid illustration of this phenomenon. To draw a somewhat odd biological simile—it is as though the initiation of the species was expensive, but once the species is realized the further generation of its individual members becomes increasingly simple. The situation with the R & D costs of scientific research technology is altogether different.

Frontier research is just that—true *pioneering*. What counts is not doing it, but doing it *for the first time*.[9] The situation of the initial reconfirmation of claimed discoveries aside, repetition in *research* is in general redundant—and thus usually pointless. As one acute observer has remarked, one can follow the diffusion of scientific technology "from the research desk down to the schoolroom":

> The emanation electroscope was a device invented at the turn of the century to measure the rate at which a gas such as thorium loses its radioactivity. For a number of years it seems to have been used only in the research laboratory. It came into use in instructing graduate students in the mid-1930's, and in college courses by 1949. For the last few years a cheap commercial model has existed and is beginning to be introduced into high school courses. In a sense, this is a victory for good practice; but it also summarizes the sad state of scientific education to note that in the research laboratory itself the emanation electroscope has long since been moved from the desk to the attic.[10]

[8] As one perceptive commentary notes:

Learning occurs as a result of the repetition of the same activity—the higher the level of cumulative output, the greater the repetition, and the greater is learning. It appears that learning is subject to sharply diminishing returns. In a much-quoted case (the production of air-frames), the number of man-hours to produce an air-frame is a decreasing function of the number of the same sort of air-frame previously produced. It appears that the function is surprisingly precise and, in fact, to produce the nth frame of a given type, the labour required is proportional to $1/(3\sqrt{n})$. (Keith Norris and John Vaizey, *The Economics of Research and Technology* [London, 1973], p. 164.)

[9] Thus in science, as in war, what matters is "gettin' thar fustest with the mostest." As his father wrote to the mathematician Johann Bolyai in 1823, "If you have really succeeded in the question, it is right that no time be lost in making it public. . . . [E]very scientific struggle is just a serious war, in which I cannot say when peace will arrive. Thus we ought to conquer when we are able, since the advantage is always to the first comer." (Quoted in Roberto Bonola, *Non-Euclidean Geometry*, tr. by H. S. Carslaw [2nd ed., La Salle, 1938], p. 99.)

[10] Gerald Holton, "Models for Understanding the Growth and Excellence of Scientific Research" in Stephen R. Graubard and Gerald Holton (eds.), *Excellence and Leadership in a Democracy* (New York, 1962), pp. 94–131 (see p. 115).

Figure 5

THE DECREASING COSTS OF MINICOMPUTERS

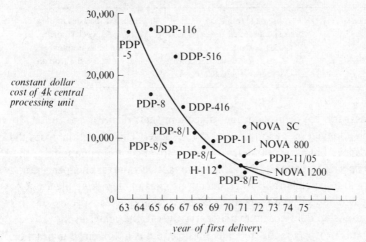

year of first delivery

From D. A. Bromley *et al., Physics in Perspective: Student Edition* (Washington, D.C., 1973; National Research Council/National Academy of Science Publication), p. 331.

The savings of mass reproduction in science are thus useless outside the context of instructional purposes. In innovative science there are no economies of scale.[11]

5. COST/CAPACITY CORRELATION AT THE TRANS-SPECIES LEVEL

Consider once more the idea of technological taxa as set out in Table 1. Our basic argument has maintained the operation of a cost/capacity correlation principle *at the technological genus level*.[12] It is accordingly

[11] Note, however, that IF the production of "basic findings" in science Q were subject to the exponential cost-decay encountered in *industrial* mass-production, THEN Q would grow exponentially even under zero-growth conditions of resource investment, and so the nature of first-rate innovation $F \propto \log Q$ would indeed remain constant, exactly as the communist theory of scientific progress demands. It is this tendency to assimilate *cognitive* production to *industrial* production that lies at the bottom of the Soviet view of science and is the source of its deficiency as seen from the standpoint of the present theory.

[12] A technological genus is (of course) defined in *functional* or *mission-oriented* terms, with reference to the nature of the task of the technological instrumentalities in question (chronometry, low-temperature cooling, particle-acceleration, etc.).

Table 1

EXAMPLES OF TECHNOLOGICAL TAXA

	Example I	*Example II*
PHYLUM	astrophysical radiation-sensors	nuclear-physics apparatus
GENUS	optical telescope, radio telescope	particle accelerator, high-flux reactor
SPECIES	Newtonian focus telescope, Cassegrain focus telescope	cyclotron, synchrotron

necessary to deal with the objection that this can be upset by technological innovation at the species level. This objection poses the prospect that as technological progress advances from one state-of-the-art species to the next, things might in fact become far cheaper—doing this so drastically that, while the log-proportionality principle $\log X \infty \log R$ is indeed maintained *within* each technological species, yet this relationship does *not* ultimately carry over to the genus level.

This prospect is theoretically feasible, but is not realized in practice. The actual situation appears as in Figure 6. The numbers here mark successive "leaps" in technological state of the art—massive increase in performance/capacity for *relatively* modest escalation in cost. Each successive stage maintains a cost/capacity ratio that is itself roughly log-linear. But—and this is crucial—the synoptic result of their overall composition is *also* log-linear. The leaps in technological progress from species to species appear (on all available evidence) to produce the effect that *a log-linear cost/capacity relationship is also maintained at the genus level in the course of technological progress.* The linear relationship at issue thus does not *block* inventiveness and innovation, but rather demands it. Yet the data indicate that this innovation proceeds within specifiable limits as regards considerations of cost-effectiveness. Our commitment to the fundamental cost/capacity relationship thus involves no denial of the reality of a process of technological leap-frogging by "break-throughs" to increasingly sophisticated levels of technological progress. It is just that this growth in effectiveness produces no savings, but—quite to the contrary—is ever more expensive.

This circumstance is perfectly compatible with a continually enhanced capacity to do less expensively what we could do before. However—as was observed above—no real advantage ensues here,

Figure 6

THE EVOLUTION OF COST-CAPACITY RELATIONSHIPS
AT THE TECHNOLOGICAL GENUS LEVEL

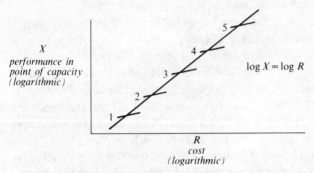

X

*performance in
point of capacity
(logarithmic)*

$\log X \infty \log R$

R
*cost
(logarithmic)*

Note One is to think of the course of technological progress as moving (by virtually
discontinuous leaps) along the successive levels of technological sophistication in
such a way that the over-all effect (on such a doubly logarithmic plotting) is
essentially linear.

because in science, as in a technological arms-race, one is simply never
called on to keep doing what was done before. Rather, a Sysyphus-like
task is posed by the constantly *escalating* demands of science for the
enhanced data to be obtained at new levels of technological
sophistication. One is always forced further up the ladder, ascending to
ever higher levels of technological performance—and of costs.

6. A LAW OF LOGARITHMIC RETURNS: THE ECONOMICS OF SCIENCE INDICATE

AN ARMS RACE AGAINST NATURE

Let us scrutinize more closely this issue of the cost of progress in
scientific inquiry at the problem-area level. The crucial step here lies in
putting together two pieces. (i) $F \infty \log X$, the Capacity/Findings
Relation of Chapter IX, and (ii) the Cost/Capacity Correlation Thesis
of the present chapter: $\log X \infty \log R$. These two relationships at once
yield the following result as regards the evolving cost of first-rate
findings: $F \infty \log R$. Thus while F advances in *arithmetic* steps, the

correlative resource expenditure R increases in *geometric* steps. We consequently obtain—at the localized problem-area level of parametric exploration—a cost-yield relationship of the same structure as the Law of Logarithmic Returns maintained in Chapter VIII above with respect to the situation in science as a whole. An exponential cost increase is required to maintain a constant pace of progress.

Subject to the explanatory rationale embodied in the parametric-space exploration model of Chapter IX, the basis for a Law of Logarithmic Returns appears as a combination of two factors: (1) the logarithmically thinning distribution of scientifically significant phenomena in parametric space as per the Findings-Distribution Assumption ($F \infty \log E$), in conjunction with (2) the ever-mounting resource-demands created by physical limits upon the interactive probing of this space as one moves increasingly far away from "home base," leading to the Exploration-Cost Relation ($\log E \infty \log R$) of the present chapter. The former thesis of findings-distribution reflects a largely epistemological view of the distribution of cognitively significant phenomena along the dimensions of parametric space. The latter thesis of technological escalation presents a physical fact: the rapidly increasing difficulty in the continually deeper probing of this space. Put together, these two theses directly yield a Law of Logarithmic Returns ($F \infty \log R$) by yet another deductive route, a route proceeding wholly within the framework of the parametric-space exploration model.[13]

The economics of scientific inquiry presents a picture of ongoing cost-escalation that is altogether reminiscent of an arms race. The technical escalation inherent in scientific research closely parallels the familiar arms-race situation of built-in technological obsolescence as the opposition escalates to the next phase of sophistication. In both cases the economic structure is the same, as new technology leads to exponential cost increases. (Consider the series of the B-bombers from the old B17 of World War II through the B-47 and B-52 of the Cold War era to the B-1 of today.)

As science endeavors to extend its "mastery over nature" it comes to be involved in a technology-intensive arms race against nature. The escalation of technological capabilities—and correlatively of costs—is the manifestation of this phenomenon.

The perspective afforded by such a model of exploration of

---

[13] For a graphic overview of the (somewhat convoluted) line of reasoning of this chapter see Figure 3 of the Appendix (p. 269).

prospecting indicates that progress in natural science has heretofore been relatively easy because we have explored nature in our own locality: not our *spatial* neighborhood, but our *parametric* neighborhood.[14] Here—thanks to the evolutionary heritage of our sensory and conceptual apparatus—we have been able to operate with relative ease and freedom. Thus the germane past has seen the combination of (1) our operating at the initial era of the scientific enterprise in our "parametric neighborhood" (thus antedating the era of seriously diminishing returns), together with (2) our being able to afford the ongoing commitment of manpower and material at an exponentially increasing rate (of antedating the ultimately inevitable era of zero-growth on the side of resource-investment). This combination of factors has forged the unique feature of the historical situation, creating a set of circumstances in the *pace* of the development of science which never again will or can be duplicated in the subsequent course of human history. Scientific innovation is going to become more and more difficult as we push out further and further from our home base towards the more remote frontiers.[15] If the present perspective is even partly correct, the half-millennium commencing around 1650 will eventually come to be regarded among the great characteristic developmental transformations of human history, with the age of The Science Explosion as unique in its own historical structure as The Bronze Age or The Industrial Revolution or The Population Explosion.

[14] Note that our assumption of the finite dimensionality of the phase-space of research-relevant parameters becomes crucial here. (Cf. p. 163.) For if these were limitless in number, one could always move on to the inexpensive exploitation of "virgin territory."

[15] The perspective adopted in this chapter opens up a promising epistemological line of approach to metaphysical method. For we see that not only *what* we know about nature but *how* we come to know it becomes a useful basis for inferences about the *modus operandi* of nature. Significant information derives not only from the secrets that nature yields to our inquiry (i.e., their specific *content*), but also from the *manner* in which she surrenders them in the face of our efforts. This suggests exploiting the historically given features of *the development of our acquisition of empirical knowledge* about the world (its rate, structure, etc.) as a basis for drawing inferences about the world itself (as, for example, with the supposition of data-technology stratification), setting out theses of an "ontological" sort (i.e., descriptive of the nature of physical reality) which both are substantively correct (insofar as we can tell) and provide a plausible account for the course of our cognitive progress. The *structure* of knowledge-acquisition thus functions as a guide to the theoretical projection of those metaphysical characteristics of the world that explain the evolution of our knowledge of it.

XII

The Cyclic Pattern of Progress at the Problem-area Microlevel: Diminishing Returns in the Restricted Context

There is a tide in the affairs of men, which, taken at the flood, leads on to fortune.

SHAKESPEARE, *Julius Caesar*, IV, iii

[Science] advances by leaps; and the impulse for each leap is either some new observational resource, or some novel way of reasoning about the observations. Such novel way of reasoning might, perhaps, be considered as a new observational means, since it draws attention to relations between facts which would previously have been passed by unperceived.

C. S. PEIRCE, *Collected Papers*, Vol. I, 1.109

1. THE MICROLEVEL: THE CYCLE OF PROGRESS AT THE PROBLEM AREAS

Consider once more the Findings-Stratification Principle of Chapter X:

In any particular problem-area of natural science, only a finite (and indeed relatively small) number of first-rate discoveries can be attained at a *fixed* level T_i of the technology for the acquisition and exploitation of the relevant data. After these findings have been realized, further first-rate discoveries cannot be obtained until the relevant data-technology is advanced to the next level, T_{i+1}.

This thesis yields the basis for a clearer picture of the structure of progress at the "microlevel" of the particular problem areas of natural science, suggesting the situation depicted in Figure 1. The incremental pattern of innovation is pretty much that of a bell-shaped curve skewed towards the initial phase of the timespan at issue. The situation

Figure 1

THE PATTERN OF DISCOVERY WITHIN A PROBLEM
AREA AT A FIXED STATE-OF-THE-ART LEVEL
OF DATA TECHNOLOGY

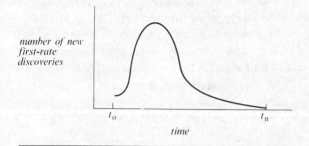

number of new
first-rate
discoveries

t_0 t_n

time

regarding significant innovation in a given problem-area has the following structure: a triggering development of technological provenience sets afoot a new phase of discovery by inaugurating a new stage in the data-technology of the problem-area. Thereupon, the major discoveries that become accessible generally tend to be realized fairly swiftly. A mutually supportive and reinforcing plurality of results is obtained, and their realization results in a really massive advance during the initial phase of new research in the problem-area at issue.[1] Accordingly, there is a marked "clustering" towards the opening phase of a cycle: so that there is an initial spurt of swift expansion—indeed, of exponential growth. For the exploitation of possibilities tends to be rather rapid: once the point of "take off" has actually been reached, the great bulk of the now-accessible findings is generally realized in a relatively short order. When some of the problems of the cluster

[1] Thomas Kuhn has described some phenomena of this sort as follows:

William Herschel, for example, when he increased by one the time-honored number of planetary bodies, taught astronomers to see near things when they looked at the familiar heavens even with instruments more traditional than his own. That change of vision of astronomers must be a principal reason why, in the half century after the discovery of Uranus, twenty circumsolar bodies were added to the traditional seven. . . . Clearly . . . the drive to look for additional planets dates from Herschel's work on Uranus. . . . X-rays were the first new sort of radiation discovered since infra-red and ultraviolet at the beginning of the century. But within less than a decade after Roentgen's work, four more were disclosed by the new scientific sensitivity (for example, to fogged photographic plates) and by some of the new instrumental techniques that resulted from Roentgen's work and its assimilation. Very often these transformations [induced by a discovery] in the established techniques of scientific practice prove even more important than the incremental knowledge provided by the discovery itself. ("Historical Structure of Scientific Discovery," *Science*, vol. 136 [1962], pp. 760–764 [see p. 763].)

occupying a given order of difficulty have been solved, the resolution of the others in their problem-area locality that are of the same order of difficulty becomes relatively simple.[2] But this soon eventuates in a period of leveling off as the now-available findings come to be realized more and more completely. And so, finally, a rapid decline sets in as the limited prospects for high-level innovation come to be exhausted (as per the saturation phenomenology of the Stratification Thesis). The initial period of relatively steep sigmoid growth, which is followed by a brief plateau which in its turn is succeeded by a final phase of exponential decay, eventuating in a final state of saturation at this T-level stage.[3] Thus if one looks at the situation from a *cumulative* rather than *incremental* point of view, there results the familiar picture of logistic growth and saturation portrayed in the S-shaped curve of Figure 2.

Figure 2

THE CUMULATION OF DISCOVERIES REALIZED IN A GIVEN
PROBLEM AREA AT A FIXED LEVEL OF DATA TECHNOLOGY

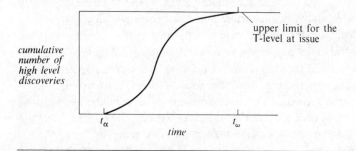

---

[2] One of the earliest studies to indicate this exponentially explosive growth-structure of a new problem-area—specifically with regard to X-ray crystallography—is Ralph W. G. Wyckoff, *The Structure of Crystals* (New York, 1924; 2nd ed., New York, 1931. Supplement for 1930–1934 to the 2nd ed., New York, 1935). See the discussion in W. H. George, *The Scientist in Action: A Scientific Study of His Methods* (New York, 1938), pp. 231–232.

[3] To be sure, the later discoveries may well be of an *intrinsic* importance co-equal with that of the earlier ones, but the early burst of innovation is particularly impressive. It makes for a quantitative difference that is virtually qualitative in nature because the significance of each result is amplified by the reciprocal illumination shed by a plurality of related findings.

It is worthwhile to look more closely at the idea of a "triggering development" that initiates such a cycle. This is usually manifested as a rather dramatic major finding in the field—a discovery of landmark proportions. The finding that heralds a fresh phase of discovery is often unexpected and seems to come virtually "out of the blue" (often the field has been relatively quiescent for a time and the finding itself serves to draw real attention to it). The new burst of activity is made available by new technology (Becquerel and the photo-plates, Michelson-Morley and relativity, pulsars and radiotelescopy, etc.). The novel and striking nature at the theoretical level of the initiating discovery sometimes tends to mask its modest origin in the item of technological innovation.

With respect to technological innovation the German economist Julius Wolf laid down four "Laws of Retardation of Progress," one of which asserts: "Every technical improvement . . . bars the way to further progress. There is less left to improve, and this narrowing of possibilities results in a slackening or complete cerration of technical improvement in a number of fields."[4] Along these lines, Fritz Machlup has written:

> There have been two schools of thought on the subject of the effect of the flow of inventions upon the ease of making further inventions. According to the "acceleration school," the more there is invented the easier it becomes to invent still more. This is deduced from the assumption that every new invention furnishes a new idea for potential combination with vast numbers of existing ideas. . . . According to the "retardation school," the more there is invented, the harder it becomes to invent still more. This is deduced from the assumption that there are limits to the improvement of technology. In its extreme form, this thesis states that the more there has been invented the less there is left to be invented.[5]

Two comparable schools of thought can be hypothesized regarding the conduciveness of *scientific* discovery to further *scientific* progress. An "acceleration school" would hold that the more there is discovered, the

---

[4] Julius Wolf, *Die Volkswirtschaft der Gegenwart und Zukunft* (Leipzig, 1912), pp. 236–237. Wolf's "law," however, will—on the present view—hold only within the restrictive confines of a particular technological state of the art.

[5] Fritz Machlup, "The Supply of Inventors and Inventions," *Weltwirtschaftliches Archiv*, vol. 65 (1960), pp. 210–251 (see pp. 236–237). This paper is a valuable study of this whole family of issues.

easier it becomes to make further discoveries, presumably because each new theory provides grist to the mill of further research.[6] By contrast, the "deceleration school" would hold that the more there has been discovered, the harder it becomes to discover still more because the pool of still available discoveries becomes dried up. On our present theory, these two views are *conjoined*. Both are held to be operative, albeit not at the same time. At the start of a cycle, the position of the acceleration theorists is appropriate, while towards the later states of the cycle, the technological limits envisaged by the retardation theorists come to the fore.

Testimonial evidence for the phenomenon of discovery-saturation that marks the closing phase of progress at the problem-area level is not easy to come by. Scientists prefer to talk about accomplishments and successes; they are understandably reluctant to dwell upon failures and defeats. And yet recurrent traces can be found in the professional literature. Thus in 1888 Simon Newcomb, the dean of American astronomers, wrote:

> If the public are disappointed at not seeing brilliant discoveries coming from all the observatories, we must remember that what are called discoveries are not the main work of the scientific man of today. It would be too much to say with confidence that the age of great discoveries in any branch of science has passed by; yet, so far as astronomy is concerned, it must be confessed that we do appear to be fast approaching the limits of our knowledge. True, there is still a great deal to learn. Every new comet that appears must be found by some one, and I do not grudge the finder the honors awarded him. At the same time, so far as we can see, one comet is so much like another that we cannot regard one as adding in any important degree to our knowledge. The result is that the work which really occupies the attention of the astronomer is less the

---

[6] The argument for this would be isomorphic with that given in another context by economists concerned with invention and technological innovation:

> The opportunity for invention therefore continually proliferates. . . . A sudden mutation, a master invention, opens up new fields both through its cross fertilisation with older ideas and through its possible crop of improvement inventions, and it further clears the ground for other possible major innovations. (John Jewkes, David Sawers, Richard Stillerman, *The Sources of Invention* [London, 1958], ca. p. 123.)

An earlier formulation of this argument with respect to science itself occurs in the 1901 presidential address of William Thomson (Lord Kelvin) to the British Association for the Advancement of Science. (Compare n. 1 on pp. 54–55 above.)

discovery of new things than the elaboration of those already known, and the entire systemization of our knowledge.[7]

This intra-level saturation helps to provide a plausible account for the recurrence of a *fin de siècle* sentiment within various scientific specialties, as noted in the opening chapter. When—towards the end of a cycle—even massive efforts yield few discernible returns it becomes easy (even for people who ought to know better) to misconstrue a temporary stoppage as a final termination. And when this happens to occur concurrently in several prominent problem-areas,[8] it becomes tempting to project this localized result across the expanse of natural science as a whole.

2. REPETITIONS OF THE CYCLE: THE PULSATION MODEL AND ST. SIMON'S LAW

A problem arises. The basic form of our theory of progress is one of steady retardation as per the Law of Logarithmic Returns: $F \infty \log R$. Now when the increase in R is exponential, how is this *linear* growth-pattern for F (on a logarithmic scale) to be reconciled with the oscillatory pulsations described in the preceding section? The reconciliation we envisage takes the form depicted in Figure 3.[9] Thus what we have portrayed as a linear curve actually represents a front of many small wavelets when the situation is viewed in closer detail. Each wavelet represents a jump or spurt of progress correlative with the opening up of a new T-level[10]—with the result of a *succession* of S-shaped configurations along the lines of Figure 2. At any given level, we have a situation where further R-inputs yield few if any additional F-outputs until the "leap" to a new (and substantially more expensive) data-technology level is accomplished.

[7] Simon Newcomb, "The Place of Astronomy Among the Sciences," *The Sidereal Messenger*, vol. 7 (1888), pp. 69–70.

[8] As can readily happen, since the pervasive nature of technological progress tends to correlate the timing of T-level accession in different problem-areas.

[9] Note that, as regards the exponential-growth past (with $\log R \infty t$), this picture agrees exactly with that of G. M. Dobrov as given in Figure 4 of Chapter V (see p. 128). Our quarrel is that he envisages for the future the unchanged circumstances of an unavoidably different past. Compare also Figure 1 of Chapter XIII (p. 224).

[10] Think again of the picture of scientific progress proposed by C. S. Peirce in the passage quoted as motto for this chapter (p. 208).

Figure 3

THE PACE OF PROGRESS WITHIN A PROBLEM-AREA AS THE RESULT
OF SUCCESSIVE SPURTS THROUGH THE ASCENT OF SUCCESSIVE
(AND INCREASINGLY COSTLY) DATA-TECHNOLOGY LEVELS

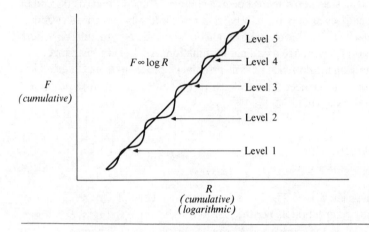

The preceding picture of progress occurring in periodic pulsations in specific problem areas implements *within the locality of each T-level stage* the basic assumption of a *fin de siècle* position. It suggests a geographic exploration model of finite progress *within* a particular problem area and under the condition of continuing operation *at a given fixed level of data-acquisition technology.* But, of course, this process only represents a single developmental phase. Viewed synoptically, such a process repeats itself over and over again as one data-technology level gives way to the next, so that the over-all pattern of progress is a structure of wave-like pulsations.[11] The resultant pattern of progress at the microlevel of particular problem-areas would look roughly as shown in Figure 4. Our theory has it that throughout this sequence of wave-like pulsations, each successive phase of active development is inaugurated (at the starred junctures) by a crucial advance in the data-

[11] The empirical reality of such pulsations has long been remarked, and various explanations proposed for it. See, for example T. J. Rainoff, "Wave-like Fluctuations of Creative Productivity in the Development of West-European Physics in the Eighteenth and Nineteenth Centuries," *Isis*, vol. 12 (1929), pp. 287–307. (Good Marxist that he is, Rainoff seeks to associate these movements with fluctuations in the business cycle!)

Figure 4

THE VOLUME OF DISCOVERY IN A PROBLEM AREA
WITH THE ADVANCE THROUGH SUCCESSIVE
STRATA OF DATA TECHNOLOGY

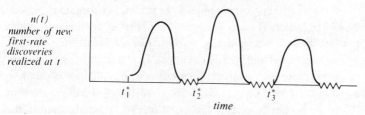

Note The t_1^* mark the "triggering events" of new spurts of innovation.

technology of the field. The pulsations themselves are correlated with the ascent from one level to the next in the ranking of technological strata. Given that there is a limited number of really first-rate results to be realized within each fixed level of such technology, one finds *at this local* level of each individual pulsation, the exhaustion phenomenon of the apple-picking model. In the absence of further breakthroughs in data-technology intra-level progress would be subject to saturation. But, of course, given a breakthrough to a new level of technology of inquiry, new vistas open up and a new crop of first-rate results become accessible. Within each pulsation the number of in principle realizable first-rate results is finite (on the apple-picking model), but taken as a whole the series of potentially available pulsations is *not* finite—on the model of endless potential progress. To be sure, breakthroughs themselves become increasingly more costly. (They must therefore themselves become less and less frequent subject to the resource-availability constraints we envisage.) On such a view, progress proceeds by way of successive spurts, each separated from its predecessor by increasingly large resource-investment requirements, and thus— ultimately, under zero-growth conditions—by increasingly long delays. For the waiting times that separate the successive pulsations will then grow longer in a geometric series.

This undulating pattern of wave-like pulsations suggests the aptness of speaking of a succession of *explosive* phases when major discoveries open up new areas of exploration in an intensive burst of activity. Such stages of rapid development are then succeeded by longer *exploitative* phases which lead to periods of relative stagnation as the newly developed prospects of major innovation become exhausted.

The French social philosopher, Claude Henri de St. Simon (1760–1825) taught that the development of people and nations involves the alternation of two phases of synthetic or "organic" periods (*époques organiques*) and analytic or "critical" periods (*époques critiques*). This principle holds in particular of intellectual culture, where synthetic periods of innovation, construction, and system-building alternate with analytical periods of consolidation, evaluation, and criticism. This "Law of St. Simon" of the cyclic alternation of synthetic and analytic phases finds one sort of exemplification in the preceding pattern of wave-like pulsations which traces an ultimately less and less rapid alternation of phases of innovation ("ascent to a new *T*-level" with its concomitant burst of discovery) with phases of consolidation and long-term exploitation in the historical development of research in the problem-areas of natural science.[12]

The present view of the structure of scientific progress stands in an interesting contrast to the picture offered in a very stimulating recent paper by Gerald Holton,[13] who presents his position in terms well worth setting out *in extenso*:

---

[12] A clear illustration of this phenomenon emerges from the recent history of physics of "fundamental" particles:

> Even a nuclear particle physicist most willing and anxious to explain his research to governments and to the public runs into major communication problems. There was a time in this research, when the field was first being explored and when new particles were being discovered every few months, when explaining research progress was not such a difficult matter. In recent years other branches of research have enjoyed similar happy periods, such as molecular biology with the RNA molecule and radio-astronomy with quasars and pulsars. However, the initial discovery of the basic entities and structures is usually followed by a long period of detailed experimentation and theoretical speculation which is far more difficult to popularize. Nuclear particle physics is now deep in one such period, very exciting and very rewarding to those working in the field but extremely difficult to explain to anyone outside, even to another scientist. No doubt when, as result of all the present research, a new synthesis appears, perhaps a new underlying structure which explains all the phenomena presently being researched, or a new theory which accounts for the nuclear force, it will once again be possible for gifted expositors to popularize the progress of this research. Meanwhile the problem remains of explaining what is now happening to those who are paying for it and it is quite evident that much more work and imagination needs to be devoted to this problem. (J. B. Adams, "Some Problems of a Big Science," *Daedalus*, vol. 102 [1973], pp. 111–124 [see p. 123].)

[13] "Models for Understanding the Growth and Excellence of Scientific Research" in Stephen R. Graubard and Gerald Holton (eds.), *Excellence and Leadership in a Democracy* (New York, 1962), pp. 94–131 (see pp. 125–126).

We are now ready to attempt a first-order approximation to improve our model for the progress of scientific research. For this purpose we examine Figure A, where curve D is simply the mirror image of I [and curve I represents the number of interesting ideas yet undiscovered], plotted in the same plane. That is, whereas I presented the decrease of ignorance, D presents the increase of total basic "discoveries" made in the finite pool of interesting ideas. The beginning of curve D indicates necessarily the occasion that launched the expeditions in this field, say the discovery in 1934 of artificial radio-activity by the Joliot-Curies while they were studying the effect of alpha particles from polonium on the nuclei of light elements. Up to this point their research had followed a fruitful line, originating in Rutherford's observation in 1919 of the transmutation of nitrogen nuclei during alpha-particle bombardment.

The new Joliot-Curie observation, however, inaugurated a brilliant new branch of discovery. We suddenly see that the previous model (Figure A) was fatally incomplete because it

---

Figure 5

HOLTON'S ACCOUNT OF SCIENTIFIC DISCOVERY

Figure A	Figure B
The Intra-Level Exhaustion of Ideas	The Trans-Level Escalation of Innovation

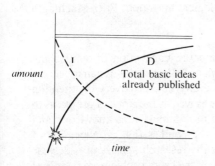 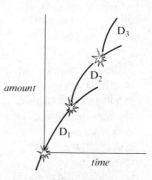

From Gerald Holton, "Models for Understanding the Growth and Excellence of Scientific Research" in S. R. Graubard and Gerald Holton (eds.), *Excellence and Leadership in a Democracy* (New York, 1962), pp. 94–131.

postulated an *exhaustible* fund of ideas, a limited ocean with a definite number of islands. On further exploration, we now note that an island may turn out to be a peninsula connected to a larger land mass. Thus in 1895 Röntgen seemed to have exhausted all the major aspects of X-rays, but in 1912 the discovery of X-ray diffraction in crystals by von Laue, Friedrich, and Knipping transformed two separate fields, those of X-rays and of crystallography. Mosely in 1913 made another qualitative change by showing where to look for the explanation of X-ray spectra in terms of atomic structure, and so forth. Similarly, the Joliot-Curie findings gave rise to work that had one branching point with Fermi, another with Hahn and Strassmann. Each major line of research given by line D in Figure A is really a part of a [limitless] series D_1, D_2, D_3, etc., as in Figure B. Thus the growth of scientific research proceeds by the *escalation* of knowledge—or perhaps rather of new areas of ignorance—instead of by mere accumulation.

If the picture of Figure A is taken to pertain to work in a problem-area *within* a fixed technological level, and the Figure B picture is taken to represent cross-level progress, then our own picture would be just like that of Holton, *with one very important difference*: namely, that for the zero-growth future, the time-scale of Figure B must be understood to be not *linear*, but *logarithmic*.

3. DIMINISHING RETURNS AT THE INTRA-CYCLE LEVEL

Writing in the context of technological invention, Fritz Machlup has said:

> Some . . . might hold that the entire conception of diminishing returns is out of place in an area as "intrinsically dynamic" as the production of knowledge. Since any new discovery or intention changes the stock of knowledge as well as the stock of problems to be solved, what sense is there in assuming that knowledge and problems are fixed? . . . [But] the point is that an allocation of research personnel that will fit the research agenda of next year need not fit the agenda of today. If the list of problems to be solved is apt to grow from today to next month, and still more to next year, this does not mean it will serve any good purpose now to employ a research staff too large for present tasks. . . . At any

moment, in other words, the production of inventions may have been pushed far into the range of diminishing returns, conceivably even into the range where marginal returns to inventive input are zero.[14]

Analogous considerations apply to pure science as well. Relative to the particular state of the art in gathering and processing of scientific data obtaining at a given time, the returns in scientific results on further resource allocations are (on our view) bound to diminish, due to the largely inflexible limits to what can be attained at this stage. Indeed, a point will be reached when the investment of further resources in inquiry on a particular problem may well be altogether futile—always supposing that inquiry is to be carried on within a fixed level of investigative technology.

This principle of diminishing returns operates in a manner different from the principle of rising costs considered above. There the topic was the massive increase in the expenditure of resources and effort needed to push from one technological level to the next level—where alone, after a certain point, major new findings could be obtained. But now we are concerned with the lessened prospects of innovation *within* a given technological level, once we reach a point where—so to speak—the cream of the level-accessible findings has been skimmed off.

In economics, the phenomenon of diminishing returns always inheres in the presence of one or more "fixed factors" necessary in production but not obtainable in increased quantity as the input of the various "variable factors" is increased. In the present case of the "production" of scientific discoveries, the element of fixity and inflexibility is located on the side of the reach of *available technique*, and is marked by the restricted interactions with nature that are in principle accessible at the given (by hypothesis, currently *fixed*) level of the technology of research, owing to the physical limitations operative here. At any given

[14] Fritz Machlup, "The Supply of Inventors and Inventions," *Weltwirtschaftliches Archiv*, vol. 65 (1960), pp. 210–251 (see pp. 240–241). Machlup has gone on to say that "the point where diminishing returns set in is apt to be pushed up as the stock of existing knowledge grows, because the number of problems on which work may fruitfully be done is likely to increase with that growth" (p. 240). It seems to be quite otherwise in our present cases, because *all* the significant problems get more difficult with the progress of science itself. This fact ultimately inheres in the nature of the "significance" at issue which differs radically in the cognitive and the technological case. (In the cognitive case an easily solved problem is *eo ipso* insignificant, while in the technological case significance is determined not by intellectual content but by causal effects.)

stage of the overall development of the technology of inquiry, there may accordingly be great differences between various problem-areas in the "returns"—in terms of significant results—that can be realized through the investment of further money and effort *at this particular technological stage.*[15] (Unfortunately, this crucial consideration is of little aid in the management of scientific resources and the determination of science policy, because the fact that a point of sufficiently gravely diminishing returns has actually been reached can in general only be determined with the wisdom of hindsight.)

[15] Over a century ago, C. S. Peirce already clearly saw that the economic idea of cost-effectiveness has a highly important role to play in the context of scientific research. See the writer's essay "Peirce and the Economy of Research," *Philosophy of Science*, vol. 43 (1976), pp. 71–98.

XIII

Aggregation to the Macrolevel and the Origin of (Scientific) Species

Immer strebe zum Ganzen, und
kannst du selber kein Ganzes
Werden, als dienendes Glied schliess
an ein Ganzes dich an.

GOETHE, *Vier Jahreszeiten*

1. THE PROBLEM OF AGGREGATION: THE TRANSITION FROM LOCAL TO
   GLOBAL SCIENCE

Two principles regarding research in natural science at the problem-area level lie at the basis of the present theory of scientific progress: (i) *The Capacity/Findings Relationship* ($F \propto \log X$) embodied in the exploration model of Chapter IX, and (ii) The *Cost/Capacity Correlation Thesis* ($\log X \propto \log R$) of Chapter XI. A principle of logarithmic returns, $F \propto \log R$, follows at once from these two relationships, as we have seen. This indicates the workings—at the problem-area microlevel—of a Law of Logarithmic Returns analogous to that which was held earlier (in Chapter V) to be operative with respect to science as a whole. But it still remains to move from this microscopic region of particular problem-areas to the larger perspective of the macroscopic situation of science in its totality, where we have also claimed a principle of logarithmic returns. Clearly, two very different levels of consideration are at issue. How is the gap between them to be closed?

To effect the needed transition, the relationship of logarithmic returns $F \propto \log R$ for *total* science can be construed as *the result of the super-*

position of many such relationships for the component problem areas of science.[1] We must examine more closely how this can be done.

2. FISSION, SPECIATION, AND THE PHENOMENON OF SPURTS OF INNOVATION

Let us begin with an economic analogy, viewing science as a whole as an economy, its branches as industries, its problem-areas as firms. Now it is one thing to deal with the microeconomics of firms and quite another thing to deal with the economy as a whole, and it may well prove to be a complex and difficult issue to aggregate the partial situations into a synoptic picture of the whole. Discrepancies can easily arise—many firms or even industries might flourish while the economy as a whole stagnates, or conversely.[2]

In discussing the rate of invention in the technological area, Fritz Machlup has written:

The predictions of acceleration or of retardation in the rate of invention, which we have mentioned above, reflect to some extent judgments about the relative frequencies of agenda-increasing and agenda-reducing inventions. . . . [S]everal writers assuming a prevalence of agenda-reducing inventions, and predicting therefore a retardation in the rate of inventive achievements, have been thinking of particular industries or particular areas of technology. Those, on the other hand, who assumed a prevalence of agenda-increasing inventions, and consequently predicted an acceleration of invention, appear to have been thinking of the entire domain of technology. Retardation of invention in particular industries would be perfectly compatible with acceleration of invention in the economy as a whole. For the economy as a whole, or for the entire domain of technology, the assumption of a prevalence of agenda-increasing inventions is probably more plausible.[3]

This poses an issue to be faced also in the present setting.

[1] Thus the point of footnote 19 of Chapter VI above (p. 107), is also germane here.

[2] Simon Kuznets has suggested (*Economic Change* [New York, 1953], Chap. 9) that technical progress will slacken after a time in each industry taken separately, insisting that this does not entail the secular stagnation of the economy as a whole.

[3] "The Supply of Inventors and Inventions," *Weltwirtschaftliches Archiv*, vol. 85 (1960), pp. 210–252 (see p. 242).

Is the logarithmic retardation we have envisaged perhaps applicable only to the local micro-situation of various "old" and exhausted problem areas, while yet failing for science as a whole? Could not new, agenda-increasing discoveries change the situation with respect to new problem areas? If new problem areas were to open up sufficiently rapidly, would the relatively rapid progress in new areas not simply offset the over-all pattern of logarithmic retardation applicable in old, "established" science? For it was maintained above that—while the production-rate of substantial new findings in an established problem-area branch of matured natural science is subject to logarithmic retardation (under the conditions of the Zero-Growth Hypothesis)—there will nevertheless be a (temporary) spurt in the pace of scientific progress when new problem areas are opened up, because it is initially easy to "pick fruit from a fresh tree." In this case, a declining growth-rate of major results within an established problem-area would be irrelevant for the larger picture of science as a whole, because—as the stock of existing knowledge grows—fertile new problem-areas are constantly opened up, with the conceivable result that discovery might proceed at an unretarded over-all pace.[4] The prospect thus enters that a sufficiently fertile development of new problem-areas might simply undo our basic thesis of the logarithmic retardation of progress in science as a whole.

In analyzing more closely the inauguration of new problem-areas in which the benefit of the "spurt of innovation" phenomenon obtains, it is helpful to think of the various problem-areas of natural science as arising as varieties within species in the natural evolutionary course of taxonomic proliferation. It is then possible to see how (under suitable assumptions) logarithmic growth of first-order findings within a whole field in accordance with $F \propto \log R$ can readily proceed correlatively with such logarithmic growth in its successfully unfolding subfields $F_i \propto \log R_i$. The situation is set out graphically in Figure 1 (which is simply a reprise of the relationships presented in Figure 3 of the preceding chapter [p. 214]). Here the turning-points of the zig-zag to a nearly vertical upwards jump indicate junctures at which a constituent component of science "fissions," creating a virtually discontinuous leap of transition to new and more fertile areas. What we have is not really a

---

[4] For examples see the discussion in Gerald Holton, "Models for Understanding the Growth and Excellence of Scientific Research" in S. R. Graubard and G. Holton (eds.), *Excellence and Leadership in a Democracy* (New York, 1962), pp. 94–131.

Figure 1

THE STRUCTURE OF PROGRESS THROUGH
THE EVOLUTION OF NEW PROBLEM AREAS

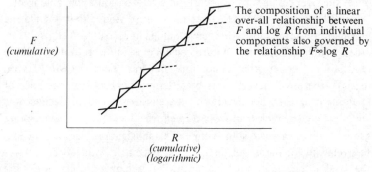

F
(cumulative)

The composition of a linear
over-all relationship between
F and log *R* from individual
components also governed by
the relationship *F*∞log *R*

R
(cumulative)
(logarithmic)

Note: It is of interest to compare Figure 3 on p. 214 above.

straight line, but a series of jumps or spurts constituting a linear, secular (long-term) trend out of a saw-toothed curve.

The linear relationship accordingly approximates a step-function each of whose jumps reflects a spurt of productivity which marks the evolutionary opening of a new taxonomic unit (problem-area). The over-all principle $F \infty \log R$ for natural science as a whole thus results from the collaboration of a whole series of analogous subprinciples for its constituent subunits. In fact, the operation of the basic log-uniformity principle $F \infty \log R$ in its *localized* form has crucial implications for our analysis. For when an old problem area gives birth to a new one, then the "charge-meter" measuring resource-investment inputs runs at the discount rate given to new customers. This means that F will (initially) increase with a quickened impetus—we are at the *initial* rather than a later stage of a logarithmic growth-pattern. The clustering of findings towards the opening phase of a new problem area is thus built into the log-proportionality principle.

3. SPECIATION: THE PRODUCTIVE EFFECT OF DISCIPLINARY
   PROLIFERATION

A crucial fact regarding natural science in its innovative aspect as a discovery-oriented domain of research is that it consists—at any given historical stage—of a (complexly interrelated) finite number of particular problem areas. If *each* of these component areas itself grows at a logarithmically retarded rate, then clearly the entire complex of *existing* science can grow no faster than this. But this argument relates to the further development of *existing* science: the progress of major innovation in the currently cultivated problem areas. Now what of the development of *new* problem areas? Clearly, *if* such new problem areas could be opened up at a pace sufficiently rapid to offset the deceleration of major findings in *existing* problem areas, then the totality of major discovery in natural science could perfectly feasibly continue at an unabated rate. (This objection seems particularly apposite because—as has been conceded, nay, stressed—there is no intrinsic limit to the new problem-areas that can be opened up, since there is no adequate basis for holding the domain of potential scientific discoveries to be inherently limited and exhaustible.) The question of the rate of scientific speciation—of the opening up of new areas of inquiry at various levels—thus becomes a crucial issue for the tenability of the thesis of logarithmic deceleration.

To begin with, it is important to recognize that *changes in the taxonomical structure of science* are an integral part of the progress of science itself.[5] As the French physicist Pierre Auger has written:

At the time of Auguste Comte, the sciences could be classified in six or seven main categories known as disciplines, ranging from mathematics to sociology. Since then, during the nineteenth century and at the beginning of the twentieth, there has been what might be described as an intra-disciplinary dismemberment, each

[5] The scientific study of the taxonomy and morphology of science itself is a virtually nonexistent enterprise. Philosophers used to deal with these matters, but they abandoned it after the late nineteenth century, when science began to change too fast for those concerned to look at truth *sub specie aeternitatis*. (A good survey of the historical situation is given in Robert Flint, *Philosophy as Scientia Scientiarun: A History of Classifications of the Sciences* [New York, 1904].) In more recent days the subject has been left to bibliographers. For the older, "classical" attempts here see Ernest Cushing Richardson, *Classification: Theoretical and Practical*, 3rd ed. (New York, 1930).

of the main categories splitting up into increasingly specialized fields, each of which rapidly assumed comparable importance to that of the actual disciplines from which it sprang. Chemistry, for example, in the days of Lavoisier formed a reasonably homogeneous entity, but chemists were soon obliged to choose between inorganic and organic chemistry; within the latter, a distinction arose during the second half of the nineteenth century between the chemistry of aromatic compounds and that of aliphatic compounds, the latter shortly being further subdivided into the study of saturated compounds and that of unsaturated compounds. Finally, at the present time, a chemist can devote a most useful research career entirely to a single chemical family. The same process can be discerned in physics and in biology.

But this very over-specialization has provoked an inverse or rather a complementary process, that of interdisciplinary synthesis; thus, from physics and chemistry there has grown up a new discipline of physical chemistry, which is influenced by both these sciences. This process has given rise to a whole series of new sciences with double or even triple names—astrophysics, biochemistry, mathematical chemistry, physico-chemical biology, etc. Thus, the diverging lines of the subjects of scientific research are connected by cross-links which restore unity to the whole.[6]

When new fields and new problem-areas open up in this way, the result is (so we have insisted) a particularly fertile period for the growth of science. Does this not bring our theory into difficulties? For could not the origination of new scientific species unfold with a speed sufficient to offset logarithmic retardation? This is a worry we must lay to rest.

Consider the example of taxonomic structure of physics. We may assume a three-layer taxonomy: the field as a whole, the branches thereof, and the sub-branches of the branches. The taxonomic situation towards the beginning of this century is given in Table 1.

It is interesting to contrast this picture of the taxonomic situation in physics with the picture of the situation in subsequent decades as given in Table 2.

These tables tell a significant story. In the 11th (1911) edition of the *Encyclopaedia Britannica*, physics is described as a discipline composed of 9 constituent branches (e.g., "Acoustics" or "Electricity and Magnetism") which were themselves partitioned into 20 further

[6] Pierre Auger, *Currents Trends in Scientific Research* (Paris, 1961; UNESCO Publications), pp. 15–16.

Table 1

THE TAXONOMY OF PHYSICS
IN THE 11th EDITION OF THE *ENCYCLOPAEDIA BRITANNICA* (1911)

Astronomy
  —Astrophysics
  —Celestial Mechanics

Acoustics
Optics
  —Theoretical Optics
  —Spectroscopy
Mechanics
Heat
  —Calorimetry
  —Theory of Radiation
  —Thermodynamics
  —Thermometry

Electricity and Magnetism
  —Electrochemistry
  —Electrokinetics
  —Electrometallurgy
  —Electrostatics
  —Thermoelectricity
  —Diamagnetism
  —Electromagnetism

Pneumatics
Energetics
Instrumentation

Note: Adapted from the Classified List of Articles at the end of Vol. XXIX (Index
  volume).

---

specialties (e.g., "Thermo-electricity" or "Celestial Mechanics"). The
15th (1974) version of the *Britannica* divides physics into 12 branches
whose subfields are—seemingly—too numerous for survey. (However
the 14th 1960's edition carried a special article entitled "Physics,
Articles on" which surveyed more than 130 special topics in the field.)
When the National Science Foundation launched its inventory of
physical specialties with the National Register of Scientific and
Technical Personnel in 1954, it divided physics into 12 areas with 90
specialties. By 1970 these figures had increased to 16 and 210,
respectively.

Table 2

PHYSICAL SPECIALTIES IN THE "NATIONAL REGISTER OF
SCIENTIFIC AND TECHNICAL PERSONNEL" FOR 1954 AND 1970

(1954)	(1970)
Astronomy (16 specialties)	Astronomy
Acoustics (7 specialties)	—Solar-Planetary Relationships (9
Optics (8 specialties)	specialties)
Mechanics and Heat (13 specialties)	—Planetology (6 specialties)
Electromagnetism (6 specialties)	—11 Further Astrophysical Special-
Solid State (8 specialties)	ties
Atomic and Molecular Physics (5 special-	Acoustics (9 specialties)
ties)	Optics (10 specialties)
Nuclear Physics (9 specialties)	Mechanics (10 specialties)
Theoretical Physics: Quantum Physics (4	Thermal Physics (9 specialties)
specialties) (= Elementary Particles	Electromagnetism (8 specialties)
and Fields)	Solids (25 specialties)
Theoretical Physics: Classical (3 special-	Fluids (9 specialties)
ties)	Atmospheric Structure and Dynamics
Electronics (7 specialties)	(16 specialties)
Instrumentation and Miscellaneous (4	Atoms and Molecules (10 specialties)
specialties)	Nuclei (3 specialties)
	Elementary Particles and Fields (6 special-
	ties)
	Physical Chemistry (25 specialties)
	Biophysics (6 specialties)
	Solid Earth Geophysics (10 specialties)
	Instrumentation (28 specialties)

Data from *American Science Manpower: 1954–1956* (Washington, 1961; National
Science Foundation Publications) and "Specialties List for Use with 1970 National
Register of Scientific and Technical Personnel" (Washington, 1970; National Science
Foundation Publications).

Substantially the same story can be told for every field of natural
science. The springing up of new disciplines, branches, and specialties is
manifest everywhere. And as though to negate this tendency and
maintain unity, one finds an ongoing evolution of interdisciplinary
syntheses—physical chemistry, astrophysics, biochemistry, etc. The
very attempt to counteract fragmentation produces new fragments.
Herbert Spencer argued long ago that evolution is characterized by von
Baer's law of development "from the homogeneous to the
heterogeneous," and manifests an ever-increasing "definiteness" and
complexity of articulation. This may or may not be correct for
biological evolution, but it does seemingly hold for *cognitive* evolution.

Table 3

RECENT EVOLUTION IN THE MORPHOLOGY OF PHYSICS

		Number of Units at this Level			Growth Rate
	Taxonomic Level	1911	1954	1970	*Per Decade*
Phylum:	Physics	1	1	1	none (constant)
Genera:	Branches of Physics (e.g., Nuclear Physics, Solid-State Physics)	9	12	16	linear (at ca. + 1)
Species:	Specialties in Physics	19	100	205	ca. 50%

Note: For details see Tables 1 and 2 and their sources.

It is clear that historically there has been a continual growth in the taxonomic refinement of natural science, a growth along the general lines illustrated by the example of Table 3. There is, indeed, every reason to think that scientific speciation has proceeded—during the past period of the exponential growth of science—in the standard evolutionary manner encountered in the biological sphere. The situation here is that the *rate* of speciation at the lower taxonomics level (species, subspecies, varieties) has proceeded proportionately with the *size* of this level (i.e., its number of its elements). Thus if $S_L(t)$ is the magnitude or size of the taxonomic level L in terms of its number of constituents at the time t, then $d/dt\ S_L(t) \propto S_L(t)$, so that consequently $S_L(t) \propto 10^{kt}$. During the past era of unhampered growth—an era which will, to be sure, come to a not distant end—the taxonomic development of science has, in short, proceeded in the same exponential pattern of natural unfettered growth characterizing the division of cells, the multiplication of microorganisms, etc.

Consider the usual inverted-tree hierarchical structure of taxonomic subordination:

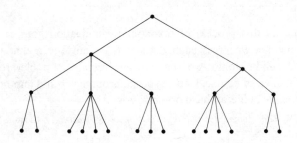

We have it here that at all the lower taxonomic levels of branches, specialties, etc., the *size* of the stratum grows exponentially, with an increasing exponent as one descends on the taxonomic scale, the entire expansion being geared to the growth rate at the very lowest level of *infima species*. Historically, scientific speciation has proceeded exponentially—at a constant per-period percentage growth-rate—doing so with increasing rapidity as one moves downward on the taxonomic scale. The resultant dynamical structure of speciation in general is depicted in Figure 2, which shows the temporal pattern of growth at each unit/subunit level throughout the lower parts of the taxonomic hierarchy. This structure of the process of taxonomic growth obtains across a wide spectrum of highly diversified cases.[7] And to all appearances it obtains with respect to scientific taxonomy as well. On the basis of the picture obtained from Tables 1–3, this phenomenon can be illustrated with respect to the morphological evolution of physics as in Table 4.

Figure 2

STRUCTURE OF SCIENTIFIC SPECIATION

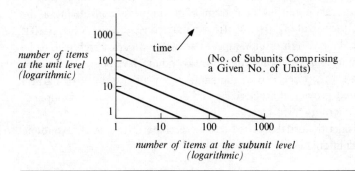

number of items at the subunit level
(logarithmic)

As long as this process of taxonomic ramification goes on—no matter how far we press such descent from any given unit to its successive subdivisions—we shall always remain in a hierarchical order. This fact, of course, lends a special prominence and importance to the principle of hierarchical organization.

[7] See G. K. Zipf, *Human Behavior and the Principle of Least Effort* (Boston, 1949), pp. 229ff.

Table 4

HYPOTHETICAL GENERAL MODEL OF SCIENTIFIC SPECIATION
IN THE HISTORICAL SITUATION OF AN EXPONENTIAL GROWTH
IN "ROUTINE" FINDINGS AT 5% PER ANNUM

Taxonomic Stratum (S_L)	Correlative Findings-Quality* Level ($Q^{\lambda(L)}$)	Growth-Rate of S_L Per Annum	Per Decade
Phylum: the whole field	——	0%	0%
Genera: branches	"first-rate findings"	linear	linear
Species: specialties	Q^{λ} with $\lambda = \cdot 8$	4%	48%
Subspecies: subspecialties	Q^{λ} with $\lambda = \cdot 9$	$4\frac{1}{2}$%	55%
Sub-subspecies: sub- subspecialties: problem-areas	Q^{λ} with $\lambda = \cdot 95$	$4\frac{3}{4}$%	59%
Infima-species: individual problems	"routine findings" (Q^{λ} with $\lambda = 1$)	5%	63%

Note: The fundamental assumption here is that the size of each taxonomic stratum (S_L) is simply *proportional* to the total volume of findings at the correlative quality-level: $S_L \propto Q^{\lambda(L)}$. The taxonomic proliferation rate (growth-rate of S_L) is thus proportional to the growth rate of the volume of findings at its correlative quality-level.

* Compare Table 1 of Chapter VI (p. 102).

On this perspective, morphological growth in the taxonomy of science is correlated with developments at the various quality-levels in scientific discovery. Specifically, the situation in physics over the exponential-growth era of the present past would have the structure indicated in Table 5.

The correlation principles at issue lock the size of a taxonomic level

Table 5

THE TAXONOMIC EVOLUTION OF PHYSICS: 1910–1970
(HYPOTHETICAL MODEL BASED ON TABLE 4)

Taxonomic Level	Number of Units at this Level 1910	1930	1950	1970	Growth Rate per annum	per decade
Physics	1	1	1	1	—	—
Branches	9	11	14	17	(linear growth)	
Specialties	20	43	95	210	4%	48%
Subspecialties (Problem Areas)	60	140	350	850	$4\frac{1}{2}$%	55%
Problems	300	800	2,100	5,600	5%	63%

(S_L) and the volume of its high-quality findings (F and Q^λ) into an inexorable lock-step. This guarantees that the effect of species-proliferation cannot undo the eventually projected logarithmic retardation of F (as per the earlier worry). To be sure, the opening phase of a new taxonomic unit assures a spurt of growth for F, but these are duly coordinated— they do not permit F to "get ahead of itself" so to speak. In circumstances where F is subject to logarithmic deceleration, S_L itself is *also* subject to a correlative deceleration—the pace of F-augmentation and that of S_L-proliferation always keep in proper coordination. It is thus infeasible, virtually as a matter of principle, to maintain that the opening up of new and initially fertile fields can proceed at a rate that compensates for a decline of first-rate findings within the existing framework of scientific inquiry.

If a principle of deceleration on the order of geometrically increasing waiting-time and logarithmic retardation is operative at the local level of particular problem-areas, it will consequently also have to be operative at the global level of science as a whole. The hopeful view that problem-areas will proliferate *de novo* at a rate sufficient to offset the logarithmic retardation of progress within existing problem-areas is therefore altogether unrealistic. For the crucial fact is that new fields and new problem-areas do not spring forth *ex nihilo*. The sorts of discoveries that open up such novel vistas are themselves among those that qualify as scientific advances of the very first magnitude. Accordingly, *new specialties and problem-areas will themselves have to emerge as the result of major innovative developments within old ones.*[8] This being so, the proliferation of new problem areas simply cannot outpace the progress of major discovery within existing ones. A deceleration of high-quality scientific findings will carry in its wake a corresponding deceleration in the taxonomic evolution of science.

---

[8] Someone might say: "True revolutions need not come from within—they can be forced from without. Physics, for example, might conceivably be revolutionized through something at present even begrudged recognition as strictly scientific, like parapsychology." But the discovery that established the physical relevancy of parapsychology would *eo ipso* be a monumental physical discovery, and one that could not gain recognition as such in the absence of an appropriate science-internal basis (though conceivably this might initially be credited as much to psychology as to physics).

4. RETROSPECT

The preceding synthesis brings to its conclusion one major phase of the present discussion, which has endeavored not only to maintain the validity of a Law of Logarithmic Returns at the problem-area microlevel, but to establish that such a law will carry over a science as a whole. Our argumentation had led to the upshot that the production function of natural science obtains in the specific form of the Law of Logarithmic Returns, $F \propto \log R$, and thus holds with respect to *cumulative* parameters, rather than in some different form—such as the Engels' Theory relationship $F^* \propto \log R^*$ for *incremental* parameters, as was mooted above. Our exposition of the mechanisms of the cost-escalation incorporated in Planck's Principle of Increasing Effort thus discharges the task (whose necessity became apparent in Chapter VII) of providing—at least roughly—a justificatory rationale for the theory of logarithmic deceleration that underlay the discussion of the earlier chapters of the book.[9]

[9] For a graphic summary of the overall course of reasoning that leads to this upshot see Figure 3 of the Appendix (p. 269).

XIV
Data Barriers, Unanswerable Questions, and the Limits of Scientific Knowledge

No man can find out
the work that God maketh
from the beginning to the end.

ECCLESIASTES, 3:11

There was a door
to which I found no key:
There was a veil
past which I could not see.

OMAR KHAYYAM, *The Rubáiyát* (Fitzgerald)

1. THE ROLE OF HUMAN LIMITATIONS

Scientific progress is in principle subject to limiting constraints of two very different sorts: there are limits on the side of interactions with nature—and thus on *data acquisition*—and there are limits on the side of man's intellect in the *exploitation* of accessible data.[1] It may perhaps seem that the preceding discussion has given duly short shrift to the oft-mooted deficiencies of the human mind in point of imagination, intelligence, insight, motivation, etc. The main stress in this connection is generally located in one place, that of man's absorptive intelligence—of an initiate's ability effectively *to master enough existing science to get to the frontiers* and thus to be able to advance them.[2] Now, to be sure, one cannot deny that such limitations may

---

[1] The analogy of a computer with its *data-banks* on the one hand, and its *programming* on the other may be helpful here—even though, like all analogies, it has its shortcomings.

[2] This capacity-oriented approach was already central in the interesting deliberations of Eugene P. Wigner, "The Limits of Science," *Proceedings of the American*

create barriers to scientific knowledge.[3] But we have postulated a suspension of disbelief in this regard for the sound methodological reason that we wish *to consider the situation regarding the limits of science that would operate at the more objective, world-characterizing level, even if this whole sector of man's strictly* INTELLECTUAL *limitations were done away with.*

Moreover, this problem of carrying the novice to "the frontiers" of knowledge appears in a less problematic light in the context of our present theory. For given the logarithmic deceleration we have envisaged, this issue is bound to become increasingly less prominent. As the pace of innovation becomes slow enough, mankind's already well-developed skills for heuristic compression will doubtless become sufficiently improved to meet the needs of the situation.[4] The orientation

---

Philosophical Society, vol. 94 (1950), pp. 422–427. The following passage from Ernan McMullin is typical of the lines of thought at issue:

> [L]ife is short and effort is precious, and the *Physical Review* keeps doubling in size. . . . We stand aghast at the difficulty of reaching the frontiers today; very few educated people do (or could, without considerable further training) understand what is going on today in quantum field theory, for example. But here we are, after only a few decades of really intensive exploitation of science, appalled already at the problems of understanding, or even finding out about, what is going on—and yet we speak glibly in terms of centuries ahead! (Ernan McMullin, "Limits of Scientific Enquiry" in *Science and the Modern World*, ed. by J. Steinhardt [New York, 1965], pp. 37–84; see pp. 76–77.)

McMullin does, however, later on in his paper, come to grips briefly with the issues that primarily concern us here:

> The experimental probing of the nucleus takes vast quantities of concentrated energy. . . . As time goes on and machines get bigger and more complex, questions arise about the focusing of energy on tiny areas, and it is obvious that such focusing cannot be indefinitely improved. There is a limit to the amount of energy available, and to the means by which we can bring it to bear. It is not a sharp limit, of course, but it does remind us that the picture of physicists probing ever deeper into the worlds within worlds runs into problems at the very first step: getting the data. (*Op. cit.*, pp. 71–72.)

[3] We are not prepared to enter into some science-fiction-like hypothesis of some large-scale quasi-evolutionary process of consciousness expansion that produced successive generations more and more amply endowed with intelligence and ingenuity—a process perhaps ultimately freeing human inquiry from material constraints in something like the manner envisaged in G. B. Shaw's *Back to Methusalah*.

[4] Peter B. Medawar's cogent observations merit endorsement here:

> May not the body of knowledge also become unmanageably large, or reach such a degree of complexity that it is beyond the comprehension of the human brain? To both these questions I think the answer is "No." The proliferation of recorded knowledge and the seizing-up of communications pose technological problems for which technical solutions can and are being found. As to the idea that knowledge may transcend the power of the human brain: in a sense it has long done so. No one can "understand" a radio set or automobile in the sense of having

of the present theory of scientific progress towards logarithmic deceleration thus operates in such a way as to excuse the neglect of specifically intellectual limitations.

Finally—and this is perhaps the most telling and cogent reason for putting intellectual limitations aside—the really crucial question in the case of a plurality of barriers relates to that which is encountered *first*. Once a barrier is reached, it does not matter about the others that lie further down the road. And the burden of the present course of argument is that the most pressing and immediate limitations to scientific progress are those operative on the side of physico-economic limits to the acquisition and processing of the data themselves, rather than those relating to their strictly *intellectual* exploitation.[5]

2. LIMITS ON DATA ACQUISITION

The issue of the strictly physical limits on data acquisition warrants further examination. In securing data regarding some facet of nature we must *interact* with it. Two things must in general be done: (1) We must act physically upon the environing world so as to create some *impact* on it, and (2) we must obtain some suitable feedback from this impact-action upon us, by way of a discernible *reaction* upon us and/or our instrumental auxiliaries. Accordingly, the limits which *nature itself* imposes on us with respect to interactions produces limitations on our capacity to secure data about it. To be sure, the case of such strictly *physical* limits on access to natural phenomena may appear to contrast significantly with that of the *economic* limits which have concerned us throughout the preceding discussion. Yet this appearance is misleading, for what is actually at issue is a matter of degree rather than one of kind. The two cases in fact lie along the same continuum. For there is a

---

an effective grasp of more than a fraction of the hundred technologies that enter into their manufacture. But we must not forget the additiveness of human capabilities. We work through consortia of intelligences, past as well as present. (*The Hope of Progress* [New York, 1973], pp. 131–132.)

[5] If our basic theory is right, even hyperintelligent beings living in distant parts of space could not produce the "scientifically more advanced civilization" dear to the hearts of science-fiction writers if their economic circumstances were not also much more auspicious, so that their access to the power requisite for larger-scale interaction with nature were also substantially greater than ours. (Presumably at least an order-of-magnitude differential would be required to make for a significant difference.)

characteristic correlation between economic costs and physical limits in this area of data-gathering, seeing that it becomes more and more difficult—and hence expensive!—to operate as one moves further into physical extremes. The physical limits represent *barriers of resistance* which create ever-increasing difficulties of approach that are reflected in ever-rising economic costs: as we have seen, it becomes exponentially more difficult—and thus expensive—to push our capabilities closer and closer towards their limits.

The idea of overcoming ever-mounting obstacles is the unifying link between the operation of physical and of economic factors in this sphere. Consider some examples: (1) the increasingly more powerful accelerators needed to push the velocity of particles ever closer to the speed of light in order to probe into the fine internal structure of "fundamental" particles, (2) the increasingly massive, complex, and powerful equipment needed to detect radiation over greater and greater cosmic distances, (3) the increasingly complex and powerful equipment needed to send out and retrieve signals (e.g., to send as sophisticated an "observation apparatus" as a man out even so short a distance as that to the moon), or again (4) the increasingly complex and powerful apparatus needed to produce very low or very high temperatures or pressures, etc. The same underlying principle operates throughout this range—that of the escalating resistance encountered in inquiry into nature, inhering in the physical limits or limitations inevitably encountered in operating our technological instruments of intervention. In particular, *physical limits are always amplified by technologico-economic limitations* so that the move into extremes encounters a penumbra of increasing resistance, as it were. The limits exert a kind of repelling force: as one seeks to operate in increasingly remote reaches of parametric space, ever more complex, sophisticated and powerful equipment is needed, so that the economic requisites become increasingly demanding. *The economic limits to scientific progress always inhere in a physical basis: increasing costs of inquiry are invariably associated with physical resistance to large-scale interactions.*

Thus consider somewhat more closely the first item of the preceding list, particle accelerators. On the subject Richard P. Feynman has written:

Beside our eight gluons and nine quarks there would still be the electron, muon, photon, graviton, and two neutrinos, so we would still leave a new proliferation of particles to be analyzed by the next generation. Will they find them all composed of yet simpler elements at yet another level?[6]

The answer here is a virtually foregone but qualified affirmative: "They will—*if they ever get there.*" And therein lies the rub. The real question is whether "the next generation" of nuclear physicists will in fact ever have the opportunity to preside over the technical resources of the monumental proportions needed for effective work at this level of the domain. Their efforts may well become blocked, not by nature *per se*, but by the economic ramifications of physical resistances.

3. POWER INTENSIVENESS VS. COMPLEXITY INTENSIVENESS: THE COMING SEA-CHANGE

Scientific problems demanding ever more massive resource-inputs can always be resolved—even in a zero-growth world where fresh resources become available at a merely constant rate—provided that the conditions of an "Installment Plan Hypothesis" are met, so that it is not necessary to pay the whole enormous bill of resource-inputs at one particular point in time. The perfectly realistic prospect must, however, be faced that there will be *some* problems in natural science with respect to which this hypothesis cannot be satisfied—problems for whose resolution one needs to have more or less "simultaneously" a nonaffordable quantity of nonstoreable resource-inputs, namely with respect to the synthetic and "power"-intensive problems. In such cases, the escalating level of resource-demands—the size of equipment, the magnitude of energy-requirements, etc.—will eventually pose a *practically* insuperable obstacle. Here we ultimately approach a decisive *de facto* limit in the attainability of data and hence in the realizability of results, a limit not of *possibility* but of *feasibility*. For the effective factorization stipulated by the Installment Plan Hypothesis is in fact only tenable with respect to one category of scientific problems: the analytic or complexity-intensive. This important point needs closer scrutiny.

Consider once more the different species of data-technology surveyed above (pp. 141 ff.):

---

[6] Richard P. Feynman, "Structure of the Proton," *Science*, vol. 183 (1974), pp. 602–611.

A. Power-Intensive ("Data Synthesis"-Related)
  I. condition-producing (physical power: high energies, low or high temperatures, etc.)
  II. observation/detection/measurement (resolving-power)
B. Complexity-Intensive ("Data Analysis"-Related)
  III. processing/combination/coordination (complexity-oriented analysis)

Now with data of category A—relating to our actions upon environing nature and discernment of its reactions on us—we will clearly always eventually be driven to the limits of the possible—the physically and economically possible—because this *synthetic* dimension of data relates to the forging of physical circumstances that must be realized *at one time*. Problems in this domain cannot be resolved on the installment plan because even then most fine-grained factorization will (*ex hypothesi*) call—someplace along the line—for synthetic data that can only be attained by a concurrent effort greater than any which can actually be generated under zero-growth circumstances. Our capacity to resolve synthetic, power-intensive problems must ultimately come to an end in the face of physico-economic limits. The resolution of these problems demands an all-at-once "burst of effort." Accordingly, the synthetic aspects of data (i.e., I and II) can only be improved "up to a point" within ultimately finite limits of feasibility. Problems become insoluble not because they are *inherently* so, but primarily because those technical measures indispensable to their resolution cannot be put at our disposition within the limits of available resources.

However, in category B this sort of blockage need never arise. The situation is quite different here, for—as was argued above—the analytical aspect of complication/compilation/complexity can always be accommodated *sequentially*. Unlike synthetic problems, analytic issues are always factorable—they can be decomposed into smaller pieces that can be resolved "on the installment plan." Thus with the analytic, complexity-intensive problems of the power-attainable domain, only the sky (or—speaking less figuratively—the horizon of time and the reach of human patience and ingenuity) is the limit.

The existence of this category of complexity-intensive problems is accordingly critical for the long-run prospects of scientific progress. With the data of the synthetic (power-relative) domain, an effectively insuperable *economic* barrier must eventually be reached.[7] But with analytical problems such a barrier can always in principle be bypassed—given sufficient patience.[8] This distinction is crucial to the issue of end-to-progress theorizing. If the only mode of progress were that of the power-intensive sphere of exploration of ever larger regions of parametric space, then scientific progress would ultimately have to approach an end. However, the analytic dimension manifests the critical fact that new scientific discoveries do not inevitably depend on an ever-deeper penetration into new parametric areas. Sufficiently elaborate exploration within the "already accessible" parametric regions can always yield more sophisticated insights into the complexity-levels of physical processes. Effects of the second or third (etc.) order can yield a ceaseless sequence of new crucial insight into relationships.

The future of scientific progress is thus bound to differ for analytic and synthetic problem-areas. This is illustrated graphically in Figure 1. An ultimate check in the direction of power-intensiveness means that, as science moves along the course of its historical development, the "curve of progress" must—for economic reasons—eventually encounter an asymptotic blockage in the upwards axis of increasing fundamentality or depth in the exploration of nature. But there is no reason of principle for its encountering such a barrier along the outwards axis of increasing complexity. With the factorable problems in the complexity-intensive sphere, the installment-plan hypothesis dispells any prospect of an absolute blockage.

This perspective does, however, indicate an eventual sea-change in the nature of natural science. Heretofore, synthetic problems have predominated, for there is little question that the course of modern science has seen an enormous escalation on the side of power-enhancement. In the future, work on analytic problems is bound to become increasingly prominent in the setting of a zero-growth world. An ultimate shift in the nature of natural science must be anticipated—away from a predominantly power-intensive, synthetic

---

[7] Here a cousin to the myth of Sisyphus is applicable, that of the giant who rolls up the mountain-side path a stone that becomes (nontrivially) heavier with each advancing step—be he ever so strong, even his most intense efforts will ultimately receive a check.

[8] Reverting to the myth of the preceding footnote, observe that there need be no limit to how far the stone could be moved by the giant if it (and its pieces) could be split into halves at any stage.

Figure 1

THE TWOFOLD GRID OF THE HISTORICAL "CURVE OF
PROGRESS" IN NATURAL SCIENCE

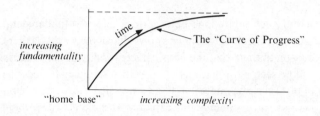

*increasing
fundamentality*

time

The "Curve of Progress"

"home base"   *increasing complexity*

phase in which ever *new* regions of "parametric space" are opened up
(the sort of scientific progress that has in fact predominated since the
industrial revolution), and towards a predominantly complexity-
intensive, analytical phase. The central issue of this latter-day phase will
be the increasingly intricate relationships obtaining in already
accessible regions, but only brought to light through increasing sophistication, relying upon increasingly refined mathematical methods in
data-utilization and theory-formulation.

One aspect of this theory deserves stress. Even when the "end of the
line" is reached in terms of man's effective capacity to further the *depth*
of penetration into parametric space, this certainly does not spell the
demise of experimental science. The work of experimentalists will (as in
empirical science it ever must) play a decisive role. But it is now a
perhaps less glamorous one. For the focal task will be an increasingly
sophisticated comparative/statistical analysis of ever vaster volumes of
data within an already "well-known" sector of parametric space—data
which can be made available only by the labor of well-conceived and
patiently executed programs of large-scale experimentation geared
towards the application of aggregative techniques.

Thus while the commitments of our theory do definitely make room
for the existence of insolubilia, it certainly does *not* envisage the
consequence that all scientific progress must eventually come to a dead
end. For even though scientific progress on the synthetic, power-
intensive side is ultimately blocked under the conditions of zero-growth
in resource-availability, the endless stock of problems on the analytic,

complexity-intensive side is sufficient to underwrite the prospect of unending discovery.

4. HOW SERIOUS ARE DATA LIMITATIONS FOR THE PROGRESS OF SCIENCE?

The existence of such limitations upon inquiry poses a fundamental question about the extendability of our knowledge of the world. Is there in fact any reason to think that the physical infeasibility of data-access to certain remote sectors of parametric space will seriously impede the expansion of our scientific understanding? After all, if for some reason certain parts of the earth could not be explored, this *merely geographic* deficiency in our information would almost certainly not retard in any substantial way our knowledge of the earth's structure, history, geology, etc.

But this analogy is misleading. With natural science it is not just some minor and venial deficiency that is at issue. The regions in which our access to data is blocked by physico-economic limits are precisely the regions where certain peculiar and characteristic sorts of physical processes take place, processes we have every reason to regard as crucial for our understanding of nature. The sectors of parametric space we are prevented from viewing is not just another random region, information about which we could pretty well bypass by extrapolation from without; by its very nature it is a region whose *phenomena* are—or may, in the face of all past experience, safely be presumed to be—different in kind from those to which we already have access.

Inaccessible phenomena entail inaccessible findings. If physical limits—and their economic amplifications—restrict the scale of our interactions with nature, they thereby limit our cognitive access to the *phenomena* of nature, and therefore—so we cannot but believe—they restrict access to its *laws* as well. If we are empiricists (as in this sphere of natural science we have no alternative but to be), then we are forced to take the view that every substantive limitation on the side of data-acquisition is a limitation on the side of the adequacy and completeness of theory. The standard empiricist posture must prevail: our knowledge of the world is *empirical*—i.e., data-dependent—and any significant deficiency in our access to phenomena must be presumed to entail a correlative deficiency in an understanding of the natural laws that govern them. Our knowledge of the world accordingly becomes circumscribed in such a manner that we must accept the humbling lesson of Hamlet's dictum that "There are more things in heaven and earth, Horatio. . . ." The existence of knowledge-impeding limitations of access to the phenomena must be acknowledged to have decisively negative implications for the claims of science to the realization of adequacy and comprehensiveness.

The economic aspect is particularly significant here. It means that certain problems are not unanswerable because nature itself somehow conceals its secrets, nor because the inherent intellectual weaknesses of man as data-processer or as theoretician mean that certain combinations lie beyond his comprehension of his imperfect intellect, nor yet because the acquisition of certain data is by their very nature beyond man's feeble powers. Rather the unsolvability at issue reaches in the fact that the technical means for the realization of the particular data requisite to the solution of certain problems lie beyond the limits of affordability. But here we are not dealing with physical limits, but with their "economic amplifications" (in the sense indicated above). The limits at issue are *nowise absolute but merely economic*: they are not limits of possibility but simply limits of feasibility. The existence of limits of this nature indicates the correlative reality of problems that are not intrinsically unanswerable but nevertheless must unavoidably go unanswered.

5. UNANSWERABLE QUESTIONS AND THE KANT EFFECT

The idea of questions that cannot be answered needs closer scrutiny. To begin with, it deserves note that some questions are not just *unanswerable*, but actually *unaskable* because—in the given state of knowledge—they cannot even be posed. Caesar could not have wondered whether plutonium is radioactive. It is not just that he did not know what the correct answer to the question happens to be—the very question not only *did* not, but actually *could* not have occurred to him, because he lacked the conceptual instruments with which alone this question can be posed. Cases of this sort are typical. In the main, today's scientific problems could not even have arisen a generation or two ago: they could not have been formulated within the cognitive framework of the then-existing state of knowledge.

Ignorance (i.e., the lack of knowledge) will accordingly be of two very different types. It prevails at a surface level when we can grasp a question but lack—under the circumstances—any means of giving an answer to it. (Think of the status of claims about mountains on the far side of the moon made in 1850.) Ignorance prevails at a deeper level when we could not even pose the question—and indeed could not even *understand* an answer should one be vouchsafed us by a benevolent oracle.

The thesis that there are unanswerable scientific questions must be clarified in the light of this distinction between unaskable *vs.* merely unanswerable questions. For this thesis can be understood in two very distinct senses:

(I) *Sense A:* There may well be some scientific questions that will never be answered because we will forever remain in a position of *fundamental ignorance* with regard to them. We do—and always shall—lack the means of probing nature at a level of comprehensiveness and/or detail *needed even to develop the operative concepts of the question* itself. Not just the answer but the very question lies beyond our grasp.

(II) *Sense B:* There are some scientific questions that will never be answered because we must always remain in a position of *effective ignorance* with regard to them. While these questions can—or will—indeed be asked (since the means of their formulation are or will come to hand), yet they will never be resolved. The means of probing nature at the requisite level of comprehensiveness and/or detail needed to answer the question lie beyond our grasp.

The first conception is the more troublesome, because one cannot, of course, adduce any example of such fundamentally inaccessible questions. But their reality is rather easily envisioned on the basis of past experience. The fact that some *current* ideas were unrealizable at all *earlier* historic stages[9] is readily generalized to the more drastic

[9] George Gore offers some illustrations:

That which is inconceivable by one man, or in one age, is not necessarily so by another man, or in another period. . . . Ideas which at one period are beyond reason, do in many cases, by the progress of knowledge, come within its domain. . . . Some discoveries which are unattainable in one age or state of knowledge become attainable in another; for instance, the laws of electro-magnetism or of electro-chemical action could not have been discovered in an

conception that some ideas may be unrealizable at *all* historic stages.

The distinction in view shows that the never-terminating open-endedness of science is perfectly compatible with the prospect that our science can eventually be completed at some particular state of knowledge. Let S_t represent the state of scientific knowledge at the time t, and let Q_t represent the correlative family of questions that can be posed at this juncture. Then it is perfectly possible that some future state $S_{t'}$ will be attained where *all* of the questions of Q_t will be resolved, while yet there are then (i.e., at t') further questions in $Q_{t'}$, which are unresolvable at t'—questions that are not members of Q_t because they could not have been envisaged from the cognitive posture of S_t. This is a condition of affairs that can in principle continue to exist *ad infinitum*.

The thesis of endless scientific progress is thus perfectly compatible with the view that *every* question that can be asked at *every* stage is going to be answered at some future stage: it does not commit one to the idea that there are any unanswerable questions placed altogether beyond the limits of possible resolution.

All that is needed for unending progressiveness is the very real phenomenon that in the course of answering old questions we constantly come to pose new ones. The situation of science is in this regard akin to that of a man walking with a lantern down a long, dark gallery. Some questions about its furnishings he can answer easily: they are clearly within the range of illumination of his light. Others he can discern dimly in the obscure penumbra of his light. Beyond this he cannot see at all—everything is shrouded in utter darkness. The problem-situation in science may be analogous.[10] We see "our own" questions very clearly; we can discern dimly those that lie a little ahead; those that lie distantly ahead we cannot see at all with any specificity (though we may conceivably be more successful in blocking out at a level of generality the broader region where they may lie).

We propose to call this phenomenon of the ever-continuing "birth" of new questions the "Kant Proliferation Effect," after Immanuel Kant

---

age when electro-currents were unknown, nor could the principle of conservation of matter and of energy have been arrived at when science was in its infancy. (George Gore, *The Art of Scientific Discovery* [London, 1878], pp. 19–20.)

[10] The analogy is imperfect—we do not (need not) lose sight altogether of the problems of the past.

who described it in the following terms of a continually evolving cycle of questions and answers:

> Who can satisfy himself with mere empirical knowledge in all the cosmological questions of the duration and of the magnitude of the world, of freedom or of natural necessity, since *every answer given on principles of experience begets a fresh question, which likewise requires its answer* and thereby clearly shows the insufficiency of all physical modes of explanation to satisfy reason.[11]

The italicized passage indicates an aspect of the phenomenology of scientific inquiry which is empirically as well established as any in our study of nature itself. This gives rise to what is, as it were, a conservation-law for scientific problems.

This line of thought indicates a fact of considerable importance for the present theory of scientific progress. The significant problems of the future need not be identifiable, nor even need they be formulable now: they may not yet exist, so to speak. One need not claim longevity—let alone immortality—for any of the *current* problems to assure that there will be problems ten or one hundred generations hence. (As immortal individuals are not needed to assure the immortality of the race, so immortal problems are not needed to assure the immortality of problems.) It suffices for the prospect of endless scientific progress to rely on the operation of the Kant effect that old problems when solved or dissolved give birth to others—no recourse to *Welträtsel* or *insolubilia* need be made. Moreover, even a theory which holds (as ours has done) that there indeed *are* such insolubilia need not regard them as being *identifiable* at any given stage of scientific development—we may never even get as far as their recognition because they may well prove to be inaccessible to scientific inquiry at any given *actually realizable* state. It is thus by no means necessary for a theory of endless scientific progress—one which envisages an inexhaustible pool of scientific

---

[11] Immanuel Kant, *Prolegomena to any Future Metaphysic* (1783), sect. 57. Compare the following passage:

New knowledge is not like a cistern, soon emptied, but is a fountain of almost unlimited power and duration. . . . The area of scientific discovery enlarges rapidly as we advance; *every scientific truth now known yields many questions yet to be answered.* To some of these questions it is possible to obtain answers at the present time, others may only be decided when other parts of science are more developed. (George Gore, *The Art of Scientific Discovery* [London, 1878], p. 27.)

problems—to accept the idea that there are certain problem-issues, identifiable *at this stage of the game*, whose solutions lie inaccessibly behind the data barrier.

This perspective also has important implications for the issue of the completability of science. Conceivably, if improbably, science might reach a fortuitous equilibrium between problems and solutions. It could be completed in the *effective* sense—in providing an answer to every question one *can* ask in the then-existing (albeit still imperfect) state of knowledge, yet without thereby being completed in the *fundamental* sense of answering the questions that would arise if only one could probe nature just a bit more deeply (as, alas, one cannot). The *perceived* completeness of science may fail to betoken its *actual* completeness.

6. TWO VERY DIFFERENT SORTS OF LIMITS

Limits or restrictive boundaries upon knowledge can function in two very different ways. Consider the analogy of a reference library of a rather unusual sort—one with an *infinite* number of volumes. Suppose, as a first possible case, that only some finite number of its shelves are accessible. Then we have the situation of what may be characterized as a *terminating* limit on the information to be obtained: since only finitely many volumes can be attained, the body of knowledge to be derived—however vast it may be—must in the end remain finite. An inquirer will, in principle, have to come to the end of the road as regards the knowledge he can eventually secure: although still drastically incomplete, it will be incapable of any extension.

By way of contrast, consider the case in which only the last volume on every shelf of the infinite library is inaccessible. Clearly this too is a circumstance of restrictive limits. But such an *excluding* limit on the information to be obtained is something very different from the preceding *terminating* limit. For despite the undoubted existence of a very real limitation, the prospects of further substantial advances in knowledge are now always open. An inquirer can evermore extend his information in any given subject-matter direction as far as he pleases.

The point at issue was clearly put in the eighteenth century by Kant, who was prepared to grant the actuality of excluding limits while vehemently denying that of terminating limits.

In mathematics and in natural philosophy, human reason admits of *limits* ("excluding limits") but not of *boundaries* ("terminating limits"), namely, it admits that something indeed lies without it, at which it can never arrive, but not that it will at any point find completion in its internal progress. The enlarging of our views in mathematics and the possibility of new discoveries are infinite: and the same is the case with the discovery of new properties of nature, of new powers and laws, by continued experience and its rational combination. . . . Natural science will never reveal to us the internal constitution of things. . . . Nor does that science require this for its physical explanations.[12]

This Kantian distinction between terminating and excluding limits is crucially relevant to our discussion. For in the context of scientific progress we must carefully distinguish two very different questions:

(1) Can we always improve (more than marginally) on the body of scientific findings we already have in hand?

(2) Does anything within the realm of the potentially discoverable lie entirely beyond our grasp, in being outside the range of what is possible for us to realize?

The former question comes down to: Does science have terminating limits? The latter to: Does science have *any* limits, be they terminating or excluding?

The issue of the prospects of ongoing scientific progress relates only to question (1)—it pertains to the question of *terminating* limits, and leaves that of *excluding* limits aside. The existence of inaccessible phenomena (and thus of "unattainable findings") accordingly has no decisive bearing on the prospects of unending progress. And so to maintain (as has been done) the essential limitlessness of science on the side of terminating limits—the feasibility of unending scientific progress—is not to deny the prospect of problems whose solution lies beyond the physical and/or economic limits of man's investigative capacities. The existence of actually unanswerable questions in science —problems whose solution lie forever on the inaccessible side of an economically imposed technological data-barrier—would *not* mean an eventual end to scientific progress. This would only be the case

[12] *Prolegomena to Any Future Metaphysic*, sect. 57.

in the implausible eventuality that a stage were reached where every unresolved first-rate problem proved to be unanswerable in this way—i.e., if we reached a data barrier on *every* major front of inquiry.

The idea of such a "check-mate" state of scientific inquiry can certainly be envisaged—a stage when each and every path to significant advance issues in the dead end of unanswerable questions. But while this stoppage of science in such a "check-mate" may represent a theoretically conceivable prospect, it is one whose reality our present position emphatically rejects. For we have argued that while one may meet barriers in *some* direction, one can always push ahead in others. As every sailor learns from the device of tacking, the end to progress in a given direction does not necessarily mean the end to progress as such. This standpoint tempers the pessimism of a preparedness to acknowledge the existence of unanswerable questions with the optimism of a theory of unending scientific progress.

The distinction between the two types of limits thus carries the important lesson—already drawn by Kant—that to accept the idea that scientific knowledge is limited is *not* tantamount to accepting the idea that science is finite or completable. The existence of unsolvable questions in natural science—of genuine *insolubilia*—will emphatically *not* entail the consequence that our knowledge in this sphere must ultimately terminate at some dead-end, issuing in a "completed" state of knowledge whose boundaries we can extend no further. Local limits to knowledge are emphatically compatible with global limitlessness. (Think of the ever more comprehensive exploration of a limitless flatland replete with high peaks that one simply cannot scale.)

·These considerations are crucial to the ideological bearing of our theory of science-deceleration. For someone might be tempted to object: "I cannot see that it makes any real difference—from a practical point of view—whether important findings in science get scarcer because there are fewer of them left, or because they are very difficult and expensive to realize. The net result is the same in either case." Now this may well be so as regards the individual scientist's immediate concerns—for him it may not matter whether one reaches the limit of the *achievable* or that of the *affordable*. But in the large doctrinal perspective, the difference is important and far-reaching. In the former case, conclusions are warranted regarding the intrinsic completeness of our knowledge which are emphatically *not* warranted in the latter. Let us explore this issue more closely.

7. PHILOSOPHICAL RAMIFICATIONS: PEIRCE AND SCIENTIFIC REALISM

In the late 1800's, that justly most celebrated of American philosophers, Charles Sanders Peirce, propounded an interesting theory about the relationship between the results of scientific inquiry and the nature of "the real truth" in factual matters regarding actual existence in the world. In the face of the philosophic sceptic's agnosticism as to the very possibility of attaining "the real truth" about nature, Peirce proposed to eliminate the problem by maintaining that here *the truth simply IS what the scientific enterprise will discover in the idealized "long run."* Once scientific progress reaches a point where a question is answered in a certain way—the answer being thenceforward maintained without any change of mind—then this in fact is *the true answer* to the question in hand. Specifically, Peirce offered two contentions:

(1) That whatever science will come to maintain over the theoretical long run is true. (Over the theoretical long run, science maintains *nothing but* the truth.)

(2) That *all* truth regarding the world will be realized by science in the theoretical long run. (Over the theoretical long run, science maintains *all* the truth.)

The deliberations of the present theory of scientific progress cast a strong shadow of dubiousness over Peirce's position. His thesis (2) appears as untenable because there will be *ignorabimus* issues— questions that science will in fact *never* be able to resolve, even in the infinite theoretical long run, because their resolution depends on a greater concurrent commitment of resources than will ever be marshalled at any one time in a zero-growth world. They involve interactions with nature on a scale so vast that the resources needed for their realization remain outside our economic reach in a world of finite resource-availability.

And even Peirce's thesis (1) must be rejected, because what science maintains over the indefinitely projected long run *could well be false*, having defects which could be discovered only on the far side of an economic "data barrier" in that a determination of the falsity of the claims at issue makes demands upon the marshalling of concurrent resources that could not be met at any stage in a zero-growth world. There is every reason to deny that what we ultimately reach is in fact "nothing but the truth," since there is every reason for thinking that—where scientific knowledge is concerned—further knowledge not only *supplements* but generally *corrects* our knowledge-in-hand, so that the *incompleteness* of our information can entail its *incorrectness* as well.

Accordingly, it is clear that the present theory of scientific progress also indicates the untenability of any version of *scientific realism* which proposes to conceptualize REALITY in terms of "what will eventually be held to be the case by science (over the long run)." On the present view, the progress of science—even at the level of the idealized long run—will never issue in a perfect representation of "authentic reality" but only in a historical succession of presumably suboptimal realities, reality-pictures on whose behalf we are not entitled to advance any claims to finality—not even that merely *approximate* finality envisaged by Peirce.

Peirce and the scientific realists who follow him hold the ill-advised view that *only the limitations of time* separate between "the-truth-about-reality" from "the teachings of science," holding that if we think of these limitations as removable *by working at it long enough* (i.e., over the infinite long run), then the gap will close.[13] They see the attainment of truth as a single-factor idealization correlative with the removal of a single limitation, that of effort maintained over time. Our own theory suggests that if one wants to move along this particular route then one must resort at least to *a two-factor idealization with respect not only to time but also (and more drastically) with respect to the availability of resources.*

The defect of Peirce's theory of the science-truth relationship is thus simply that it abstracts too far from the limitations of human finitude under which scientific work must actually be done. It may well be plausible for the science of a community of sufficiently powerful disembodied intelligences whose capabilities and efforts at inquiry are unimpeded by the operation of any economic constraints upon mastering the resistances of nature: beings whose observations are obtained by cost-free processes, for whom computations and data-processing operations are to be had for the asking, and whose experimental interactions with nature can be carried out by acts of will

[13] *Collected Papers*, Vol. VII (Cambridge, Mass., 1958), 7.78.

alone. But creatures constituted as we are, who must carry on their scientific efforts subject to crucial disabilities in regard to the utilization of resources, cannot be confident that *their* science must in principle ferret out "the real truth" in the course of time. In the actual circumstances of the case, the Peircean vision of a total cognitive victory over nature achieved by the scientific enterprise in the idealized long run is essentially visionary in the sense of being *unrealistic*.[14]

[14] This is particularly striking because Peirce was in other contexts acutely (and pioneeringly) alive to the economic aspects of science. (Indeed—as we have seen—Peirce may be viewed as the founder of the still underdeveloped discipline of "the economy of research.") However, the reason is easy to see. For while Peirce presciently discerned the cost-escalation of science, he thought this did not matter because later science simply dealt with the increasingly insignificant differences of the nth decimal place:

> This value increases with the fullness and precision of the information, but plainly it increases slower and slower as the knowledge becomes fuller and more precise. The cost of the information also increases with its fullness and accuracy, and increases faster and faster the more accurate and full it is. It therefore *may* be the case that it does not pay to get *any* information on a given subject; but, at any rate, it *must* be true that it does not pay (in any given state of science) to push the investigation beyond a certain point in fullness or precision. (*Collected Papers, op. cit.*, vol. I, 1.122. Compare footnote 22 of Chapter V above, pp. 88–89.)

Peirce's commitment to asymptotic convergence thus neutralized the impact of his cost-escalation theory.

XV

Implications and Nonimplications of a Deceleration of Science

Since we live in an age which endeavors to go deeply into things, those who care for the general good must make an effort to take advantage of this tendency which may not last long among men, especially, if it happens by misfortune or by heedlessness that they are not contented, which would one day make them relapse from curiosity into indifference and finally into ignorance.

G. W. LEIBNIZ, "Nouvelles ouvertures" (in *Opuscules et fragments inédits de Leibniz*, ed. by L. Couturat)

1. ON NOT AWAITING THE END OF HISTORY

The stage for these concluding deliberations is set by Henry Adams' somber speculation that human intellectual history has developed through a quickening sequence of successively briefer historic phases, rushing towards a final *Götterdämmerung* of intellect—a juncture when man's scientific intelligence will have attained the limits of its reach, bringing "thought to the limit of its possibilities," as Adams picturesquely put it.[1]

Various thinkers have been beguiled by this prospect of a radical discontinuity in intellectual history which sees an initial period of explosively rapid development of scientific progress succeeded by a final period of deadlock, stagnation, and frozen stability. All concerned see the key to this discontinuity in the idea of power. Francis Bacon was the grandfather and Henry Adams the father of the thought that human *progress* is correlative with the ever widening extension of human *power*. And in strict consonance with their thinking, the historian Carl Becker projected the idea that if—nay *when*—the historic process of a continual enhancement of our access to power comes to an end, this

[1] For Adams' thought see the works cited in footnote 4 of Chapter IV.

circumstance spells the end to the progressive development of the human condition. An era of sterile fixity will then set in:

> It seems indeed unlikely that the adjustment [of men to their environment and to one another] can ever be more than clumsily effected so long as the multiplication of implements of power continues to increase the complexity and to accelerate the tempo of social change. But it is conceivable, even probable, that the possibility of discovering and applying new sources and implements of power will in the course of time gradually diminish, or even be altogether exhausted. In that event the outward conditions of life will change less and less rapidly, will in time become sufficiently stable perhaps to be comprehended, sufficiently stable therefore for a relatively complete adjustment of ideas and habits to the relatively unchanging body of matter-of-fact knowledge of man and the outer world in which he lives. In such a stabilized and scientifically adjusted society the idea of progress would no doubt become irrelevant as progress itself became imperceptible or nonexistent.[2]

Becker's line of thought seems to be that the processes of historic change must eventually grind to a halt with an ultimate stabilization in the utilization of power-deployment. Adopting and extending this perspective, Roderick Seidenberg has anticipated a transition to a *posthistoric* era, maintaining that:

> [T]he ultimate stabilization of human relationships toward which man is drifting implies a gradual reversal and slowing down of the tempo of his history: in place of an accelerating rhythm of change he will experience a gradual abatement and exclusion of all change and variation, until at length he will find himself in an ever more securely established milieu—in a period of unchanging continuity. He will have passed through the transitional, historic phase of his evolution, and attained at length a post-historic stage.[3]

[2] Carl Becker, *Progress and Power* (New York, 1949), p. 112.
[3] Roderick Seidenberg, *Posthistoric Man: An Inquiry* (Chapel Hill, 1974), p. 237. Compare the following passage:

That the vast drama of human history should eventually find its denouement in the sterile perspectives of a world at least analogous if not similar to that of the social insects may seem to us at once forbidding and incredible. But that, moreover, such an apparently blind and aimless state of fixity should finally crown the triumph of intelligence seems like a bitter and ironic anticlimax to all our efforts, reducing the long travail of our development to a kind of ultimate *reductio ad absurdum*. (P. 194.)

Now for all that has been said in these pages, it is possible—though surely implausible!—that the Becker–Seidenberg stagnation thesis should correctly describe the structure of human development in point of *material* progress. And this in turn *may* even have the consequence—though not inexorably, save for Marxists—of an ultimate fixity in the structure of man's *social* arrangements. But the present analysis indicates that such a socio-economic stabilization need certainly not carry over to intellectual—and specifically not to *scientific*—progress.[4] Our argument has it that even in a zero-growth world as regards power-exploitation, science, while necessarily slowing the historic pace of its change, need certainly not eventuate in the crystallization of a changeless pattern.

The orientation of the present analysis is thus diametrically opposed to the view of a termination of scientific progress in a condition of absolute fixity. In the altered circumstances of a zero-growth future, our theory foresees an era of *slow-down*, not one of *stoppage*. To be sure, it anticipates a marked deceleration of the process of historic change from the established pattern of exponential growth (and *linear* progress) to which we have become accustomed from past experience. But this slowing is *not* seen as ever issuing in a crystallized condition of unchanging fixity—not even in an asymptotic limit. It is, after all, a crucial aspect of the mathematics of logarithmic deceleration that *it allows for a continual slowing that yet will never eventuate in a final halt*. The structure of scientific progress in the future is accordingly seen to differ from that of the past only in degree, and not in kind. Given logarithmic deceleration, the pace of change will, to be sure, become slower, and eventually even glacial, but nevertheless the prospect and the reality of drastic change is always ineliminably present. Our analysis thus indicates that there is no need to anticipate an "end to history"—be it with joy or with sorrow—when it is the history of *scientific inquiry* that is at issue.

2. ON NOT WRITING THE OBITUARY OF SCIENCE

The opening chapters showed that an impressive array of Nobel-prize winners—E. P. Wigner, R. Feynman, MacFarlane Burnet, *et al.*—have

---

[4] Let alone *cultural* change, an issue which goes outside the confines of our present considerations.

expressed views that indicate a return to the *fin de siècle* position by some of the most experienced and creative scientific professionals. Once again we seem to be entering an era where perceptive students of the subject incline to the view that the progress of scientific discovery may be nearing its end.

This melancholy judgment was adumbrated by that large-minded student of the idea of progress J. B. Bury, who mooted an eventual demise of the ideal of progress itself:

> Will not the process of change, for which Progress is the optimistic name, compel "Progress" too to fall from the commanding position in which it is now, with apparent security, enthroned? . . . A day will come, in the revolution of centuries, when a new idea will usurp its place as the directing idea of humanity. Another star, unnoticed now or invisible, will climb up the intellectual heaven, and human emotions will react to its influence, human plans respond to its guidance. It will be the criterion by which Progress and all other ideas will be judged. And it too will have its successor.[5]

Now such a prospect may possibly—perhaps probably—represent the ultimate fate of man's material and his *moral* progress. But does the prospect of *cognitive* progress also call for such *sub specie aeternitatis* resignation to an inevitable sunset? The whole tenor of our present analysis suggests otherwise. In the long run there may be cycles of decline and fall, but the prospect of phoenix-like renovation always lies ahead—even if distantly. If the present view of the matter is but approximately correct, science need never encounter an absolute check in its attempts to penetrate more deeply into the secrets of nature. There are obstacles, to be sure, but their impact is one of retardation not blockage, of slow-down rather than stoppage. The horizons before us are literally limitless and the prospects of new achievement are in principle endless. The ultimate question is not that of the *feasibility* of advance, but of the *will* to do so in the face of increasing difficulties and mounting obstacles.

---

[5] *The Idea of Progress* (New York, 1973), p. 353.

3. ON NOT SELLING INTELLECT SHORT

One oft-encountered objection against the idea of limits to scientific progress goes as follows: "All this attention to limits of inquiry and boundaries of knowledge is gloom and doom thinking. Do not sell human intelligence short! Man's intellectual creativity will ultimately prevail to overcome all these apparent obstacles to smooth scientific progress. What looks like an insuperable limit from our present-day perspective may well crumble down under the next breakthrough that lies just around the corner."[6]

But this is surely wishful—and highly unconvincing—thinking. The obstacles that have been canvassed in our discussion are *technological limits* on data-availability which are themselves inherent in the very nature of the physical world, as best science itself depicts it for us. Natural science is *empirical* science—it indispensably needs data. Only a rationalist of an extreme and doctrinaire stamp could think that sheer intelligence can surmount data-barriers in mastering the "secrets of nature." To hold that pure thought and unaided intellect can overcome the physical limitations correlative with data dependency is alien to the very nature of empirical science. (However great its reliance on imagination and creative thought, natural science is something very different from imaginative literature or pure mathematics, where creative force of intellect can operate alone, without the constraining restrictiveness of material limitations.) These limits manifest themselves to us in a fundamentally *economic* manner. Our physical interventions in the course of nature are everywhere subject to the limitation of economic constraints upon the availability of resources. There is—and can be—no adequate reason to think the case is otherwise in the domain of empirical inquiry, where our *interaction* with nature is a driving force of the enterprise.

The position presented here is thus not a matter of "gloom and doom thinking" at all, but simply one of being *realistic*—of "facing the facts" as best we can make them out. It accepts squarely and honestly the

---

[6] The idea that "everything will be different" after the next breakthrough is tempting, but is clearly no very scientific way of defending the interests of science. Scientific rationality demands adoption of a methodological uniformitarianism between the seen and the unseen. And we should surely use the same ground-rules of explanation and method in discussions *about* science that apply in discussions *within* science.

inexorable implications of the economic limits upon the progress of inquiry in a context where the deployment of technology in the acquisition and processing of data represents an unavoidable fact of life.

4. ON NOT BEING PESSIMISTIC

It is sometimes said that to maintain the existence of limits or limitations to scientific progress is to succumb to an unwarranted pessimism. This poses a delicate question—one which depends heavily on the vagaries of attitude and expectation of the sort implicit in the anecdote of the half-filled barrel. But surely—and quite seriously—a *deceleration* in scientific progress is nothing all that unhappy or unfortunate. Would an unending combination of the recent pace of scientific advance really conduce to our human interests and concerns? Would it really be to anyone's advantage to continue *ad indefinitum* the science-explosion whose exponential expansion has characterized the past 300 years of history in the West? Is this expansion in fact not rather something that is a cause for common and reiterated lament—the explosion of information; ever narrower specialization; the crushing burden of literature and information; the creation of a situation where the teaching and the learning of science become increasingly unmanageable?

Et quasi cursores vitae lampada tradunt. The light of learning—in the superb simile of Lucretius—is handed down from generation to generation like the torch brought by the relay runners to the stadium at the opening of the Olympic games. But if the weight of the torch grows substantially with each transmission, the runners will at last become immobilized. There is plainly something self-defeating about this. Surely no one would welcome a pace of scientific progress that assures the collapse of the enterprise under its own weight—a science that becomes unteachable because it becomes unlearnable save in subdivisions that ultimately become so narrow as to lack any element of wider significance.

Surely the most desirable condition is one that sees a reasonable balance between what can be absorbed and what must be transmitted, a balance that provides both for learnability and for innovation. In this regard, the present theory of logarithmic retardation is in fact an invitation to optimism rather than its reverse. It offers us the very best of both worlds. In combining open horizons for unending progress in discovery with a pace of advance that is sufficiently sedate to be manageable on the side of learning, teaching, and intellectual exploitation, it enables us to have our cake and eat it too. If there is error here, it surely lies on the side of optimism, not pessimism.

This optimism is indeed very marked. It is convenient to develop this point in opposition to the following interesting statement by the American biologist Bentley Glass:

> Let us keep clearly in mind . . . that progress cannot continue indefinitely. Indeed, so awesome is already the accelerating rate of our scientific and technological advance that simple extrapolation of the exponential curves shows unmistakably that we have at most a generation or two before progress must cease. . . .[7]

This passage suffers from the fatal lack of a due distinction between *material* and *intellectual* progress. The fact that "progress" in the augmentation of human population on the planet and its exploitation of physical resources must eventually come to a stop clearly affords no convincing reason why *scientific* (or technological) progress should cease in the resulting world of a zero-growth equilibrium. If our deliberations are anything like correct, there is no need to join with Henry Adams' brother Brooks in anticipating in the context of science itself "a huge, an awful tragedy . . . the end of mankind's struggle with nature."[8] Indeed, the decisively optimistic aspect of our present discussion is its insistence upon the prospect of an open future for *scientific* progress even in the face of an ending to that *material* progress which has to date always accompanied the course of scientific advance.

5. ON NOT DEPRECIATING ACHIEVEMENT

Even though the circumstance of a deceleration of science may thus be regarded with relative equanimity from the broader aspect of human concerns, must not the tendency of our theory be seen as being disastrous at any rate from the standpoint of the practicing scientific

---

[7] Bentley Glass, "Science: Endless Horizons or Golden Age?", *Science*, vol. 171 (1971), pp. 23–29 (see p. 26).

[8] Quoted in E. Samuels, *Henry Adams: The Major Phase* (Cambridge, Mass., 1964), p. 439.

researchers themselves? Is it not a dire misfortune for them that the task of major discovery becomes ever increasingly difficult?

Surely not. Scientific fame and fortune do not—or *should* not—depend solely on the magnitude of the *discovery*, but on the difficulty of the task overcome and so on the magnitude of the *accomplishment*. But in a situation where discoveries are getting increasingly difficult, the ingenuity and effort needed for a second or third magnitude result will *at that stage* be every bit as great as that needed for a first magnitude result earlier on. Think of a geographic-exploration analogy—the discoveries of Columbus and Magellan vs. those of the searchers for the sources of the Nile or—still later—the climbers of Everest. Not just the *size* of the find, but the *magnitude of the achievement of its finding* should be—and largely are—determinative of achievement and deserved fame. On this basis, the later discoverers need have no fear of invidious comparisons.

There is, moreover, every reason to expect that deep-rooted tendencies in human nature will support this standpoint. To be sure, the theory of deceleration contains the prospect of longer and longer periods of elapsed time between the realization of really first-rate discoveries—a situation of continually increasing waiting times for equal progress. But all this is by *absolute* standards, while men in fact tend to make their judgments on a relative and comparative basis. We incline to esteem as first-rate the best findings realizable under the working conditions of the day, esteeming scientific greatness by the relativistic standards of the researcher whose work figures massively in the citation-indices and whose labors are held up as latter-day exemplars to his colleagues. The natural human tendency is to construe "the best" as "the best that can be expected in the circumstances." Suppose, by way of analogy, a gradual increase in strength of earth's gravitational field. The time would arrive when the runner who runs a four-minute mile would be a great athlete. Reputations would still be made. The age of heroes will not have come to an end: the heroes of the day will still be those who win its races.

6. ON NOT OVERGENERALIZING THE ANALYSIS

The present considerations have throughout been geared to the *natural* sciences: to physics, chemistry, biology, and their congeners. The question naturally arises: Does this theory of retardation carry over from natural science into other domains?

This question must be answered in the negative. For one thing, the analysis does not apply in the *social* sciences. For these study the lawful aspects of the organizational structure of human activity, and such laws will differ as the modes of organization themselves change. Novelty in the *types* of objects being studied offers the prospect of unending innovation in the cognitive exploration of these objects. Physical nature, however, does not usually put such novelty at our disposal—carbon atoms, unlike men, do not devise new modes of collective interaction.

Again, the premisses of our analysis do not apply to the *formal* sciences (mathematics and logic). These fields do not hinge on the availability of factual data that can be had only by interacting with nature. There is no intrinsic limitation to the development of new theoretical formalisms. Their independence of the whole issue of data-exploitation shields them against any prospect of a breakdown due to increasing obstacles encountered in bringing this sort of grist to their mill.

In particular, the process of technological escalation indicates a decisive difference between the sciences of nature on the one hand and the strictly formal sciences (mathematics, logic) on the other. In natural science there must be a steadily deeper or more extensive penetration into the parametric structure or the complexity of nature—it will not serve the requirements of progress to do more of the same *sort* of thing that was done before. Such further journeys of exploration demand the overcoming of continually greater physical obstacles and requires ever more potent instrumentalities of intervention. But in those sciences whose *modus operandi* is purely intellectual (be this on the side of analysis or synthesis), and where no *physical* resistance need be overcome, this technological escalation does not enter in. And with its absence one also removes the mechanism whose operation is the sum and substance of the present analysis of the limits of science.

Finally, the present analysis does not apply to the *humanities*. These are hermeneutic in methodology. They envisage the ongoing prospect of reinterpreting finite materials from new points of view. There is thus no end to innovation here as long as there is no end to the formation of intellectual perspectives that afford the combinations and the emphases through which new humanistic interpretations always become possible. And there is no reason to think that the range of such interpretative perspectives is finite. Think of the endless products of, say, Shakespeare scholarship, which generates each year a written corpus several times larger than the *opera omnia* of the master himself, gaining new insights from developments in branches of knowledge (e.g., Freudian psychology or statistical linguistics) that did not even exist in his day.

Thus in other fields of learning (*Wissenschaft*) the situation is sufficiently dissimilar from that of natural science (*Naturwissenschaft*) that the considerations of our present theory—geared as they are to the economic penumbra of the physical limits to the acquisition and utilization of data—will not have bearing upon these other domains. (This, of course, is a nowise *compensatory* advantage—since these disciplines are mute on the vital subject of the physical universe that is man's home.)

7. ON NOT EXPECTING MIRACLES

The lay public has by now become altogether accustomed to the latter-day situation of perpetual revolution in science. As science moves more and more deeply into its eventual phase of deceleration—as we have argued it must—an era of disillusionment and disappointed expectations on the part of the nonscientific laity becomes virtually inevitable. For as the rapid succession of major results begins to slow to a trickle, the flood of science-initiated technological miracles will also abate. A deceleration in *scientific* progress can be expected ultimately to bring in its wake a corresponding slowing of the rate of *technological* progress. The intimate interdependence of the two enterprises is such that the *application* of scientific innovation must proceed at a rate more or less in step with that of scientific innovation itself. Accordingly, it is reasonable to expect that decelerating rate of scientific progress will also ultimately lead to a corresponding deceleration in .the rate of technological innovation.[9] Our present view of the prospects of

[9] Consider one rather typical illustration:

A [significant] . . . pressure is the growing demand by corporate managements for increased productivity for their research departments, as these activities take a growing share of corporate revenues. In my own organization [Borg-Warner], for example, the total revenues of the company have gone up 22 percent per employee in the last five years, while the overall cost of doing research has gone up 29 percent per employee. The high hopes of management during the 50's and 60's for a cornucopia of new products and exciting new business ventures to come tumbling out of their research palaces have not been fulfilled. (Donald W. Collier, "The Future of Industrial Research Establishments" in P. C. Ritterbusch [ed.], *Scientific Institutions of the Future* [Washington, 1972], pp. 91–99 [see p. 93].)

scientific progress thus indicates it to be decidedly dubious that the technological explosion of the recent past represents a permanent facet of the human condition, and that technological "future shock" will in times to come present as notable a phenomenon as in the past.

A connected point deserves stress. Note that the steady-state posture we have assumed to be operative eventually on the side of scientific *effort* (albeit not *progress!*) nevertheless postulates a condition of undiminished investment. Our theory of logarithmic deceleration still envisages an unabatedly massive ongoing input of public resources into science as a research enterprise. There are scant grounds for unqualified optimism here. For such an approach effectively ignores the prospect of public frustration, of a mounting resentment of people objecting that scientists are now merely boondoggling because—despite massive investment—the resulting returns seem comparatively modest, judged by the standards of the past.

One analyst has conjured up the following bleak picture:

It is not difficult to imagine a change in economic organisation which . . . might easily so distract attention from technical and scientific work as to depress recruiting among the rising generation below that necessary for the maintenance of efficiency. A Kelvin, a Leonardo, and even an Edison might very well not concern themselves with science at all; the only scientists and technicians, apart from those merely there to earn a living, would be true narrow-minded cranks. . . . Spengler predicts such a turning-away from science and technology is due to happen to ourselves within a century or two. . . . For us, the urge towards material invention and power over matter is intimately bound up with our cast of mind; our God is the Great Artificer, the 'maker of Heaven and Earth'. Other civilisations have had their cosmogonies, their accounts of how the world came to be; but they have rarely regarded the creator, to whom the pioneer invention of the Universe has been ascribed, as the important ruling power to be supplicated and conciliated. They seem, in fact, to have had a better insight than ourselves into the fate of pioneers.[10]

The clear lesson emerges from our present discussion that a great deal of public information and education is necessary in this regard. People

[10] H. Strafford Hatfield, *The Inventor and His World* (West Drayton and New York, 1948), see pp. 106–107.

who incline to complain about slackness, inefficiency, or incompetence in scientific work—complaints nowadays heard with increasing frequency—simply have no real idea of what natural science is up against in its ongoing attempts to penetrate the "secrets of nature."

Human undertakings and enterprises generally either grow or decay. It is thus vastly difficult to achieve the situation that is the basic postulate for the present analysis: the maintenance of a stable effort in the face of increasing obstacles. Nevertheless, the prospect we have envisioned here is a perfectly feasible one, which a judicious combination of common sense, enlightened self-interest, and higher aspiration can combine to bring to realization.

8. ON NOT EXCUSING INADEQUATE EFFORTS

One critically important final point deserves stress. Even if it were certain that mankind had pushed its effort at scientific inquiry deep into the region of diminishing returns, one should not suppose that this had gone too far. The evaluation of the *costs* of scientific knowledge in terms of material and intellectual resources must be offset by recognition of the *benefits* of scientific work. And these "benefits" should not be construed in the narrowly utilitarian, gadgetry-oriented sense of *panem et circenses*. It is important to recognize that not just *material* but *intellectual* benefits are involved. For while scientific progress has indeed produced an immense benefit in terms of physical well-being, there remains the no less crucial fact that it represents one of the great creative challenges of the human spirit.[11] Man's intellectual struggle with nature deserves to be ranked as a key element of what is truly *noble* in human life, together with our social efforts at forging a satisfying life-environment and our moral strivings to transcend the limitations of our animal heritage.

A society that spends many billions of dollars on a varied cornucopia of deleterious trivia, to say nothing of untold billions on military outlays, assumes an uncomfortable moral posture in deciding that science—even big and expensive science— is a game that's not worth

---

[11] On this line of thought compare sect. 2 of Chapter 9 ("Social Goals Beyond Welfare") of the author's *Welfare: The Social Issues in Philosophical Perspective* (Pittsburgh, 1972), pp. 155–166.

the candle.[12] The scientifically and technologically most advanced countries nowadays spend some 2–3% of their GNP on research and development and some 3% of that on basic science.[13] This allocation of roughly one-tenth of one percent of GNP to pure science is certainly not exorbitant—perhaps not even seemly, considering the size of our material and intellectual stake in the enterprise. We may thus end this discussion of the difficulties of scientific progress on the splendidly affirmative note struck by Sir Peter Medawar: "To deride the hope of progress is the ultimate fatuity, the last word in poverty of spirit and meanness of mind."[14]

[12] The moral aspect aside, it is probably not even a matter of prudentially enlightened self-interest. Compare the cogent discussion in Stephen Toulmin, "Is There a Limit to Scientific Growth?", *Scientific Journal*, vol. 2 (1966), pp. 80–85.

[13] See Keith Norris and John Vaizey, *The Economics of Research and Technology* (London, 1973), p. 56.

[14] Peter B. Medawar, *The Hope of Progress* (New York, 1973), p. 137.

Appendix
The Formal Structure of the
Argumentation

To clarify the over-all structure of the lines of reasoning developed in the preceding discussion, it will help to set out the deductive connections among its principle theses in diagrammatic form. This is done in Figures 1–3. Figure 1 outlines the argument for the contention that the historical structure of scientific progress indicates a law of logarithmic returns on science-committed resources which entails the onset of logarithmic retardation in the zero-growth future. Figure 2 shows how the basic model of progress through the technologically facilitated exploration of the phase space of physical parameters (in terms of a capacity for power-access or complexity-handling) gives rise to a log-uniform distribution of findings relative to this capacity. Finally, Figure 3 shows how the economics of the situation means that this capacity /findings relationship serves to rationalize the principle of logarithmic returns which underlies the logarithmic retardation thesis.

The following abbreviations are used throughout these figures:

R: resource investment in scientific work [cumulative]. See pp. 63–69 and 113–116.

F: number of *first-rate* findings [cumulative]. See pp. 82 and 90–94.

Q: number of *routine* findings [cumulative]. See pp. 98–103 and 119–120.

E: range in the phase-space of physical parameters. See pp. 153–157.

P: "power." See pp. 74–77 and 158–159.

C: "complexity." See pp. 74–77 and 170–172.

X: "capacity" (in terms of C or P). See pp. 172–173.

$*$:   indicates time-derivatives. (Thus $R^*(t) = \dfrac{\mathrm{d}}{\mathrm{d}t} R(t)$.)

$\propto$: indicates proportionality. (Thus $x \propto y$ iff $x = cy$.)

∞ : indicates quasi-proportionality (q-proportionality) amounting to *linear relatedness*. (Thus $x \infty y$ iff $x = cy + k$.) What is at issue here is simple proportionality subject to a suitable adjustment of the origin.

Figure 1

THE STRUCTURE OF ARGUMENTATION (Part I)

(See Chapters IV-VII)

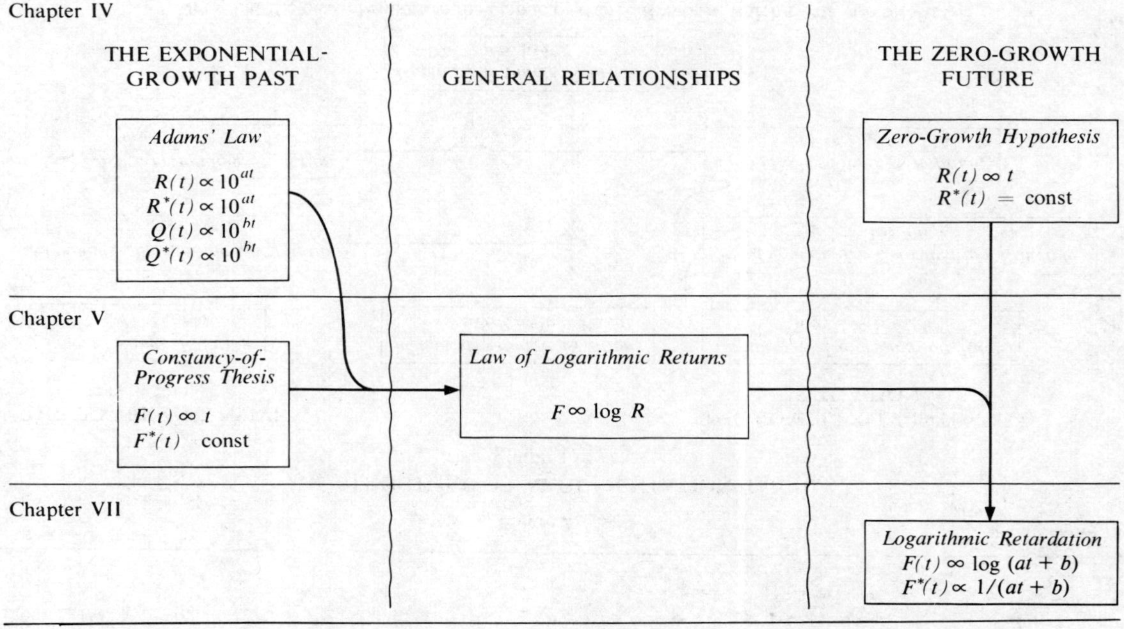

Chapter IV

THE EXPONENTIAL-GROWTH PAST

GENERAL RELATIONSHIPS

THE ZERO-GROWTH FUTURE

Adams' Law

$R(t) \propto 10^{at}$
$R'(t) \propto 10^{at}$
$Q(t) \propto 10^{bt}$
$Q'(t) \propto 10^{bt}$

Zero-Growth Hypothesis

$R(t) \propto t$
$R^*(t) = $ const

Chapter V

Constancy-of-Progress Thesis

$F(t) \propto t$
$F^*(t)$ const

Law of Logarithmic Returns

$F \propto \log R$

Chapter VII

Logarithmic Retardation

$F(t) \propto \log (at + b)$
$F^*(t) \propto 1/(at + b)$

Figure 2

THE STRUCTURE OF ARGUMENTATION (Part II)
(See Chapter IX)

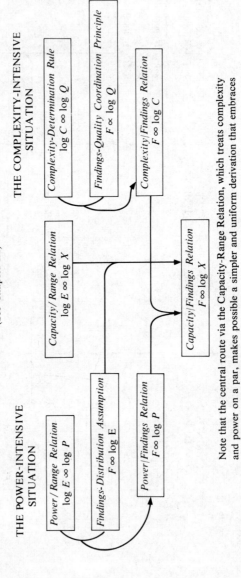

THE POWER-INTENSIVE SITUATION

THE COMPLEXITY-INTENSIVE SITUATION

Power / Range Relation
$\log E \propto \log P$

Findings-Distribution Assumption
$F \propto \log E$

Power / Findings Relation
$F \propto \log P$

Capacity / Range Relation
$\log E \propto \log X$

Capacity / Findings Relation
$F \propto \log X$

Complexity-Determination Rule
$\log C \propto \log Q$

Findings-Quality Coordination Principle
$F \propto \log Q$

Complexity / Findings Relation
$F \propto \log C$

Note that the central route via the Capacity-Range Relation, which treats complexity and power on a par, makes possible a simpler and uniform derivation that embraces alike the power-intensive case.

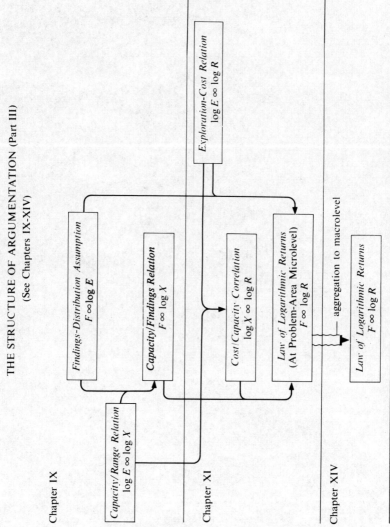

Figure 3

THE STRUCTURE OF ARGUMENTATION (Part III)

(See Chapters IX-XIV)

Chapter IX

Findings-Distribution Assumption
$F \infty \log E$

Capacity/Findings Relation
$F \infty \log X$

Capacity/Range Relation
$\log E \infty \log X$

Exploration-Cost Relation
$\log E \infty \log R$

Chapter XI

Cost/Capacity Correlation
$\log X \infty \log R$

Law of Logarithmic Returns
(At Problem-Area Microlevel)
$F \infty \log R$

Chapter XIV

aggregation to macrolevel

Law of Logarithmic Returns
$F \infty \log R$

Name Index

Subject Index